Exploring Therapy, Spiritua

# Exploring Therapy, Spirituality and Healing

Edited by

William West
*Reader in Coumselling Studies, University of Manchester, UK*

First published 2011 by
PALGRAVE MACMILLAN

Palgrave Macmillan in the UK is an imprint of Macmillan Publishers Limited, registered in England, company number 785998, of Houndmills, Basingstoke, Hampshire RG21 6XS.

Palgrave Macmillan in the US is a division of St Martin's Press LLC, 175 Fifth Avenue, New York, NY 10010.

Palgrave Macmillan is the global academic imprint of the above companies and has companies and representatives throughout the world.

Palgrave® and Macmillan® are registered trademarks in the United States, the United Kingdom, Europe and other countries.

ISBN 978–0–230–55406–1

This book is printed on paper suitable for recycling and made from fully managed and sustained forest sources. Logging, pulping and manufacturing processes are expected to conform to the environmental regulations of the country of origin.

A catalogue record for this book is available from the British Library.

A catalog record for this book is available from the Library of Congress.

10   9   8   7   6   5   4   3   2   1
20   19   18   17   16   15   14   13   12   11

Printed in China

*This book is dedicated to Clem Pinder*

# Contents

# List of Figures and Tables

**Figure**

**Tables**

# Notes on Contributors

**Revd Dr Terry Biddington** was formally a mental health advocate, director of a large mental health charity and chaplain to a National Health Service psychiatric unit, and was previously the coordinator of the North Midlands Spirituality Network. Currently he is Anglican chaplain to the Manchester Higher Education Community and a co-Director of the Manchester Centre for Urban Spirituality.

**Fevronia Christodoulidi** is a Greek counsellor and has just been awarded a PhD by the University of Manchester, UK. She trained as a spiritual healer in her home country and has conducted research projects on the spiritual dimension in therapy, therapists' spiritual development and the process interaction among counselling, spirituality and culture.

**Christa Gorsedene**, born of a Second World War British soldier and a German mother, has always sought understanding across boundaries, history notwithstanding. After degrees in Physics (BSc) and Environment (MSc) her chequered career has included teaching, life modelling and cycle-touring writing. She is now a 'normal' person-centred/integrative prison counsellor and 'strange' working doctoral researcher at the University of Manchester.

**Dr Peter Gubi** is Principal Lecturer in Counselling, and Divisional Leader for Counselling and Psychological Therapies, in the School of Nursing and Caring Sciences at the University of Central Lancashire. He is a BACP Senior Accredited Counsellor/Psychotherapist and a BACP Senior Accredited Supervisor in Private Practice. He is author of *Prayer in Counselling and Psychotherapy: Exploring a Hidden Meaningful Dimension* (Jessica Kingsley, 2008) and has researched and published in peer-reviewed journals on the subjects of prayer and counselling, and spiritual abuse.

**Dr Chris Jenkins** is a priest and psychotherapist based in Stockport. As well as working in a parish he is on the staff at St Luke's Centre, Manchester (www.stlukescentre.org.uk) and is Chair elect of APSCC, the division of the British Association for Counselling and Psychotherapy concerned with spirituality and pastoral care. Chris also edits the journal *Thresholds* for counsellors 'working with spirit'. In his spare time he plays tenor sax.

**Dr Roy Moodley** is Associate Professor in Counselling Psychology at the Ontario Institute for Studies in Education at the University of Toronto. Research and publication interests include traditional and cultural healing; multicultural and diversity counselling; and race, culture and ethnicity in psychotherapy and masculinities. His books include *Carl Rogers Counsels a Black Client: Race and Culture in Person-Centred Counselling* (co-edited with Colin Lago and Anissa Talahite, PCCS Books, 2004), *Integrating Traditional Healing Practices in Counseling and Psychotherapy* (with William West, Sage, 2005) and *Race, Culture and Psychotherapy: Critical Perspectives in Multicultural Practice* (with Stephen Palmer, Routledge, 2006).

**Olga Oulanova** is based at the Ontario Institute for Studies in Education at the University of Toronto.

**Dr David Paul Smith** is Chief Psychologist and Director of Training at St Bernard's Hospital in Chicago, Illinois. He holds a master's and a doctorate from the University of Chicago. He is a member of the Society of Psychotherapy Research and a member as well as editor of the newsletter for the Society of Clinical and Experimental Hypnosis.

**Dr Barbara Thompson** is Assistant Professor, Counseling Program, Graduate School of Education and Human Development, George Washington University and is in private practice at Towson, Maryland.

**Professor Brian Thorne**, recently retired from the University of East Anglia, is a key figure in the development of counselling in Britain, especially person-centred counselling, and is well known for his work and writing around counselling and spirituality.

**Dr Barbara Vivino** maintains a private practice in psychology in Berkeley, California. She previously worked as the Director of Clinical Training and Associate Professor of Clinical Psychology at the California Institute of Integral Studies in San Francisco, CA.

**Dr Marie Wardle** is a counsellor, supervisor and researcher in adult mental health with South Staffs and Shropshire Healthcare NHS Foundation Trusts, working in both primary and secondary care services. Her research interests are in parapsychology, spirituality and psychiatry. She is a member of BACP and SRF (Spiritual Release Foundation).

**Dr William West** is a Reader in Counselling Studies at University of Manchester where he directs the Counselling Studies programme, including a Professional Doctorate in Counselling. He is Chair of the Culture and Psychotherapy section of the Society for Psychotherapy Research (International) and is a Fellow and practitioner member of BACP and a former Chair of its research committee. He is well known for his research and writing (3 books, 22 peer-reviewed papers and 14 book chapters) on spirituality, culture, traditional healing, supervision and qualitative methodologies.

**Dr Dori Yusef** had a background in fine art before moving into health and social care and then psychotherapy. Her training encompassed the transpersonal, body psychotherapy and supervision, all of which she teaches to diploma, degree and research levels. Understanding the integral and interconnectivity in the therapeutic process is paramount to her practice, teaching, research and creativity.

# Acknowledgements

Early in 1992, during a tutorial with Professor John McLeod at Keele University, I tentatively raised the question of doing a PhD with him. I was more than half expecting to be turned down. But he encouraged me and soon I was researching therapy and spiritual healing, trying to bring these two traditions from my own clinical practice into some kind of better relationship. I wanted to do a PhD because 'it was there' and because 'I always secretly wanted to do one'. What I never expected was to become an academic and have some extraordinary students working with me at doctoral level, as well as the chance to meet up with talented colleagues from all over the world. These people are truly the co-authors of my work, whether they would wish to claim this honour or not. Apart from the gifted contributors to this book I must acknowledge Linda Ankrah, Liz Ballinger, Allen Bergen, Jeni Boyd, Dee Brown, Francisco Cavalcante Jr, Louise Drage, Dawn Edge, Terry Hanley, the late Pittu Laungani, Lynn Learman, Clare Lennie, John McLeod, John Morris, Greg Nolan, David Orlinsky, Brother Mathew Panathanath, Abdullah Popoola, Wayne Richards, John Rowan, Ann Scott, David Spence, Richard Summers and Mary Swale.

The editor and publisher would like to thank the following for permission to reproduce copyright material. Chapter 5 is an abridged and modified version of 'Compassion in Psychotherapy: The Perspective of Therapists Nominated as Compassionate' (Vivino et al. 2009), published by *Psychotherapy Research* and used with the kind permission of the publisher Taylor and Francis, http://www.informaworld.com. Nightingale Conant for permission to quote Rumi in Chapter 7.

Some material from Chapter 10 has previously been published in a different form, as follows: C. Gorsedene (2007) Agnostic counsellor and spirit guide: can such an unlikely team ever help? *Thresholds* Spring 2007, reproduced here with kind permission of the publisher.

Every effort has been made to trace all copyright holders, however if any have been inadvertently overlooked the publishers will be pleased to make the necessary arrangements at the first opportunity.

# Foreword

*Brian Thorne*

It was Stanislas Grof who wrote: 'A recognition of our own divine nature, our identity with the cosmic source, is the most important discovery we can make.' This bold statement – made by a contemporary psychiatrist – exposes in a sentence the poverty of much that passes for psychotherapy and counselling at the present time. Many therapists and therapeutic orientations, if Grof is right, are still selling their clients culpably short by failing to acknowledge, let alone attend to, the central aspect of what it means to be truly human. Even a convinced atheist might well be suspicious of those therapists who seem to regard as irrelevant a perception of reality to whose rejection he or she may have devoted much intellectual and emotional energy.

It is perturbing to reflect that 30 or so years ago this book would have been unlikely to find a publisher. The reluctance of therapists to accept spirituality as not only a legitimate but an essential area for their concern was at that time so widespread that those who ventured into such terrain were regarded as wildly eccentric or probably covert proselytizers. It was not so long ago that, as a therapist who openly affirmed his religious allegiance and by definition the importance of the spiritual dimension in therapy, I experienced myself as something of a St Sebastian figure. I imagined myself on a bridge over a river with my fellow therapists shooting arrows at me from one bank and my co-religionists from the other. Therapists regularly saw religion, and by implication spirituality, as a source of disturbance or indeed of psychotic tendencies, while members of faith communities regarded therapy as an activity prompted by psychological theories which were for the most part antagonistic to spiritual wisdom.

The situation today is markedly different. Life on the bridge is by no means so lonely – indeed, at times it feels quite crowded – and the distinction between religion and spirituality is now more likely to be understood so that even the concept of atheistic spirituality is not altogether incomprehensible. Disturbingly, however, this book reveals that for clients and therapists alike there are many battles still to be fought. We read of clients who have found their medication increased when they have talked of their spiritual convictions or who have quickly learned to conceal their most important feelings in the light of the evident disapproval of their therapists. We read, too, of therapists who search in vain for supervisors who are sympathetic to their spiritual insights and practices. Others ensure that this vital aspect of their work is kept safely off the supervisory agenda. There is continuing evidence, in short, that there remains deeply entrenched in the therapeutic professions a suspicion of and even hostility towards both clients and practitioners for whom spiritual reality constitutes their primary source of meaning and motivational energy. When this state of affairs is placed in the context of a society where recent surveys reveal that the vast majority of people believe in God and profess to have spiritual experiences, this is a situation which could legitimately be deemed abusive. It is wholly appropriate, therefore, that beneath the measured and reflective contributions to this book there sometimes simmers a permeating anger. The trainers of therapists are the rightful recipients of some of the more overt expressions of such anger, for the responsibility rests with them for ensuring that future generations of therapists no longer dismiss the spiritual insights and yearnings of their clients as evidence of psychological disturbance or harmful delusion. Many contributors to this book, either directly or by implication, record their dismay that so few trainers seem to recognize their responsibility in this respect.

William West is to be congratulated on bringing this book to fruition. His accomplishment is not confined to his editorial competence. His own stimulating chapters are the latest addition to an impressive array of books and articles which seek to give the spiritual dimension in therapy the central place it merits. Many of his fellow contributors are former or current students for whom his work at the University of Manchester has been inspirational and his support crucial to their own research investigations. Spiritual experience lends itself readily to poetic expression, prophetic utterance and powerful rhetoric. It does not sit so comfortably with the patient sifting of evidence and the sensitive participation in interviews where the subject matter often verges on the inexpressible or demands respectful silence. It is to the enormous credit of editor and contributors that this book constitutes, at one and the same time, a fine repository of research enquiry and a source of encouragement for those who daily, as therapists or clients, have the demanding privilege of engaging with the infinitely fascinating world of spiritual experience.

# Introduction

*William West*

> When I was ill, I certainly learned *very* quickly to keep the spiritual side of myself separate from the rest of myself whenever I met with any of the 'professionals'. (Counselling client in Jenkins 2006: 80)

I think it is crucial to begin this book with these words of a client, disempowered and feeling forced to deny the importance of spirituality in her life. I would invite you, the reader, to remain engaged with the clients' perspective as you read this book. Spirituality remains at the heart of the human condition for the vast majority of humans who believe in the Divine in some form or other. Even for those without such a belief, the language and cultures of religion and spirituality retain a deep communicative expressiveness.

The issue of spirituality and its relationship to therapeutic healing is a profound one and spirituality remains a word that is evocative and resonant. When a good friend of mine was compulsorily detained in a mental hospital a few years ago, her consultant, while not sharing my friend's religious faith, was moved to describe her as 'a soul in torment'. Was this merely the use of a powerful metaphor by this mental health physician, or was he pointing to the limits of a secular treatment; that is, to the point at which a spirituality-informed approach needed to take over? Indeed, John Swinton (2001) refers to spirituality as the 'forgotten dimension in mental health care'. Regrettably, the physician in this case did not explore this spiritual dimension for my friend, for he was blind to her strong religious faith.

Sometimes my colleagues in the fields of counselling and psychotherapy question my view that there is a problem around therapy and spirituality in the western world. Some deny that there has ever been a problem, while others insist that there was a problem but that it is less apparent now. Certainly, more and more is being written about therapy and spirituality, as will be apparent in this book. It has become easier in recent times for more clients to speak about their spirituality in therapy sessions.

Out of my research and research supervision, therapeutic practice and clinical supervision, I have an ongoing interest in the often cutting-edge work that arises when spirituality and healing are able to take their rightful place within the therapeutic encounter. To work in this way can be very challenging to the therapist. Indeed, in some of this work it feels that the boundaries of counselling are being creatively and ethically tested to benefit the client.

John McLeod suggests:

> Psychotherapy can be viewed as a culturally sanctioned form of healing that reflects the values and needs of the modern industrial world. As such, it has not been 'invented' by scientists but has evolved from the healing practices employed in various historical periods by ordinary people, and necessarily contains within it the residue of these earlier forms. (1997: 2)

These earlier forms of healing practices largely occurred within a religious or spiritual context. Such healing continues to this day within all communities, whether in industrialized societies or not (Moodley and West 2005). Such practices are to be found within forms of pastoral care offered by most, if not all, religious groups.

So this engagement between spirituality and healing practices predates modern forms of therapy. Indeed, many therapy clients today will also access traditional and spiritual forms of care concurrent with their therapy sessions. In Chapter 9 in this book, Roy Moodley and Olga Oulanova discuss two such examples from clinical practice, exploring the challenges that such actions can represent for the therapist involved. Of course, such initiatives may well remain unknown to the therapist. On the other hand, this raises the question of whether the therapist should ask about such matters in the initial contracting and assessment process.

The broader debate around religion, spirituality and society is highly charged and increasingly polarized; witness the popularity of books that attack religion by Dawkins (2007) and Hitchens (2007). This polarization has been a feature of much discussion post 9/11 and the tensions around the spiritual and the secular remain huge. Any efforts to integrate and welcome spirituality into the therapeutic encounter are inevitably set against this societal and cultural backdrop.

I struggle at times to convince my colleagues in the therapy world that there is a problem around therapy and spirituality. I have played a modest part in the whole process of making it more possible to talk about spirituality within therapy. Most of the contributors to this book have bravely researched topics relating to spirituality and therapy, sometimes working without colleagues' support.

## What is spirituality?

At this point it would be helpful to begin to define spirituality and the related concept, religion. Most people seem to use the word 'religion' to cover the organized group of people, religious leaders and buildings that are used by a faith group. In contrast, 'spiritual' is often seen as being about the individual's personal beliefs and experiences, which may well be in some kind of tension with the faith group they belong to, if any.

Not everyone accepts these distinctions. For instance, I have met some African Caribbean Christians and Jewish rabbis who equated the word spirituality with religion. So it is important for therapists to hear how clients use these words. However, a distinction between religion and spirituality does seem to reflect much common usage and dictionary definitions. For example, the *Compact Oxford English Dictionary* defines religion as '1. the belief in and worship of a superhuman controlling power, especially a personal God or Gods. 2. a particular system of faith and worship'. In contrast, spiritual is defined as '1. relating to or affecting the human spirit as opposed to material or physical things. 2. relating to religion or religious belief'.

If we choose to equate religion and spirituality, we can be doing people a disservice. John Swinton warns us:

> A view of spirituality that does not look beyond institutional religion risks missing out on some of the very significant spiritual needs that are experienced by people with no formal religious interests, on a daily basis. (2001: 12)

It is precisely this group of people, who are awake to their spirituality but not contained within organized religious groups, who might well access therapy.

From my own viewpoint and for the purposes of this book, I would define religion as the formal structures and frameworks provided that enable people to belong to a religious group. These structures consist of buildings, religious services and other meetings and frameworks for religious instruction and pastoral care of members. In contrast, I regard spirituality as relating to the individual's personal beliefs and lived experience of things of the spirit. Such spirituality might remain relatively private to the individual, or the individual may be engaged in individual or group practices that they regard as developing spirituality, for example yoga, Tai Chi, meditation or prayer. For some people, their spirituality will be contained and expressed through organized religion.

In Chapter 1, I will further explore definitions of spirituality that are pertinent to therapeutic practice. The whole question of spirituality and its role in the therapeutic process continues to remain a problematic, and controversial, area for practitioners, despite their interest in the topic (West 2000a, 2004a). In my view, it has received less development in terms of clinical practice, supervision, training and research than it warrants.

It seems, particularly in the US, that this picture is changing (Richards and Bergin 2005), somewhat encouraged by the generous funding made available for research into forgiveness (Worthington 1998) and by the many research studies into the use of meditation, mindfulness and other spiritual practices derived from eastern religions in therapy. (See Barbara Vivino and Barbara Thompson's discussion in Chapter 5 of this book, for example.) A further example of this is the work of the Melbourne Academic Mindfulness Interest Group, which is a collaboration between academic staff from Monash University and the University of Melbourne who reviewed the evidence for mindfulness-based psychotherapy in 2006. (Mindfulness involves a concentrated awareness of one's thoughts, actions or motivations and is an essential part of the practice of Buddhism.)

There is therefore a developing interest in spirituality among practising therapists and questions around spirituality continue to have a high profile among clients and in the wider society.

## What is healing?

A focus on healing and therapy might appear to be a natural topic for practitioners. Indeed, it could be argued that healing is what all therapy – indeed, all caring work – is about. However, there are other uses of the word 'healing' to apply to the therapeutic encounter that are much more controversial. It can be linked to extraordinary moments of change within the therapeutic encounter, described by Buber (1970) as 'I/Thou'. Buber contrasts this I/Thou experience with the more usual I/It encounters in which people treat each other as objects.

Somewhat similarly, Rogers (1980) discussed a way of being with that he called 'presence', which he described as 'an altered state in ...iich his inner spirit has reached out and touched the inner spirit of the other... Profound growth and healing and energy are present.' Brian Thorne (1991) introduced a concept he called 'tenderness', which in many ways overlaps with Rogers' presence. Thorne's discussion of tenderness includes:

> It seems as if for a space, however brief, two human beings are fully alive because they have given themselves and each other permission to risk being fully alive. At such a moment I have no hesitation in saying my client and I are caught up in a stream of love. (1991: 77)

Such moments as Buber, Rogers and Thorne are describing are also often talked about as 'spiritual'. The word 'healing' could also refer to the use of specific healing techniques such as aura work or the laying on of hands. There are chapters in the second section of this book that specifically address the use of healing techniques alongside therapy. For example, Marie Wardle explores psychic energy and healing; Christa Gorsedene considers how counsellors might be guided in their work; and Roy Moodley and Olga Oulanova discuss examples of therapy clients also consulting traditional healers.

## Summary of chapters

All of the contributors to this book have been engaged in research and practice around their areas of expertise. This is therefore a research- and practice-informed book organized around therapy, spirituality and healing. It is a unique book because theory, research and practice are not separated out, with each contributor drawing from their own and others' research and from their practice as therapists and clinical supervisors. This fits within the tradition of the practitioner–researcher in which research is linked to practice and vice versa. Contributors also offer guidelines or pointers towards best practice and relevant points for discussion.

It should already be apparent that there are differing ways of viewing both spirituality and healing. Indeed, from a therapist's point of view it is important to honour and respect the client's view of both. The contributors to this book have researched their topics in their own particular way. There is plenty of overlap in how each views therapy, spirituality and healing; in fact there has been much dialogue among the contributors. Some of the differences will also be apparent in the research methodologies chosen and this extends to the voice and style of writing of the contributors. These differences allow us to be aware of the varying ways in which we all make sense of the world.

The book is divided into three sections. The first section consists of seven chapters that focus on therapy and spirituality. In Chapter 1, Spirituality and Therapy: The Tensions and Possibilities, I begin by considering a recent example of a trainee counsellor experiencing difficulties around a spiritual moment in counselling. Particular aspects of her experience are used in order to explore a number of relevant issues relating to spirituality and counselling. This is followed by a consideration of what is meant by spirituality and the part it can play within the therapeutic encounter, including the notion of implicit and explicit spirituality. Some key questions are then addressed around culture and spirituality, including ethnic matching of client and therapist. The human urge to evangelism is considered, and finally some promising developments around the use of spiritual interventions in therapy, such as meditation, yoga, forgiveness and compassion, are acknowledged.

In Chapter 2 Chris Jenkins explores When the Client's Spirituality Is Denied in Therapy. Chris draws on his research and practice to consider the clients' experiences of having their spirituality denied in counselling and offers a model for counsellors to work integratively with spirituality. In focusing on the clients' voice in this way, Chris alerts us to the challenge of facilitating the client's therapeutic process, including their spirituality. His chapter provides further evidence of therapeutic failure, including the human consequences for the clients involved, when this does not happen.

In Chapter 3, Counselling and Pastoral Care, Terry Biddington draws on research and practice to explore the differences between counselling and pastoral care provided in faith communities. He offers a most useful exploration of pastoral care within the main religious traditions, teasing out its relationship with theology. He brings the practice of pastoral care alive by offering three brief case studies. In conclusion he asks: What are the interfaces and overlaps between counselling and pastoral care; when is referral appropriate – and to whom; and what are the possibilities of joint working? Clearly, this can only be achieved on a basis of mutual understanding and respect. Such questions are very pertinent to anyone working with spirituality in therapy and the answers enable us to locate therapeutic work with clients' spirituality in relation to pastoral help from organized religion. This may well prove to be the most challenging but also the most useful chapter to read in this book.

In Chapter 4, Integrating Prayer in Counselling, Peter Gubi presents his mixed methods research that reveals the surprising amount of prayer that is done in counselling, much of it covert, and not explored in supervision. Peter's work challenges the notion of how secular counselling actually is in practice. For those therapists who choose to use prayer, he provides safe and appropriate recommendations for safe practice in the use of prayer within counselling.

In Chapter 5, Compassion in Psychotherapy, Barbara Vivino and Barbara Thompson present the findings of their qualitative study into psychotherapists' understanding and use of compassion in their practice. Compassion is one of those key concepts that are able to bridge both secular and spiritual cultures, and represents a way of discussing spiritually informed therapy without getting too caught up on definitions of what spirituality is, or what language we need to use to discuss it.

In Chapter 6, Counselling, Spirituality and Culture, Fevronia Christodoulidi challenges us to reflect more deeply on issues of culture and spirituality in therapy. Her research is into the problematic but potentially highly creative area of counsellors working across cultures and spiritualities with clients. Drawing on her considerable experiences of practising and researching cross-cultural and spiritual work with clients, Fevronia presents guidelines for such work.

In Chapter 7, Embodied Spirituality and the Therapeutic Encounter, Dori Yusef takes us on a heuristically informed research journey into embodiment. She draws on her research conversations and her own story to explore issues for the client and therapist that deal with the fundamental realities of human spiritual experience and the intangible alternative realities that can emerge. Dori invites us into her exploration of liminal spaces and encourages us, in turn, to explore both the macro and micro levels of human existence. She addresses such questions as: How are these expressed in the therapeutic relationship and what are the implications for our ethical responsibilities?

Dori writes in a style that bridges the personal encounter and the profoundly spiritual and philosophical questions that relate to existence. Her work can be a challenge to read and engage with, but the experience, I find, is always fruitful. Her kind of research – heuristic – that lends itself to a disciplined personal as well as professional journey, has a particular relevance for researchers exploring spirituality, where there will always be a personal agenda however well disguised or hidden. Such a heuristic approach is also followed by Christa Gorsedene in Chapter 10 and Marie Wardle in Chapter 11.

The second section of this book has four chapters focused on therapy and healing. In Chapter 8, When Counselling Becomes Healing, I explore the varieties of healing that can happen within the therapeutic encounter. I consider the vexed questions of how to deal with, and make sense of, experiences of healing when they arise within the therapeutic encounter; what kind of experiences can arise and how they can be explored in ways that benefits the clients involved; and how to maintain appropriate boundaries and the best use of supervision.

In Chapter 9, Traditional Healing alongside Counselling and Psychotherapy, Roy Moodley and Olga Oulanova draw on a rich range of relevant research literature and clinical practice to consider how to work with clients who also consult traditional healers. They consider how to deal with the boundary and other issues involved, including making sense of such consultations within the counselling framework and facing the possible challenges and dilemmas that arise. They present a rich case vignette of a client who sought traditional healing alongside counselling and they provide us with an exploration of relevant ethical issues and implications for practice.

The final two chapters in this section take us into even more challenging waters and the authors involved are to be applauded for their courage in highlighting and exploring their research topics. In Chapter 10, Assessing a Counsellor's Use of a Seemingly Spiritual Gift, Christa Gorsedene addresses the issue that many counsellors do feel helped or guided in their work with clients but few will talk about it. Christa draws on her own innovative research work with an apparent spirit guide to provide guidelines for such work and reflect on the potential client benefit involved.

In Chapter 11, Psychic Energy and the Client, Marie Wardle invites us to understand the extraordinary work of a spiritual and/or healing nature that can occur in counselling in terms of a psychic energy framework. Marie draws on her years of research and practice to present a unique view of psychic energy and counselling. She considers what is meant by psychic energy within a counselling context and explores the ethical and supervisory issues involved, before finally offering some very relevant guidelines for practitioners.

The third section of the book has three chapters which focus on research and practice. In Chapter 12, Research in Spirituality and Healing, I suggest that while the question of research into spirituality and healing can be regarded merely as a problem area, it also offers possibilities of using innovative methodologies. I explore some of these possibilities before offering guidelines for researching the counselling of spirituality and healing.

In Chapter 13, Emergent Spirituality, David Paul Smith draws on historic and current descriptions of spiritual experiences, including those of the author and other contributors to this book, to argue for an approach to such phenomena that does not rely on medical or religious classification. He suggests instead that there is much to be gained by adopting an experiential, phenomenological viewpoint, which could open the door to more collaborative work between traditional healing and modern psychotherapy.

In Chapter 14, Practice around Therapy, Spirituality and Healing, I focus on the challenges faced by the practitioner, including possible models for working with spirituality and healing. I conclude with guidelines for training and practice around counselling, spirituality and healing.

## Who is this book for?

This book is intended for and should appeal to practitioners of therapy and related disciplines, including psychotherapists, counselling psychologists, counsellors, religious pastoral care, youth and community workers, social workers, probation officers, teachers involved in pastoral care and health care practitioners. It is also a book for practitioner–researchers. There is plenty of rhetoric about reducing the gap between researchers and practitioners and developing the notion of practitioner–researchers. This book is a fine example of such work. However, the gap between researchers and therapy practitioners largely remains (McLeod 1999).

This is also a book for researchers. The focus is research done by practitioners, choosing topics that appeal to them with congruent methodologies. Such research may not be the focus for all mainstream researchers, but some interesting dialogues could result. It is also a book for interested others. Therapy, spirituality and healing all attract their own audiences outside the role of professionals. This book is written in a way that is intended to be accessible to this wider group.

## A question of style

As editor of this book, it has been important to me to encourage my contributors to find and use their own voice. As a result, I have not imposed a strong house style but have instead offered my contributors a framework to write within and have given them feedback on earlier drafts of their chapters. I hope that, as a result, their voices come through clearly and that any change of style between chapters will alert the reader to the diversity of approaches expressed here. Therapy, spirituality and healing are such important topics that we need to maintain a diversity of perspectives, since this reflects the human condition.

Note that in what follows we will tend to use the word 'therapy' to cover both 'psychotherapy' and 'counselling' and the word 'therapist' to cover both 'psychotherapist' and 'counsellor', except when we separate the terms for the purpose of quotation or to emphasize possible differences between counselling and psychotherapy.

# Part One
# Therapy and Spirituality

# 1
# Spirituality and Therapy: The Tensions and Possibilities

*William West*

## Introduction

This chapter begins by using a recent example of a trainee counsellor experiencing difficulties around a spiritual moment in counselling. I use the particular aspects of this experience to explore a number of issues relating to spirituality and therapy. I then further consider what is meant by spirituality and the part it can play within the therapeutic encounter, including the notion of implicit and explicit spirituality. There are some key questions around the whole area of culture and spirituality that are addressed in a way that includes drawing on my own experiences, including visits to Kenya and India. It seems useful then to consider the thorny issue of evangelism in religion and therapy. Finally, I acknowledge some promising developments that point to a more hopeful view of the part that can be played by spirituality in the therapeutic encounter.

### A spiritual moment in therapy

Despite the signs of real progress being made around spirituality and therapy, the tensions, problems and possibilities remain. Indeed, let us be mindful that there is a tension between therapy and spirituality. If I had any doubt about this matter, an email I received from Louise Drage, a counsellor struggling with these issues in this case in a training context, illustrates the difficulties. With her permission, I am quoting from her email at some length to put the issue into a clear context:

> I was having a discussion with my client at the end of a counselling session when something happened. In that moment it was as if we were both suddenly 'held'. I had never felt anything like it before. Neither of us said anything, but we both knew that something had

occurred... like an imperceptible seismic shift. It was as if I had stepped out of normal time and space and suddenly felt connected with everything that was, is and would be. I had a feeling of joy and I remember thinking that if I died there and then, it would be OK, because I had experienced this and that was all that mattered! Bizarre. In that moment I felt Blessed and as if we had both received some 'healing' at the same time.

When we discussed it the next week, my client described it as feeling some great need of wanting to get back into the room and be back with me immediately. However, I don't think it was 'me'. I think he needed to be back in the experience which, to me, felt like 'unconditional love' coming from someone or something other than me. It was difficult to discuss and describe, almost as if we didn't need to. To have experienced it was enough.

Later, I found a description of 'presence' presented in a book by McLeod and also read an article in the *Thresholds* magazine, in which a psychotherapist was discussing with another person the internal struggle that she was having with her Christian faith and her psychodynamic work. During their encounter, the therapist talked of experiencing a sense of feeling 'met'. These examples seemed to describe my experience exactly. I then took it to supervision, in great excitement and looking for some help on interpreting it. However, we did not discuss it as being a spiritual experience. As a group we described it, in psychodynamic terms, as the client becoming 'attached' to me, which he undoubtedly was, but I felt it was more than that. I felt that something else had happened, that wasn't created or facilitated by me or my client. So, without getting much further in being able to talk about it in spiritual terms, I put the experience to the back of my mind then, thinking that it wasn't valid and that it wasn't helping my psychodynamic training or supervision. During the session with my client that day, I truly felt that, for a few moments, the counselling room really did become a 'sacred space'.

To me there are three aspects of considering spirituality and therapy: the role of spirituality in the life of the client; the role of spirituality in the life of the therapist; and spirituality within the therapy session itself, including spiritual experiences. The above account encapsulates a spiritual experience occurring within the therapy encounter. To the therapist it is clearly a spiritual experience, since she is talking in terms of Grace and healing. We are not, however, told whether the client viewed the experience as spiritual, though it was clearly of some import to the client.

Then occurred that strange but regrettably all too common experience of a lack of acceptance – indeed, understanding – of such experiences within supervision. This is where I believe there is both a training issue and an issue for the professional bodies. Without committing ourselves to a spiritual or even religious agenda, can we not accept that there are experiences that happen inside and outside of counselling that will often be labelled 'spiritual' and that in most cases are beneficial or even life changing? If this is the case, then let us consider how to integrate such experiences into our theories, training, supervision and practice. Let us remember that we live in a world in which the vast majority of people do believe in God, do have spiritual experiences (Hay and Hunt 2000). It is high time that our therapy theories and practices were more respectful, more accepting of the healthy part that spirituality plays in many people's lives. Yes, there are problems, and spirituality can be entwined with some very real mental health issues, but so can sexuality and that does not lead most people to lives of celibacy!

I can hear a small voice say to me, 'OK, suppose you are right. But are these experiences that are best left to the experts in these matters, namely the religious leaders, the priests, imams, rabbis, gurus and so on?' If only this were true, for as Louise went on to say: 'I found it hard to describe my experience in a Christian setting too and to find clarification of what, I felt, had been a moment of Grace.'

There are three further problems related to leaving these matters to religious leaders. First, should we be hiving off this aspect of human experience as being not a fit matter for therapeutic practice? Secondly, even if religious leaders were well equipped to do such work (and Terry Biddington's Chapter 3 in this book discusses this very issue), many people would probably not visit them even though many people remain interested in, and awake to, their spirituality. Thirdly, I suspect your average therapist would run a hundred miles rather than involve a religious leader in the therapeutic process for a client. (Such work does happen from time to time in the US, according to Richards and Bergin 2005.)

I find it hard to accept that many therapists are still so arrogant in their attitudes to spirituality and religion. For all the rhetoric on training courses about stepping into the client frame of reference and the use of empathy, many secularly minded therapists struggle with having a positive view towards any religious faith, however liberally minded their client's faith might be. In truth, some of the more fundamentalist believers make such prejudices easier to hold and maintain. Nonetheless, I have met some healthy, lovable people of strong religious convictions, many of whom wrestle with their more rigidly minded fellow believers.

So clearly the problem is not sorted, the tensions remain. But merely to focus on the tensions would itself be to do a disservice to the many therapists who are working with a due regard for the part that healthy spirituality can play in the lives of their clients.

## What is spirituality and how does it relate to therapy?

It is important to define what we mean by spirituality and define it in relation to therapy. However, before I do that, I wish to make clear that spirituality is what people say it is, that I have no desire to control or direct our discussions about it. Also for me spirituality is essentially about experiences – some of which are truly beyond words – so to get caught in arcane arguments about what spirituality is, or is not, seems especially unhelpful. The pragmatic philosopher Rorty (1991) urges us to avoid those questions which cannot be answered.

A better discussion could be had about healthy and unhealthy spirituality, though Allman et al. (1992) found that prejudice occurred even among therapists. In their research they presented a vignette or brief case study to full-time practitioners who were members of the American Psychological Association. The case study included material showing that the client had had a mystical experience but also demonstrated some signs of psychological disturbance. Respondents were asked how they would work with such a client. A number of their respondents who favoured mystical experiences ignored the psychological disturbance shown in the vignette, while those less accepting of mysticism focused only on the psychological disturbance. In other words, the practitioners' own view of mysticism was biasing their responses to the client. Practitioners who had themselves had a mystical experience, who valued their own spirituality and who were of a humanistic orientation were more likely to view such experiences as healthy.

With these caveats, I wish to offer the following definition of what spirituality is in a therapeutic context. This view draws a lot on the work of Elkins et al. (1988), whose research emphasized spirituality as something people experience; John Swinton (2001), who affirmed the sense of connectedness that is part of spirituality, including belonging to a faith community; and John Rowan (1993), who clarified the relationship between spirituality and our various levels of the self:

- It is rooted in human experiencing rather than abstract theology.
- It is embodied.
- It involves linking with other people and the universe at large.

- It involves non-ordinary consciousness.
- That active engagement with spirituality tends to make people more altruistic, less materialistic and more environmentally aware.
- It deals with the meaning that people make of their lives.
- It faces suffering and its causes.
- It relates to God/Goddesses/ultimate reality.
- It often uses the word 'soul' or 'higher self'.
- Techniques such as prayer, meditation, contemplation, mindfulness, yoga and Tai Chi are often used as spiritual practices.

The above is likely to resonate with any clients actively exploring their spirituality, likely who may have issues arising from these areas and from residual childhood and adult interactions with organized religion. Many people, including some readers of this book, might think so what, if a few people are concerned about spirituality that is for them. However, this ignores the work of David Hay (Hay and Morisy 1978; Hay and Hunt 2000), who has compiled some impressive evidence to show that a majority of people in Britain and world wide have had some kind of spiritual or religious experience.

In his most recent survey (Hay and Hunt 2000) David Hay reports a cumulative total of 76% of his British respondents experiencing religious or spiritual experience. Although such experiences are often life changing and sometimes very challenging, Hay found that people in Britain are often reluctant to discuss them. This reticence has caused people to assume that British society is more secular than it is. The understating of the British interest in spirituality has been encouraged by the decline in Christian church attendance, especially among white people, but as Davie (1994) made clear, this is a matter of 'believing but not belonging'. That is, people in Britain still have spiritual faith but choose not to express it through organized religion.

I have always been struck by the paradox that we could see the whole of life as sacred, as spiritual; we could also reserve the word 'spiritual' for special moments; or we could do both. So the whole practice of therapy could be seen as spiritual; or again, we could reserve the word 'spiritual' for explicit moments in therapy when spirituality is discussed or the therapeutic encounter itself becomes, or feels, explicitly spiritual.

When questions are raised about how therapist training relates to spirituality, we could view it in the same manner. Namely, it is possible to view training as a spiritual process, even if it is not framed or talked about in that way; or spirituality could be the focus of a particular part of the course; or an experience in therapy or personal development;

or both. Valda Swinton has done some interesting research work into counsellor training in Britain that explores both these aspects.

There are several key elements emerging from Valda's work:

- Spirituality is important for many counsellors in training.
- There is dissatisfaction among some trainees about how spirituality is explicitly addressed, or not, within counsellor training.
- A number of trainees experience their training as spirituality whether this is voiced or not.

Valda concludes:

> Person development and spiritual development could be viewed as one and the same process, it may not be explicitly named as a spiritual process. In the connections and interactions; in the thirst for knowledge of self and others; where there is search for meaning and purpose for one's existence; where there is a struggle to grow and change something profoundly spiritual is taking place. (Swinton, 2007: 19)

## Therapy, culture and spirituality

> Nevertheless, there is no escape from the fact that the activities that we know as counselling and psychotherapy are the indigenous remedies of people in Judaeo-Christian urban industrial societies; therapy is part of Western indigenous psychology. There are many cultures in which therapy as we know it has never taken hold or had only a marginal impact. (McLeod, 1997: 25)

If it is appropriate, and above all useful, to follow John McLeod (quoted above) and consider therapy as an activity between people that occurs within a culture, then some questions clearly arise:

- In what way might therapy be an expression of our culture; and what do we mean by 'our'? At a basic level, this challenge invites us to think about what our culture is. For example mine is British, white, male, middle class by education, heterosexual, politically left of centre, environmentally aware, religious.
- What is the culture of therapy itself and what message does that give to clients, for example acceptance, autonomy, self-actualization? Despite its pre-industrial roots in religious pastoral care, therapy is

generally presented in the West as secular. It also embodies values which are traditionally regarded as female, and most therapists and most clients in Britain are women. It is usually done one to one and client autonomy and empowerment are encouraged.

- How does our would-be client relate to 'our' culture and to the culture of therapy? Most people in the West value their spirituality and believe in God, even if quite a few avoid religious services. Therapists usually operate in a secular framework and are not usually well trained to support clients exploring spiritual issues. (I am well aware, of course, of both the transpersonal therapists and other spiritually and religiously minded therapists, as well as the existence in Britain of groups such as the Association of Christian Counsellors.) Indeed, in my experience significant numbers of therapists have unresolved issues relating to religion.

John McLeod further suggests that we view counselling as a social and cultural process rather than a psychological one:

Counselling represents one of many ways in which cultural norms and values of a society are affirmed, and operates as a means of helping individuals to negotiate their own relationship with these cultural norms. (McLeod 2001: 589)

While I find this definition helpful as a way of reframing counselling, not as a medical or psychological activity but as social one, it does raise some important questions in my mind. First, which culture or society is John referring to when he suggests that counselling affirms the norms and values of a society? Is it the one the client feels they are part of, or the wider dominant culture? Secondly, in our postmodern multicultural society, what are the cultural norms? This is especially true at a time of huge cultural change. Thirdly, how can we support our clients living with cultural and subcultural tensions?

It seems to me there is a state of hopefully creative tension, but sometimes destructive tension, between the various groups and subgroups one belongs to. For example, tensions between extended family and nuclear family, local subculture versus national culture, workplace culture and the wider society, spiritual or religious groups and the wider society. For particular groups at particular times these tensions become extra powerful, for example arranged marriages among ethnic minority groups; gay people and Christianity; young people and adult society.

Research (discussed in Edge and Rogers 2005; Farsimadam et al. 2007) shows us that people from ethnic minority groups in Britain are less likely to access talking therapies and more likely to receive drug treatment and hospitalization for their mental health needs. (As Pittu Laungani pointed out to me in a conversation in 2007, there is never talk of white people being an 'ethnic minority group' in, say, Africa or India. To be an ethnic minority group is to be Other and usually disadvantaged.) When ethnic minority people do get access to counselling, they usually have similar outcomes to white people. Research shows that those who specifically want to be counselled by people from their own ethnic background do have better outcomes than those who are not ethnically matched (Farsimadam et al. 2007).

There is a simple, elegant and empowering solution to this whole question of matching clients and therapists, namely asking the clients what they want. Such an approach is practised by PSS Counselling in Liverpool, which works with asylum seekers. The clients are invited to choose which gender of counsellor they want, which gender and community they wish the interpreter to come from and which language the session will be conducted in. Such an approach fits with the person-centred view of the agency and also models to the asylum seeker that they matter and that what they want is heard and acted on.

However, when we think of matching client and counsellor, we also need to consider class, religion and gender (see discussion in Farsimadan et al. 2007 and Laungani 1999). Indeed, ethnic minority people do not expect white counsellors to be culturally aware and this is an important factor in why such people do not seek counselling (Edge and Rogers 2005). So the solution might seem simple, namely to train more counsellors and psychotherapists from ethnic minority groups.

This is a good idea, but it is not enough. If we truly want more ethnic minority clients, we need to explore what counselling and psychotherapy currently mean to them – rightly or wrongly – and where these might fit in for them. It would be useful also to pose the question: Is it necessarily a good thing for more ethnic minority clients to access therapy? Is therapy as it is currently practised the best that can be offered to all people at all times?

Does one size fit all? Can therapy, which culturally represents white, western, middle-class, educated and arguably female values, be applied to all people on a 'one-size-fits-all' basis? Or can we begin with humility and with what people actually perceive their needs to be, and then figure out would most help that community? The needs of a particular community might be better met if we could recognize the web of professional and 'below-the-radar' support systems that may be currently available to that community. We could explore where the gaps are, how they might be filled and what part, if any, counselling does play, or could play, for that community.

Dawn Edge established that: 'Black Caribbean women [in the UK] are apparently less likely than women from other ethnic groups to be diagnosed or treated for perinatal depression' (Edge 2006: 646). She found that black Caribbean women were more likely than white women to draw on spiritual sources for emotional support. All 12 black Caribbean women in the qualitative part of her study referred to the necessity of drawing on spirituality in adversity, although only three were regular church attenders. They drew on prayer and the Bible, and faith communities were used as potential sources of practical and emotional as well as spiritual support.

> In this study, beliefs that 'counselling' was unlikely to be culturally sensitive and therefore incapable of meeting their needs were also evident... Although women's own sense of agency, and self-efficacy appeared to be effective coping strategies, importance was placed on spirituality both for enhancing a sense of well-being and for receiving practical support... some observers... compare elements in Black church services to group psychotherapy. (Edge and Rogers 2005: 22–23)

I have recently returned from my first visit to India, and while it was only a brief visit to Bangalore, a modern city in southern India, my experiences there had an impact on my view on therapy, spirituality and culture in a very different way to my frequent visits to Kenya. It is useful to bear in mind that I visited India as a white British male attending a professional counselling conference and this obviously influenced what I noticed and how people in India treated me.

The dominant religion in the Indian subcontinent is Hinduism. Hinduism at its best is an inclusive religion. This is helped by it already having so many gods and goddesses, any of which could be called on or prayed to, so the idea of using gods from other traditions is not always seen as such a strange thing to do.

Indeed, Pittu Laungani advises:

> India itself, as you know, is a multicultural country. There are over 40 different languages and over a thousand dialects spoken in India. To this you must add different religious groups: Hindus, Muslims,

Buddhists, Parsis, Sikhs, Ba'hais, Catholics, non-worshippers; and within each group are several denominations, several splinter groups, that it is best to refer to India as a multicultural, multi-faith country, rather than a country with a predominantly Hindu population although statistically that is true. (in West 2004b: 421)

The dominant Indian culture seems to be religious rather than secular. This culture goes back thousands of years and has mostly not been significantly changed by a whole series of invaders, including the British. Even though India has a secular constitution religion still permeates every aspect of life. As Pittu Laungani comments, India is

a paradox of contradictions. Poverty and opulence reside side by side. Health and illness work hand in hand. Science and religion are as inseparable as enjoined identical twins. Appearance is often indistinguishable from reality. (in West 2004b: 421)

This situation may well be changing with globalization, especially within the westernized cities. Nonetheless, even at a counselling conference in Bangalore in 2008, I was struck by how comfortable Indian people were using religious terms. Indeed, a common greeting is saying 'Namaste' while holding one's palms together and bowing. This greeting apparently translates as 'The god in me salutes the god in you'.

It is as if, in India, there is a default position that assumes a religious faith or at least a religious upbringing, whether Hindu, Islam, Christian, Buddhist, Sikh, Jain or some other faith. This seemingly enables Indian therapists to sit comfortably within their own faith. I noticed that this acceptance of religion had the effect on me of drawing that side of my nature more to the fore. I felt less split, less careful than I usually have to be in speaking about my life and faith. Not having to be so careful in what I said, I tended to speak more simply, more directly. It was as if being in India invited me to engage more directly as a spiritual being. I subsequently noticed this ease with one's religious faith among second-generation counsellors whose parents came to England from the Indian subcontinent.

While staying in Bangalore, I was staggered to see cows walking in the main roads in the rush-hour traffic. Since cows are sacred to Hindus, they walk unchallenged and remain unharmed. Indeed, the traffic takes great care to avoid them. At first I thought this was so illogical, so crazy, why not ban cows from such busy roads? But then I thought why not? Why not value the spiritual, the sacred in everyday life, in the traffic and other chaos of that (post)modern Indian city. Pirsig (1974) insisted that the Buddhahood could, and should, be found in a motorbike and Gandhi warned us, 'If you don't find God in the next man that you  meet you won't find him anywhere else.' So why not treat cows – in fact all life – as sacred?

Apart from its impact on my understanding of my own spirituality and issues relating to culture and therapy, my visit to India also caused me to view people in Britain of Indian descent somewhat differently. I could see more clearly the challenges they face living in modern secular Britain while simultaneously drawing on an ancient religious culture.

After my visit to India I used the phrase 'the cow in the room' for a while instead of the in-vogue words 'the elephant in the room' when something, in this case spirituality, was present but not talked about. Religion and spirituality are frequently sidelined in therapists' training programmes in Britain, and race itself is often difficult to discuss. Instead the word 'diversity' is usually used. This has the drawback of encouraging religion to be discussed as something ethnic minority groups do. Consequently, being white and Christian is not often explored, rarely deconstructed. White identity – and white culture as a whole – is also not usually explored, although an excellent book by Ryde (2009) does just that.

Admittedly, there are people like Roy Moodley (see Chapter 9, co-written with Olga Oulanova) who are using the word 'diversity' in a creative way to take us forward from what he regards as the confusion created by the use of 'multiculturalism'. However, I remain troubled by the use of the word 'diversity' if it involves a reluctance to visit racial and religious differences.

It seems apparent that today's therapy trainers were themselves probably trained about 10 or more years ago and will be drawing on their own experience of training, and may not have updated themselves sufficiently through continuing professional development activities since. We know that practitioners mostly do not read research (McLeod 1999) and I suspect the same still largely applies to trainers. I also have some doubt as to how well today's therapists-in-training are being equipped to work with either race or religion. I am aware that I am being rather robust here in my criticism of trainers, and I am myself still actively involved with training therapists, but these matters are too important not to be discussed.

Part of the problem is the fear that surrounds these issues, not helped by the war on terror and the consequent increase in, and almost legitimization of, Islamophobia. What is missing from these approaches to cross-cultural understanding is the possibility of pleasure. When I meet people Other than me there is always the potential for curiosity, for enjoyment. People from different cultures bring the potential to share their food, music, spirituality, clothes, ideas about life and so on. Why miss out on this through fear? I am not denying the downside to such encounters, nor idealizing such meetings. But this question of encountering the Other is a challenge that predates history and has, I believe, a profoundly spiritual and human meaning.

I do not expect the situation with regard to religion and spirituality to change in the West in the near future, though there may perhaps be the birth of a new mass religion some time this century. I am of the opinion that Christianity in its current form may not thrive in the West, despite people's undiminished spiritual and religious needs. I can say this while still acknowledging the good work done by many people in the Christian churches.

It does cause me to reflect that I work among people most of whom by and large do not value their spirituality; or if they do, they do not talk about it. Sometimes it feels like I am part of a misunderstood, marginalized group. This is a good learning experience for me, reminding me of what it feels like to be part of a minority group, including being feared in some quarters. I know that there is a fear of religious evangelism or attempts at conversion, but I am more aware of conversions to therapeutic theories happening around me than to religious beliefs. Indeed, I see therapy in many ways as meeting some of the same needs as a religion: something to believe in, something to belong to, something that explains human problems and how to deal with them.

## Evangelism in religion and therapy

The whole question of belonging to either a religious group or a therapy school can be problematic. I am deliberately linking both together because a rigid attitude of evangelism, of a need to spread the good word and involve other people in one's group, can apply to both. The process of training as a therapist can be seen as akin to a religious conversion process. Indeed, Halmos (1965) coined the phrase 'the faith of the counsellors' and wrote of the coming of the counsellors, capturing the mood of the early spread of counselling in the US.

In comparing religious evangelism with its therapy counterpart, I am not writing this to be offensive, but more to point out that the humanness of the power of belonging to a group seems to have the answers to life's difficulties. Remember that Carl Rogers (1980) wrote a book entitled *A Way of Being*. So the person-centred approach was then no longer a useful form of therapy but could be applied to education in the form of student-centred learning; applied to group and racial conflicts; indeed was a way of being.

Doubt in evangelical groups is often dealt with by seeking to win others over. And of course the 'other' group – other Christian and religious groups, other therapy groups – is the one with all the faults. It is all too easy to denounce evangelical Christians as rigid and fundamental, but being non-religious does not mean that therapists cannot be equally rigid or fundamentalist.

Recently Jacqui Moulton did Master's research in Britain into the experience of some Christians made unemployed by their church. She described the experience of one young woman who she refers to as Carol:

> Carol... initially started working as a receptionist in a hospital. At the outset Carol found her job difficult, because in the ministry her main source of contact with non Christians was through evangelism – meeting people for the purposes of them coming to church and becoming Christians. She had to learn 'how to be in the normal world, the real world, the world outside church'. Although this was a challenge at first, Carol says she loved her job and enjoyed being around people. Her job also changed her perception of non Christians, that they were 'actually not that bad', in fact that there were great people who did not necessarily believe in God or go to church. (Moulton, 2007: 43)

I am especially struck by Carol's realization that non Christians were actually not that bad; in fact there were great people who lacked religious faith! So it is possible for a Christian living in Britain in the twenty-first century to have this attitude, to be so cut off from mainstream society, to believe that only those of one's own faith are any good. Such a sheltered life is of course possible within the counselling subculture.

When I reflect on the 400+ forms of therapy that have been developed (Karasu 1986), on the tensions for example between Californian and Chicagoan person-centred therapists, on the ongoing tensions between the various Christian groups, or on the tensions among various political groups, I see human beings not doing group dynamics very well. I see therapists unable to model healthy group relating. We can all be like Carol and see non-Christians or practitioners of other therapies to our own as bad or evil.

## Some promising developments

However, it would be wrong to focus merely on the challenges and diffi-culties faced by those of us who feel that working with clients and their spirituality in therapy and the resulting healing that occurs is of great import. Most, if not all, chapters in this book underline the value and importance of such spiritually informed work. I wish here to highlight these and other relevant developments.

One of the most curious and interesting developments in the western world over the past 40 or 50 years has been the huge increase in yoga, meditation, mindfulness, Tai Chi and other physical health-promoting practices drawn from eastern religions. It is striking that most of these classes are taught outside of a religious context and sometimes even devoid of any spirituality.

The popularity and widespread usage of such approaches have inevi-tably led to exploration of their use within a psychotherapy context. Gilbert speaks of how 'efforts to integrate Eastern psychologies and mind training practices with Western forms of psychotherapy have also advanced greatly in the past few decades' (2005: 3). In more recent times the use of prayer and religious imagery drawn from Christianity, Judaism and Islam has also been considered (see Propst et al. (2002) as a particularly good example, discussed in Chapter 12). Richards and Bergin (2005) provide a very wide-ranging and informative summary of spiritual interventions in therapy, albeit from a theistic perspective, which is explored further by Chris Jenkins in Chapter 2. Peter Gubi's Chapter 4 on prayer also provides us with a useful example of the use of prayer within counselling.

Apart from the application of techniques derived from religious traditions, I am interested in the use of notions such as compassion, which I feel bridges the secular and the spiritual. I will not repeat here the fascinating material on compassion and psychotherapy covered in Barbara Vivino and Barbara Thompson's Chapter 5. However, in my own therapeutic practice I have on occasion invited clients to reflect compassionately on themselves. This has usually proved to be most useful and sometimes profoundly moving, particularly with those who care so passionately about others but somehow leave themselves out of such care. It is as if such people are not doing to themselves what they are doing for others.

Another powerful form of spiritual intervention is the use of forgive-ness (Worthington 1998; West 2001a; Richards and Bergin 2005). I have been struck in my own clinical practice how frequently Christian clients need to experience self-forgiveness. They can find forgiveness of others a challenge, although they mostly see it as a religious duty, but for some reason self-forgiveness is ignored.

I regard the increasing willingness within psychotherapy and counselling to use these spiritually derived techniques as a most hopeful sign. I would be even happier if such practice was more linked, where appropriate, to the client's own spiritual or religious worldview. However, the very application of such techniques is encouraging.

It does seem as if the tide in the therapy world may be turning towards a greater acceptance of the client's spirituality and its role in successful therapeutic practice. Perhaps Freud's legacy to psychotherapy of a distrust of religion is waning. Certainly, the impact of a multicultural approach which inevitably respects religious beliefs has been helpful, as has the pioneering work by some brave souls willing to practise, write and research around these matters.

## Conclusion

In this chapter I have sought to open up some questions and challenges in relation to spirituality and therapy. In the next six chapters the authors will share their research and practice experiences relating to aspects of spirituality and therapy. The aim of this chapter, indeed of the whole book, is not to produce a new orthodoxy about therapy and spirituality. My intention has been to offer some information, some thoughts and some pointers in the hope of stimulating a creative response in the mind, body and spirit of the reader.

### Discussion points

1. What would you find most challenging from a spiritual or religiously minded client and how would you work with that issue?
2. If the West can now be seen as 'post-Christian', what does that mean to you?
3. What are your own beliefs, if any, about religion and spirituality and what challenges arise for you as a practitioner?

# 2
# When Clients' Spirituality Is Denied in Therapy

*Chris Jenkins*

## Introduction

This chapter describes a research process (Jenkins 2006) that focused precisely on the experience of clients who had found their spirituality either excluded from therapy or pathologized within it. It begins with a brief discussion of the context of the research, followed by the findings from the research, then implications for practice and a model for integration of spirituality into therapy.

The aim of this research was not to see how often such exclusion or pathologizing happened, but to seek a fuller understanding of what it was like for clients when it did happen. This question, originally stirred up in me by the experiences of my own clients, became a long journey.

## Background

In the enormous expansion of writing on spirituality and therapy in the last decade, both in the US and the UK (see the surveys in Sperry 2001; Sperry and Shafranske 2005; West 2004a), there remains a dearth of writing and research into clients' experience. While this is true of therapy more generally, it is strikingly true in the area of spirituality; Knox et al. (2005) surveys the few studies available.

A qualitative methodology, primarily heuristic, was used in the research being discussed and 16 extended interviews, plus many other encounters and a thorough review of other studies, helped open up this experience. The names of all participants have been removed, along with some other identifying details, to protect their confidentiality. Participants included Christians, Muslims and those who described themselves as spiritual but not religious; most were from the UK but two were from the US and one from Canada.

At the outset I want to let you hear just a couple of the experiences participants shared with me and I invite you to engage your imagination, to enter empathically into their experience:

> Imagine being in a psychiatric unit, so ill and confused you aren't even sure of the year. Imagine, as the confusion begins to subside, having one source of clarity, an awareness of divine care and love. Imagine meeting your therapist and mentioning this and seeing her reaction, noticing your medication has been increased... and is increased whenever you talk about your spiritual awareness. Then being in a therapy group when another patient names their sense of God, the group shutting them up and hearing, at the break, the patient being told: 'Don't talk about that stuff in here, you'll never get out...' Slowly you are learning to play the game, to leave a vital spark of yourself outside the therapy room door.

> Imagine being a bright young PhD student, overwhelmed with work and then overwhelmed in a relationship that went wrong; having a termination under pressure from all sides and feeling dreadful afterwards, only your practice of meditation providing a peaceful space to be in. You seek help from an experienced therapist, feeling at once a sense of safety and relief, then you are told to stop meditation because it would open you to psychosis, that your abortion was 'like having a tooth out' and not to go on about it... Increasingly you drink to numb the pain and, aware of your family history of alcoholism, bring this to therapy only to have your concern dismissed... why stay with such a therapist? Recognise the fear of losing the support there was...

## Clients' experiences of self-censorship and self-disclosure

Precisely because spirituality is at the heart of how people understand themselves in the world, an attack on someone's spirituality or its denial is an attack on the heart of the person, on their integrity, their wholeness. To refuse to take someone's spirituality seriously is to refuse to take them seriously. To seek to convince someone that precisely what helps them hold themselves together is 'immature', 'psychotic', in need of medicating away or has no place in their healing is to do great violence. As we continue to explore the key themes raised by the research, we need to keep that context in view.

The dyad 'Playing their game and not being myself' seems to focus a good deal of what the participants shared. In both psychiatric settings and in private practice, these men and women found that what was happening was 'not about me' but about the prejudices and beliefs of their therapists, and that they needed to split themselves into what was and was not acceptable to their therapists, which developed or deepened patterns of self-censorship. Some continued in 'therapeutic relationships', which were no longer therapeutic but, at least partly, 'abusive'. Others walked away and either did, or didn't, eventually find help elsewhere.

For me, part of the strength of the image of 'playing the game' is that it seems so innocent. Yet, as Eric Berne emphasized (Berne 1968), games can be sinister as well. When I first heard participants say 'I just learnt to play the game' I felt a shiver down my spine. Here was therapy splitting people, or at least deepening splits in them. In both the hospital and the private counselling room, the message had been received that part of them was unacceptable and needed to be hidden, or left 'outside the door'. In different words and with more or less subtlety, this experience was echoed again and again. To take just two examples:

> I always felt ashamed like I couldn't really talk about it, and I think too, when somebody's in a powerful position and looks down on or in some way censors you, you don't really, at least I don't often question, if it's something that means a lot to me and I think they could somehow damage it, take it away from me, I don't know, sanction me or whatever, you know you just don't, they're not the kind of things I would confront people on.

> I didn't feel very sure of myself. I felt very vulnerable and very low and that is the tragedy. I felt, well he is probably right, so I won't say anything; I'll try to play the game.

Sometimes the imposition of the therapist's viewpoint led to the client walking away and yet, again and again, the participants described struggling on, splitting themselves so as to be acceptable. Often they talked about vulnerability, or being young, inexperienced, not knowing better. As the PhD student we have already met said, 'I thought she was probably right.' Also, particularly highlighted by her but also echoed by others is the issue of not wanting to let go of the positive benefits of the therapy: 'She was helping me in many ways.' Many of them, from where they are now, wonder why they ever tolerated their therapist's behaviour. I heard many variations on 'If it happened now I would just walk away'. But young, vulnerable or uncertain clients are scarcely rare and that only deepens the responsibility of therapists to 'handle with care'.

Another aspect of 'playing the game' is self-censorship, even sometimes when the therapist *is* explicitly open to issues of spirituality in therapy. Participants linked this with broader cultural messages, or messages received in training or more personal factors. In terms of cultural messages one participant said:

> In certain circles... religion and spirituality don't come into it. You know it's just not talked about or addressed,... it embarrasses people, people don't like to talk about things like that, and certainly psychotherapy fits into that milieu... where I come from if you say that you're a Catholic it's the same as saying you're stupid.

Another echoes this:

> Some people if I said very much about it they would think 'Oh you know she's been born again, she's going to try and convert people', so there were loads of people who even though they were quite close friends, I just never discussed that very important area of my life with.

Remarkably, one of the most striking examples of self-censorship occurred almost in spite of training. One of the participants had been on a training course about 'Therapy and Spirituality' and later went to the trainer for therapy. However, he withheld from the therapy powerful spiritual experiences he was having at the time. This was despite not only the training but also many other positive messages about spirituality from his therapist's home setting, his demeanour – 'a prayerful attitude' – and what he knew of the therapist's spiritual background. He described his reasons for withholding as 'multi-layered' and talked about concern that his spiritual experiences weren't 'the right kind of spirituality', and about the influence of his training. It was only when he reviewed the analysis of his interview that he went further and named a fear that these precious experiences of a 'beautiful all-encompassing sense of love and light and forgiveness' might be 'analysed and explained away' *even by such a therapist.*

At the same time, some of the participants had positive experiences with other therapists. For one, a growing understanding of what went wrong in her first therapy has been greatly helped by other therapeutic experiences, especially that with her current therapist. Whereas with her first therapist she often felt the agenda was not hers, now the therapy is 'all about me':

> She's real and I've never had such an intimate emotional encounter with a therapist, as I'm having with her. It's deeply challenging because what she's doing is helping me get underneath my intellectual defences... and encouraging me to go into my heart so it's the antithesis of what happened in the past and what's happening is this tremendous... accelerated process of healing around very very deep stuff... it's painful but I feel very held and supported by her... it's all about me... she's there completely for me, a bit like God is really, or how I feel God is... because of her deep acceptance of me... I feel more and more confident and able to be myself... she's not out to pathologise or analyse things... it's about what this means... what does it mean for you... nothing is split away, nothing at all, she encourages me to bring everything into the room with me.

Another participant also had a very positive experience where her therapist worked with her spiritual journey. In response to my question: 'Do you think the counsellor realized that was what you were doing, exploring spiritual issues?' she answered:

> Yes I think she did. I don't, I mean she never told me what her beliefs were but she was very supportive in terms of talking about these issues, I mean for instance I got a sort of thing at one point, and I connected it to wanting to move from the place where I live to somewhere else and I kept talking about how I have this vision of myself somewhere where it was very light and I had this real thing about being somewhere where there was pure light and also I think about wanting everything to be very simple not to be cluttered with lots and lots of possessions and stuff which may not be obvious from this flat but anyway I do have that thing. And I kept thinking it had to do with where I was going to live but as I explored it with her I think she was very helpful in actually assisting me to come to the realization that I was looking for some kind of light or enlightenment or whatever but actually it wasn't really to do with where I lived, it was to do with a personal view of the world.

Most fundamentally, her counsellor did not echo the reaction of many of her contemporaries to talk about faith and 'freak':

> When I was with the counsellor, when I started saying things like that, she didn't respond, she didn't freak when I said that, and that was really positive because it meant I was able to explore those sorts of issues.

Perhaps that is the strongest contrast with so many of the other participants' experiences. Their therapists did, in one way or another, 'freak', with the consequences we have seen. And what this participant's therapist offered her was simply good therapy. She didn't play the spiritual guru or try to convert her to her view, but allowed her space and time to explore as she needed to without imposing her agenda.

## Implications for practice

Some clear implications for practice emerge, both from this research and from a broader review of the literature (Jenkins 2006). The major implication is that therapists need to be aware of how easily their own stance with regard to religion and spirituality can be imposed on clients, especially those who are particularly vulnerable. This highlights the need for therapists to have explored their own possible countertransference or prejudicial reactions to religious or spiritual issues (Lannert 1991; Wyatt 2002) so as to be freer to work with the client's understanding of these issues. Otherwise, the imposition of the therapist's understanding can lead to the premature termination of counselling or, perhaps more damaging still, to counselling continuing but with the client playing the therapist's game and pretending to go along with them. Such game playing undermines the therapeutic relationship and can leave clients feeling 'split' and 'abused'. This danger is heightened even more in settings where therapists have power over their clients, which can be enforced by medication or sectioning under the Mental Health Acts. In such situations they truly have their clients' lives in their hands.

This research, in line with that of Swinton (2001, 2005) and Macmin and Foskett (2004), argues that a focus on the meaning that beliefs have for the client, on their understanding, not only of spirituality but of their life and, if this word is appropriate, their illness, is not only ethically appropriate but also therapeutically effective. Working with clients' deepest beliefs enhances healing (cf. Propst et al. 2002).

Therapists also need to be aware that clients are likely to be nervous about sharing their spiritual understanding (Hay and Hunt 2000), fearing that it will be judged, analysed away or even diagnosed as illness. This may have been heightened by the experiences of friends or by the client's own experiences with previous counsellors. Because of this, counsellors need to pay close attention to the messages they give, both explicitly and implicitly, about these issues. What do we communicate to new clients? Do we give any messages about spirituality at all; or at least any we are aware of? Because, as we have seen, to keep silent is not to be neutral, it does give a message.

There are differing views about including religious/spiritual questions in assessment. Richards and Bergin (2005) argue for this precisely as a way of normalizing these issues. Knox et al. (2005) expressed caution about this, given their finding that if the therapist introduced spiritual issues the clients were less likely to feel they were appropriate. On the basis of this research, I would argue that if we are going to conduct an assessment at all, there should at least be a question about a person's beliefs, even something as simple as: 'Is there anything that helps you find meaning in life?' Counsellors who take more detailed histories would need to be equally detailed in exploring religious/spiritual background and beliefs. Of course, any such assessment process to a degree introduces issues into the therapy that the client has not explicitly brought. However, if the assessment is done in such a way as to clearly be exploring the client's understanding it could be more permissive – opening up areas that are okay to explore – rather than restrictive.

There are many approaches to the issue of assessment and how to approach first sessions with clients. My argument here is that to ask about many other things, such as family history, physical health, past therapeutic experience and presenting concerns, and then not to ask about spirituality/meaning is likely to be heard as saying, however unintentionally, 'we don't talk about that here'. The meaning question does not seek to determine the shape of the therapy. It does open up the therapeutic space to spiritual issues and suggest that such issues will be handled respectfully.

Messages about the acceptability of spirituality will not only be given verbally. I can remember as a nervous diploma student writing an essay about how I would set up my counselling room and what messages would, hopefully, be conveyed by things like the position of chairs. In ten years of counselling practice, in five different spaces, I have only once been able to set up a room exactly as I wanted it. And sometimes our cherished and carefully placed symbols are not even noticed by clients, or certainly not consciously. However other clients, and perhaps especially someone who has had a powerful negative experience, will be looking for signs of our views. If books are on display, what kind of books are they? What sort of art, if any, is there? Does our appearance convey a message about spirituality (a cross around the neck, or a talisman, a piece of crystal and so on)? Not to mention things we cannot do much about but which clients may interpret, such as our ethnicity, our name or our accent. (Imagine the assumptions that might be made about the spiritual views of a therapist with a Northern Ireland accent whose name was Paisley.) At the least I think counsellors can aim not to give clearly misleading messages.

Of course, we also need to be careful that our symbols do not feel like impositions on our clients. Having an open Bible on display (Richards and Bergin 2005) or even a copy of the Qur'an (Nielsen 2004) might be okay for some clients but highly difficult for others, evoking all kinds of memories and issues. Richards and Bergin (2005) urge great caution in displaying books and symbols so as to not to alienate clients who come from different standpoints. Similarly, having a candle available that clients can choose to light – if they find it a help to focusing or appropriate to their spiritual sense – is different from them walking into a room with an already lit candle. Surely the real issues are about congruence, appropriateness and choice.

Now I want to address the question of handling spiritual expressions by clients. It is worth restating at this point that these considerations do not necessarily exclude therapists who are atheist, agnostic or committed rationalists. If such therapists are willing, as those in the study by Propst et al. (2002), to work with the client's understanding whatever their own views, there is no reason for them not to work very effectively with their client's spirituality. Indeed, their lack of assumptions may, as Propst et al. (2002) noted, make them *more* effective than counsellors who are fellow believers. Of course, there will be counsellors who, from their own firm convictions, feel unable to work with these issues. Brian Thorne noted two reasons for such 'non-engagement':

> The therapist can reject the reality of spirituality and see so-called spiritual phenomena as ultimately explicable in psychological terms and therefore not requiring an alternative framework for their conceptualisation. A second position is to acknowledge the validity of spiritual experience but to exclude it from the therapeutic arena on the grounds that counsellors and therapists are not equipped to respond to it and have more pragmatic behavioural, cognitive and affective objectives to achieve. (1997: 11–12)

Thorne judged both of these positions to be ethical. We will take each of them separately. A therapist who 'reject(s) the reality of spirituality' and sees spiritual issues as being reducible to psychological interpretation would, I hope, be able to take on board the results of this study and other studies of clients' views. We have seen that it is precisely this 'explaining away' of their spiritual experience and beliefs that clients fear and reject (Ankrah 2002; Nicholls et al. 2002; Knox et al. 2005). And given the client's right to appropriate self-determination and non-discrimination on the grounds of beliefs (cf. BACP Ethics Code 2002; APA Ethics Code 2003), it is not ethical for therapists to impose their views in some desire to 'free... clients from the fantasy of God' (Stokes 2006). What would be ethical, I would argue, is for such therapists to be clear with clients about their views and, if they could not work from the client's perspective, to refer. Otherwise they are, in fact, working beyond their competence (BACP 2001; APA 2003) and at risk of working abusively.

It should also be noted that these cautions do not only apply to those who reject spirituality completely. It is just as damaging to use our locus of evaluation as the criterion for what is good or bad spirituality and to impose that view on clients. Here again, if we are clearer where we stand we are more likely, as Wyatt (2002) argues, to be able to let our clients stand where they stand and to truly listen to them.

What about the second group that Thorne identified, those who accepted spirituality as valid but refused to work with it in therapy because of a lack of skill or because there were other 'more pragmatic behavioural, cognitive and affective objectives to achieve' (Thorne 1997: 12)? Thorne also regards this position as being ethical. However, I would want to qualify that acceptance. According to most of the participants in this study, what clients need from us is not for us to be highly specialized spiritual experts. They need us to be good counsellors. To listen carefully, not to judge, to work with and build on their understandings, not impose our own.

Counsellors work constantly with people whose culture, sexuality, ethnicity, social class and so on are different to our own. We are often not experts; nor do we need to be. There may come a stage when a client feels the need to seek more expert guidance for their spiritual journey. However, as we saw with one of the participants above, her non-expert counsellor had very fruitfully helped her explore what she needed in spiritual terms for over a year before she reached the point of moving on. Her counsellor's openness to where she was and gentle exploration of her understanding (for example what a 'house filled with light' would mean for her) were precisely what she needed. This is not to say that there is no room for training (see further below), but this is the kind of training that therapists do around many issues they encounter – from suicide to eating disorders – to deepen their awareness and develop their competence to practice. It is not that only experts dare venture onto this territory.

Similarly with there being other 'objectives to achieve' (Thorne 1997). Who decides which objectives are important? One participant's words about her therapist – 'we spent a lot of time on what she considered important' – stand as a warning. If the client needs to work with their spiritual understanding, who are we to say it isn't a priority? If a therapist truly believes they are beyond their competence or that they cannot go where the client's priorities lie then, ethically, they need to seek referral (cf. BACP 2002; APA 2003). It is not ethical to say 'This is therapy, not spiritual direction so we won't look at those issues' or, more subtly but equally destructively, always to psychologize spirituality as, for example, one of Wyatt's participants did:

> I always just tried, not to keep off the subject, but to relate... always to bring it back to me and him, or his (feelings). How did he *feel* about the vicar... who does that remind him of? ... What would it have been like if your father had been that sort of role [i.e. as the vicar]? (2002: 180–81)

I wonder if her client thought that she wasn't trying to keep off the subject!

Of course, this critique can also be applied to those who work with spirituality and neglect the psychological. As Clarkson notes, both therapists and spiritual directors need to 'Learn to differentiate between the psychologization of spiritual hunger and the spiritualization of psychological problems' (Clarkson 2002: 39). And, I would add, while such discernment does require training, it also requires an openness to recognize that some issues are spiritual and some are psychological. The danger comes when we don't follow the client's need but apply the skills we feel competent in come what may: 'When you have a hammer in your hand everything around you starts to look like a nail' (Pargament et al. 2005: 162).

If therapists are ready to work with clients' spiritual issues if they arise in therapy, what further issues need to be looked at? Some points emerged clearly from this research:

- The need to avoid simply confusing spiritual beliefs – especially those that strike us as 'way out' – with unreality, especially when clients evidently are confused to a greater or lesser degree.
- The importance of exploring the role spiritual beliefs play in the client's life rather than assuming what that role would be.

- The importance of recognizing that certain spiritual practices, while they may raise concerns, may also be of great importance for the client (e.g. the PhD student and meditation) and that the counsellor may need to seek appropriate supervision or consultation in order to understand them more fully rather than just saying 'Stop doing that'.
- The need not to impose a spiritual practice on a client without their consent and understanding, e.g. meditation or prayer.
- If a client uses spiritual symbols or scriptural imagery, to treat them with great respect and care.
- To avoid in any way expressing judgements on a spiritual choice clients make (e.g. conversion).
- To be aware of client deference (Rennie 1994a), especially when working with vulnerable people, and to be appropriately cautious about expressing views which clients may feel they need to, or at least seem to, accept, leading to game playing.
- To be sensitive to signs of client self-censorship around these issues.
- To be ready to acknowledge that, while we may not share clients' beliefs, this does not mean that we cannot accompany clients in working with those beliefs without, vitally, putting on a pretence.

It should be noted that none of the above require specialized knowledge, though they do require the openness to seek others' expertise if we need it. What they do require is a willingness to work with the client's beliefs and 'what it means' for them (cf. Swinton 2001, 2005).

We will now turn briefly to two other areas of practice: the use of specific spiritual interventions (Richards and Bergin 2005) and therapist spiritual intuition (West 2004a).

## Using specific spiritual interventions

In *A Spiritual Strategy for Counselling and Psychotherapy*, published by the American Psychological Association, (1997, 2005 2nd edn), Richards and Bergin offer an extensive review of the use of 'religious and spiritual practices as therapeutic interventions' and the ways in which they are applied by contemporary therapists. Their work is of great value because it not only raises questions about whether and when such interventions are appropriate, but also looks at the available research on how effective they can be. Among the interventions they review are:

- Praying for clients
- Encouraging clients to pray

- Discussing theological concepts
- Making reference to scriptures
- Using spiritual relaxation and imagery techniques
- Encouraging repentance and forgiveness
- Helping clients live congruently with their spiritual values
- Self-disclosing spiritual beliefs or experiences
- Consulting with religious leaders
- Using religious bibliotherapy (Richards and Bergin 2005: 251ff)

Both from this research and from the literature reviewed, some comments can be made about using such interventions in practice. The clearest issue arising from this research is the need for the client's voice to be heard in considering using such interventions and for them to fit with the client's understanding, to be part of a 'congruent narrative' (Frank and Frank 1993) for them. One participant's first counsellor used the intervention of prayer. More specifically, she prayed for her to be delivered from the evil that was gripping her. Whatever the counsellor's understanding of this intervention, it was lost on her client:

> I said I remember playing with a Ouija board once, so she said 'I'm going to have to do a deliverance prayer on you, it sounds as if you've let Satan in'. She went on about Satan and all that, which I did not understand. I thought well I'll go along with all this... (but) I didn't feel as if I was getting anywhere, I think that put up a barrier for me.

She 'did not understand' what was being done to her. She went along with it but felt she got nowhere and that 'put up a barrier'. This fits into the research about deference (Rennie 1994a) which we looked at specifically above. She wanted to get help and so, even though she didn't understand what the counsellor was talking about, went along with her. However, when she didn't feel helped this created a barrier. Instead of the spiritual practice being done with Julia's involvement, it was imposed on her. Again, this issue is not limited to specifically spiritual interventions.

There are many therapeutic techniques that can be done to clients without their having been given the opportunity to really understand and consent to them. I am aware of times I have done the very same thing with clients, neglecting to check that my brilliant idea actually made any kind of sense to them. However, spiritual interventions may demand greater caution precisely because they enter into the sacred space of someone's deepest beliefs. To say to a client that they need to be delivered from Satan is on a different level to saying that, for example, they might want to let go of seeing themselves as lazy. Especially for someone for whom the language of possession by Satan was deeply engrained in their belief system, such a statement could be profoundly harmful.

Richards and Bergin (2005) propose a number of criteria for assessing the appropriateness of spiritual interventions with particular clients. In particular, they note four criteria that would exclude such interventions:

- Clients who have made it clear they do not want to participate in such interventions
- Clients who are delusional or psychotic
- Clients for whom spiritual issues are clearly not relevant to presenting problems
- Clients who are minors whose parents have not given permission to... use spiritual interventions (Richards and Bergin 2005: 209)

The first criterion is particularly relevant to the case above. This participant had asked to see a counsellor who was a Christian. For her this was about having something in common ('well I go to church'). However, her counsellor may well have understood this choice as opening the way for prayer in their work. Certainly the client had not 'made it clear she did not want to participate in such interventions' (Richards and Bergin 2005: 209). Of course, she had no reason to as she had no warning that such interventions might be part of her counselling. So she slips through the broad criteria that Richards and Bergin propose. She would also pass their criterion that such interventions are 'more effective... with less disturbed clients' (loc. cit.). She was seeking help because of her distress, but was also coping with her day-to-day life.

The point where her counsellor went wrong, according to the criteria put forward by Richards and Bergin (2005), was her failure to 'work within clients' value framework and be careful not to push spiritual beliefs... on clients' (Richards and Bergin 2005: 214). Although she had told her client what she was going to do and at least obtained tacit consent (it is not clear whether she explicitly consented or if her 'going along with' her counsellor was tacit), she had pushed onto her the belief that she was in need of deliverance. This was not the client's understanding.

I would argue that this is the fundamental point for good practice in this area. As counsellors we need to be aware of our power and to be very careful not to impose our understandings or to override the client's understandings. If we do, even if our clients seem to consent and 'go along with' our proposals, we risk losing contact with them and, at the least, creating a barrier. In order to avoid this, therapists need to keep clearly in mind the guiding principles that Richards and Bergin set out:

- Deep respect for clients' autonomy and freedom
- Sensitivity to and empathy for clients' religious and spiritual beliefs
- Flexibility and responsiveness to clients' values and needs (Richards and Bergin 2005: 214)

Used cautiously and within the principles they have set out, Richards and Bergin argue powerfully that such interventions can be highly appropriate and effective.

### The role of spiritual intuition on the part of the therapist

West (2004a) places considerable emphasis on the spiritual awareness of counsellors and has raised the question of whether working with such awareness moves beyond what can be called 'counselling'. This question may best be illustrated by an example further explored in Christa Gorsedene's Chapter 10 in this book. A counsellor, Peggy, believes that she is accompanied by a spirit guide, who sometimes makes suggestions to her during therapy sessions. What is she to do with these suggestions? Share them with the client? Keep them to herself? Explore them in supervision as countertransference? (Which she may have to if she can't find a supervisor prepared to work with her belief in spirit guides.)

A number of elements need to come to bear here:

- The fundamental focus on the needs of the client
- Whether such sharing would fit with the client's beliefs (culturally congruent narrative; Frank and Frank 1993) and could be heard by the client in a helpful way
- The nature of the suggestion (is it beneficial to the client, is the client's autonomy respected?)

It should be noted that similar issues are raised by a Christian counsellor who believes they receive 'words from the Lord' during counselling and that the very language of 'spirit guide or 'words from The Lord' probably makes it very hard to really hold an autonomous and free space for the client.

Broadly, we can say that the focus on the clients' beliefs and the research that indicates clients' discomfort with counsellors introducing spiritual issues into therapy (e.g. Knox et al. 2005) would argue for great caution in sharing such an insight with a client. On the other hand, if the client's beliefs clearly included the possibility of spirit guides (or words from the Lord) and the specific message was likely to be helpful, there could be cases when to withhold it would be unethical. And, of course, if the counsellor is withholding a vital part of themselves and their beliefs, this too could lead to an inauthentic therapeutic relationship. As so often with ethical considerations, we are not dealing with simple, clear-cut criteria but a process of responsible reflection (BACP 2002; APA 2003).

West (2004a: 80ff) writes about the 'explicitly spiritual experiences' in his therapeutic work with a client he calls Matthew. He notes feeling that this experience – for example being on the edge of going so deep as to lose ordinary consciousness – was 'risky but very important' (West 2004a: 84). For him, disclosing his spiritual beliefs and experiences was 'an important aspect of trust building, especially in the early stages of our work' (ibid.: 88). It should be noted here that West's openness to working with spirituality was known to Matthew and, indeed, that Matthew saw his therapy as at least potentially spiritual: 'I did not go to seek the realisation of God through psychotherapy – but I was not willing to deny the presence of the transcendent should it have occurred' (ibid.: 85).

Matthew had also spoken early in their work together about his sense of 'being afraid of the spiritual intimacy' in their sessions. West explored this with him, not just in terms of its content (silences, synchronous words and images arising, feelings of interconnectedness) but also what it meant in and for the therapeutic relationship. In this case spiritual openness seems to have facilitated Matthew's own growth, especially in terms of forgiving both others and himself (ibid.: 85).

It seems to me that the context here made it okay for West to self-disclose as he did and helped that to be helpful for Matthew. In another situation, to tell a client you were entering such a deep place you were losing ordinary consciousness would clearly not be helpful, especially if, for example, the client was very vulnerable and needed a sense that you were anchoring them in here-and-now reality. However, when clearly negotiated, checked out with the client and congruent with the client's beliefs, such disclosure can be helpful. But, to return to the question West (2004a) raised, is it counselling? Has such work not moved over into areas more properly labelled as spiritual healing or spiritual direction? For the moment it may well be too soon to settle these questions. A debate needs to go on, as West notes, about:

> What the limits of counselling are, who sets them and why, and how some of the growth points happen at edges or boundaries where courageous counsellors creatively draw on what is available to them to help their clients move on. (Jenkins and West 2006: 199)

## A model for integration

Having looked at some of the implications for practice arising from the research, I want to propose a model that therapists could use to integrate working with clients' spirituality, including specific interventions and spiritual insight, into their practice.

I would propose using Clarkson's (1995) model of the five facets of the therapeutic relationship to provide the broad framework we require. One of the particular strengths of her model is the incorporation of the transpersonal as a normal element within the therapeutic frame. Clarkson's model is open to practitioners of almost any counselling school (unless they are determined to be purist; see Clarkson 1998; Hollanders 2000a, 2000b describes the increasing movement towards integration/ eclecticism and the issues it raises) and focuses on the therapeutic relationship, which is increasingly recognized as the most vital single therapeutic factor (see the review in Horvath 2005, and also Hentschel 2005).

Using Clarkson's model to facilitate a spiritually inclusive therapy does not only mean a focus on the transpersonal facet of the relationship. Spirituality will enter into every facet. To illustrate this, we will take each of the five facets and raise a few possible questions and areas of reflection. However, it should be noted that Clarkson does not propose each facet as an entirely separate entity. The reality of the therapeutic relationship will often display overlap and interplay between the various elements. The strength of the model is the possibility it offers for clarity in reflection, without a corresponding rigidity in practice.

1. Within the working alliance issues could include:
   - Whether to include openness to spirituality within the issues raised in the contract and or first meeting, including any assessment process – and what a decision not to include spirituality/ faith/meaning questions would convey
   - Boundary issues around possible spiritual interventions, such as prayer, rituals, guided meditation

- Possible dual-relationship issues, for example if a therapist also ran courses or retreats, or was a religious minister (a recent professional conduct case heard by BACP focused on just these issues: *CPJ* October 2003, *Therapy Today* February 2006)

2. The transference/countertransference relationship might include:
   - Clients' relating to counsellors as quasi-religious authority figures
   - Clients' possible transferences onto God, making God in their own image, God representation issues, cf. Jung 1964
   - Therapists' reactions to clients' spiritual/religious views, cf. Lannert 1991; Wyatt 2002, including therapist's own unresolved issues around religion and spirituality

3. The reparative/developmentally needed facet of the relationship might raise:
   - Clients' woundedness from their religious upbringing (though, crucially, not the assumption that anyone who had a religious upbringing would be wounded by it). This might include revisiting key texts, for example of scripture, and letting them speak afresh (e.g. someone who had had the fear of God beaten into them might need to sit with a text like 'I love you with an everlasting love', Jeremiah 31:3; Wansbrough 1985)
   - Spiritual development needs and possible ways for deepening spiritual practice
   - The potential for counsellors to be called on to be a reliable loving presence, such as to make it possible to believe in, and choose to accept or reject, the gift of divine love (standing in loco dei) where any kind of reliable and consistent love has been absent in someone's life history

4. The person-to-person relationship might well involve:
   - Counsellors' congruence with regard to their own faith and struggles with faith and, *where appropriate*, a degree of self-disclosure (remembering Hay and Hunt's 2000 finding that self-disclosure could give respondents permission to risk sharing their own spiritual experiences)
   - Recognition that, whatever therapists do or don't say to clients, we disclose our attitudes in many ways; many of the participants in this study recognized their counsellors' discomfort or disapproval more in their body language than in what was said
   - Counsellors being rooted enough in our own spirituality – even that of a devout atheist – to let clients be where they are, however different that understanding

5. Finally, the transpersonal relationship may include all, or none, of:
   • Moments of profound silence
   • Recognition that healing happens and is not dependent on us
   • Sensed presences, spiritual intuitions
   • An openness in both client and counsellor to what is 'beyond all names'

Naturally, some counsellors will be happier with some parts of this map of the therapeutic relationship than others. Person-centred counsellors are used to talking about the person-to-person aspect but may well be wary, as Rogers (1951) himself was, of the use of 'transference', especially in rigid ways that reinforce the distance between therapist and client. However, the phenomena named 'transference' do occur, as Rogers acknowledged, 'in a considerable portion of cases' (Rogers 1951: 200; see also Merry 1995). Some analytic therapists emphasize the transferential and would be highly dubious about the person-to-person relationship, though Clarkson notes that such a position is not consistently maintained: 'From Freud onwards there has been... acknowledgment of the role of the real relationship' (Clarkson 1995: 147). Different therapists, either because of their theoretical orientation or their personal style, will move more easily in one or other facet of the relationship, hopefully in interaction with the client and their needs. This variability need not affect the suitability of Clarkson's broad framework for our purposes here.

Within Clarkson's framework we can incorporate both Richards and Bergin's work on spiritual interventions and West's attention to therapist spiritual awareness.

These three elements – the broad frame; spiritual interventions; and utilizing therapists' spiritual insights – are not presented as ascending stages. It is not necessary, for example, to embrace working with spiritual practices in the manner proposed by Richards and Bergin (2005) in order to draw on spiritual insight (West 2004a) or 'meta-empathy' (Richards and Bergin 2005). Even the broad frame is only one possible integrative framework. There are others available (Corey 1996 reviews several of them, as does Hollanders 2000a, and others continue to arise, e.g. Nelson-Jones 2002). However, I am arguing that whatever frame is chosen needs to integrate the client's spirituality fully into the counselling process, or at least be open to doing so.

Taking Clarkson, Richards and Bergin and West's contributions together, what do we have? Perhaps we can best express it visually (see Figure 2.1). In other words, within a broad model of the therapeutic relationship, which includes spirituality as a normal element, there is also

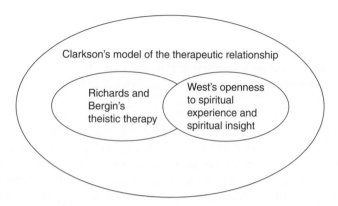

*Figure 2.1*   A model for integrating therapy and spirituality

room for more explicitly faith-based therapy (whether denominational or ecumenical) and, to a degree overlapping with them, for therapy that is open to spirituality beyond both religion and theistic belief, and therapy that includes the spiritual insights of therapists. All therapists, I would argue, can at least be invited onto the territory mapped by Clarkson. Whether they choose to visit the areas mapped out by Richards and Bergin and West will be up to them.

However, ethically, I am arguing that they need to be open to the possibility that their clients may need to visit those places. And if they do, they may need to refer them to practitioners willing to go there. We have seen throughout this chapter what happens when, because of their beliefs, therapists refuse either to accompany their clients into these areas or to help them find someone else to work with. To say to a person of faith that, because of my views as a therapist, I cannot work with them, and to offer appropriate referral, may well be the *most* ethical thing to do. To work with them while imposing my views and excluding their faith is not.

## Conclusion

This chapter has only been able to begin to open up clients' experiences and to suggest some issues for therapists to consider. In line with the whole emphasis of this project, it is appropriate to listen again to the participants:

• Spirituality is where the healing is... unless that's... engaged with [and] accepted then I think we remain alone and isolated and unwell.

- Any healing I experienced undoubtedly came from my fellow patients; the truth was raw, real, untouched... There was no fear of speaking the truth; after all we were all 'mad' anyway so there was nothing to lose.
- I think it's quite helpful when you say 'what does that mean to you?'
- The more I became who I was, healthier and happier and more free in myself and more alive, the more I seemed to displease her.
- Don't impose your thoughts about faith on an individual, accept them as where they are at and as a totality.
- A lot of counsellors had anti-religious feelings, and I got all that crap from them really.
- He was embodying what God had to offer, love and acceptance. He found it extremely difficult to stay with me where I wanted to go, in fact I made him go where I needed to be.

Few of us, as counsellors, would dream of saying we 'embody what God has to offer' and such humility is wise. At the same time we can offer a welcoming, open and freeing space to the whole person who sits before us, body, mind and spirit – even if we don't believe in spirit!

## Discussion points

1. How do you respond, both empathically and intellectually, to the stories shared by the research participants?
2. What experiences of religion and spirituality have shaped your understanding in these areas?
3. In what ways is your own spirituality a resource for you in your work with clients?
4. How helpful do you find the model proposed?
5. How would you integrate working with client spirituality into your understanding of therapy?

# 3
# Counselling and Pastoral Care

*Terry Biddington*

## Introduction

This chapter begins with a brief overview of the extensive practice of pastoral care within the world's religions. This is followed by sections on findings from research in which three critical texts – on shame, images of God and the assumptions underlying pastoral practice – will be laid alongside three illustrative case studies from real life. Subsequent sections consider the implications both for counsellors, who may choose to take an individual's beliefs into account, and for faith leaders, who may not always acknowledge that belief systems can have negative as well as positive impacts on a person's wellbeing. The chapter concludes with some suggested guidelines for practitioners of both kinds.

## Background

For centuries the pastoral care offered by the church was delivered through an assortment of activities ranging from the sermon, prayers and sacraments of the liturgy to the clerical concern for economic, educational and social interventions within the local community, so that the church was, theoretically at least, concerned with caring for all aspects of human life and existence. With the rise in the nineteenth century of alternative secular state provision for many of these activities, the consequent 'shrinking' of the role of the clergy caused many to reconsider what exactly it meant for the church to offer effective pastoral care.

In the US, where the church is associational and – unlike the Church of England – not committed in the same way to the care of the entire nation, there was from the 1920s a wholesale movement towards psychotherapy and pastoral counselling as the preferred paradigm for pastoral care. Every good Christian minister was primarily a pastoral counsellor, trained (after Freud, Jung, Rogers, Fromm or Berne) to respond to any crisis that might arise in the life of a member of the congregation. The vestiges of this are seen, to this day, in the close attention to individual guidance and analysis of motivation and aspiration that accompanies the extensive – by UK standards – marriage preparation procedures that the American churches impose on their (potentially litigious) members. The Frank Lake 'school' was the most important British equivalent of this movement, although pastoral counselling was never to the same extent a mainstream part of clerical training and practice, and even remained somewhat ill regarded by a church that preferred the more traditional nurturing activities of its 'professional amateur' clergy.

By the mid-1970s, even in the US, the pendulum had begun to swing away from secular pastoral counselling towards the exploration of more overtly Christian forms and understandings of pastoral care that were brought into critical dialogue with secular psychotherapeutic practice. This juxtaposition of two diverse traditions resulted in a bewildering range of definitions of Christian pastoral care. Thus, while Arnold talks of 'bringing *good news* to bear in relationships... and caring sensitively to persons... and faithfully to theological commitments' (Arnold 1982: 10), Clebsch and Jaekle perceive the tradition in more concrete terms as involving a varying mixture of 'healing, sustaining, reconciling and guiding' (Clebsch and Jaeckle 1975: *passim*) and Wright focuses on the eternal dimension of caring under God, the 'awareness of a path to wholeness and the transcendent reality of God' beyond, behind and above, where the pastor's sensitivity makes her the person of 'distinctive vision and perception' rather than an endless source of good Christian acts (Wright 1980: ch 1).

Campbell, writing somewhat critically of the American professionalization of the pastor, also seeks to broaden pastoral care into the activity of *every Christian*, rather than just of the traditionally assumed white, male, ordained pastor: 'pastoral care is, in essence, surprisingly simple. It has one fundamental aim: to help people to know love, both as something to be received and as something to give (Campbell 1985: 1). This recalls Deeks, who talks of pastoral care as expressing the basic obligations of the biblical *shema*: love God, neighbour and self (Deeks 1987: 3–4). Pattison, however, attempts to have the best of all possible worlds and to bring 'clarity, finitude [and no] undue restrictiveness' to his definition: 'pastoral care is that activity, undertaken especially by representative Christian persons, directed towards the elimination and relief of sin and sorrow and the presentation of all people perfect in Christ to God' (Pattison 1988: 13).

This desire for critical dialogue between secular therapeutic and faith-based practices is not limited to Christian approaches to pastoral care, however. For a long time the training of rabbis and increasingly of imams has required the study of the canon of psychoanalysis and pastoral counselling, as well as critical engagement between secular understandings of the make-up of human identity and personhood and the role and impact of traditional forms of pastoral care, such as the recitation of the Torah or Holy Qur'an as aids to recovery and wholeness.

Since the rabbinic period within Judaism, the figure of the *shoteh*, the deranged person who inhabits cemeteries, has come in some sense to signify both the archetypal sufferer of psychological distress and the way in which the mental, spiritual and physical aspects of ill-health and wellness are interconnected in the human person. Moreover, the fact that the *shoteh* is generally discussed within the framework of the interpretation of the Torah as moral 'law' illustrates how the suffering of the individual cannot be considered in isolation from the demands of pastoral care incumbent on the family or community.

Such 'legal' and creatively dialectical (*midrashic*) reflection on the stories of scripture within a social context enabled rabbis to arrive at the idea of there being two divergent inclinations within the human psyche: one towards the good, the other towards the ill, that could be influenced by the teaching and example of individuals. Integral to the pastoral development of this insight was the custom that arose in Hasidic Judaism, well over a century before Freud and Klein, whereby a rabbi might meet with a follower for 'holy' conversation. This dynamic therapeutic relationship between master and disciple was to influence Martin Buber in the evolution of the 'I/Thou' principle of mutual openness integral to much person-centred psychotherapeutic practice.

This concern with introspection is, within Muslim pastoral practice, perhaps more manifest within Sufism than in mainstream Islam. While the meditation techniques of Sufism (which developed the Enneagram in the Middle Ages) aim to promote self-awareness and are practised with the support of a teacher as a 'spiritual director', for most Muslims pastoral care is found through the observance of *sharia*. Knowledge and practice of *sharia* – the Qur'an plus the Sunnah, or Hadith, the stories of the Prophet Muhammed's life – offer the fullest expression of all that is needed to live islamically according to the will of God. Wellbeing consists in a continual submission or reorientation of one's life to the principles revealed to Mohammed. At times of pastoral need, therefore, the recitation of particular words and passages from the Qur'an are considered efficacious and may also be worn about the person.

The spiritual and psychological impact of the scriptural text on the *nafs* – the multilayered self or psyche as understood within Islam – as well as the benefits of prayer, fasting, pilgrimage and membership of the Muslim community, are bound up with a worldview that sees God's presence everywhere and is at ease with the idea of accepting the inescapability of the divine plan for each individual. Muslim pastoral care, while engaged in a fruitful conversation with the very different premises and practices of western psychiatry (see the imam training of the Markfield Institute, www.mihe.org.uk), is essentially a matter of allowing the word of God to flow into the heart and mind and so of living out the practical implications of the command to 'lighten the sorrow of the sorrowful and to remove the suffering of the injured' (Hadith of Bukhari).

The question of worldview is significant too in the pastoral care offered within Hinduism, which, like other eastern religions, eschews western models of psychiatric care and the concept of the development of the psyche in favour of the notion of spiritual enlightenment. Siva is regarded as the founder of the Sidhic or Siddha school of medicine and pastoral care is associated closely with Ayurveda – the knowledge of long life – which also has divine origins. Ayurvedic texts such as the Atharva Veda view mental illness as result of contempt for the gods, divine curses and disregard for the divinely ordained social order and caste system.

Caraka Samhita, the primary text of the Indian medical tradition, advocates spiritual enlightenment on the basis of a holistic view of life. Wellbeing consists in a concern for self-preservation and the desire for wealth and a happy future, and is promoted by an emphasis on a balanced diet, the practice of spiritual disciplines such as yoga, meditation and the use of mantras, charms and appropriate rituals. Stories from the Vedas, recounted individually or in groups, serve to put individual human suffering in the context of a preordained universal order and therapeutic, life-giving relationships are commonly found between gurus and their followers.

Similarly in Buddhism, suffering is not viewed as existentially problematical, as in the West, but as part of the givenness of life. The key, therefore, to effective pastoral care lies in the ability to minimize or even eliminate suffering by achieving detachment from all craving, pain and the desires of the ego. The 'Noble Eightfold Path' of Theravada (or early) Buddhism seeks to guide the individual to attain the *arahant* state of 'perfection' or nirvana, and the text Abhidhamma Pitaka offers a remarkable depth of psychological insight into human motivation and behaviour. The tool for personal development, behavioural change and self-care is 'spiritual mindfulness', achieved through *samatha* or serenity meditation, but more effectively though the practice of *vipassana* or 'insight' meditation. Mindfulness may ultimately lead to awareness of the transience of all phenomena and, thereby, to enlightenment. Much research has been done into the applications of these techniques to a wide range of mental health conditions, pain and stress control regimes and psychotherapeutic approaches (see Kutz et al. 1985).

## Three critical issues for contemporary pastoral care

Since the 1980s, the impact of feminist, black, queer and disabled theologies has brought about a comprehensive reconsideration of the problematic nature of aspects of religious pastoral care. Particular concern has been shown both for the tendency among some Christian, Jewish and Muslim practitioners to prioritize strong soteriological goals over the need for wholeness in the here and now – that is, to show greater concern for a person's ultimate wellbeing in the eternal afterlife than in their embodied existence in the real world (see Pattison's definition above) – and also for the propensity of many practitioners to refuse to recognize that religious traditions of pastoral care operate not only within, but against and despite, competing theological and doctrinal frameworks of 'discipline' and care that can serve not only to proffer, but also to withhold or even deny, healing and integration to individuals and groups. Ready examples of this would, of course, be the continued uncritical insistence of some in referencing, say, obscure or dubious passages of Jewish and Christian scripture that relate allegedly to same-sex practices, purity laws, the treatment of outsiders or the divine causes of suffering, in the presence of people seeking the unconditional support and understanding that was evident in the ministry of Gautama, the Sikh gurus, Jesus, Mohammed and so on.

Some important milestones have been reached in the research of many contemporary theologians and practitioners of pastoral care, but of particular interest in the English-speaking world must be the work of Stephen Pattison (2000) on shame, James Alison (2003) on forgiveness and atonement and Elaine Graham (1996, 2002) on the need to transform pastoral practice. I discuss these works below.

Pattison's *Shame* is a fascinating book and its cross-disciplinary nature makes it invaluable to faith-based practitioners and secular psychologists and counsellors alike. The section on 'shame and Christianity' begins by recognizing how the very doctrines and practices of the faith can easily contribute to the creation of unhealthy attitudes concerning sin, shame and the perpetuation of guilt. Each Christian act of worship begins with a space for the confession of sin and guilt, and in this short space of time people may well need to confess what troubles and injures them in order to unburden themselves. Yet all too often the reality is that people search their memories for 'something to say', however trivial and unwarranted, and thus effectively only anticipate and increase their sense of unworthiness and guilt. And while the remedy for sin may indeed be confession, there are many things that are unable to be spoken – even in the silence – because of certain dominant understandings of the nature of God and 'how salvation works' and so remain ever hidden and unaddressed. This compacted and destructive shame needs not confession but the nurturing of a sense of self-worth, respect and value. However, such a theology of nurture and flourishing remains far from the minds of the majority of religious practitioners, who are entrenched in the proclamation of a faith in thrall to notions of the perfection and purity of God as an appropriate aspiration for human living.

It is here that Alison's work serves to demonstrate how the Christian church – and there are clearly implications for the other world faiths – has tended to radically 'colour' or even misrepresent how we might understand God, preferring, in reality, to see God as 'just a god like other gods', secure in the easy attributes of divinity (all-knowing, all-present, all-powerful and so on) and content to require violence, vengefulness, bloodlust and sacrifice (perpetuated, for example, through particular interpretations of the meaning of Jesus' crucifixion) as the effective means by which people can find wholeness, salvation and eternal fulfilment. But Alison is keen to point out that God is altogether different: that God is unconditional love and does not demand repentance as a precondition to receiving forgiveness, that salvation is a process of the discovery of being loved and 'liked' by God.

Alison emphasizes that traditional notions of atonement – the process by which individuals are enabled to be 'at one' or at peace with God, through Jesus' self-sacrifice for the sins of others and to satisfy the outraged honour of God – are in fact *only theories*, constructed with the express purpose of creating a theological link that enables the crucified Jesus to redeem humanity from the effects of the 'Fall' of Adam and Eve in Eden. This attempt to right the wrong done by two mythical figures who never actually existed is one thing as a theological exercise; but to insist that such a theory should become the effective mechanism for shaping and offering pastoral care is to put stumbling blocks and hurdles in front of people and to deny that the need for the embodied and felt experience of acceptability and self-worth has to precede any intellectual, creedal or formulaic expression of regret or remorse. We all have to *experience* ourselves as being freed from what binds us, freed to eschew violence to self and others and freed to be loved, loving and creative, if we are to fulfil the real potential that Jesus – and other religious leaders, gurus and prophets – is held to demonstrate for humanity.

Elaine Graham, writing from a feminist perspective, is concerned to articulate the possibilities for a 'critical theology of Christian pastoral practice', one that not only questions the theological basis that informs pastoral practice, but also scrutinizes the nature of the practice itself. Graham rightly suggests that, whatever our faith, we can no longer rely on the uncritical reading of foundational doctrines as certain, stable and valid for all time since, in the postmodern world, truth and value are not eternal but provisional and highly contextualized. Truth has to be not theoretical, creedal and timeless, but contingent, discovered and enacted within contexts of a practical and embodied struggle for justice and empowerment for individuals and groups. Moreover, notions of self, knowledge and values all need to be treated within a 'hermeneutics of suspicion' in so far as they have been normatively based on a white, male, straight, middle-class, western-ordained or clerical perspective.

What Graham hopes to create is a wholesale debate and revisioning of the norms, values and practices of (Christian) pastoral care; one that seeks not to maintain traditional hegemonies, but is rather based on the radical notion of nurture and flourishing for all people. Again, there are clear implications here for the pastoral practice of all the world's religions, in so far as they have shaped the cultural expectations and social norms and disciplines of pastoral care for the so-called minorities within them, not least women within many religions, gays within Islam and some forms of Christianity, *dalits* within the Hindu caste system, the mentally ill or those with learning disabilities within traditional non-Taoist Chinese and African religions and so on.

## Examples from practice

It would be appropriate now to flesh out this theoretical discussion of critical issues in pastoral care with some pertinent, anonymized case studies from real life.

## Case study: 'Peter'

Peter was in his mid-50s when I encountered him at a project for the homeless and needy. For a long while he presented as nervous, timid and very hard to engage; he would take his tea and sandwiches into a corner, looking around anxiously before making a quick exit. Over several weeks I edged closer and the relationship began to unfold. He had worked in the media industry and had enjoyed an affluent lifestyle – parties, travel, fast cars – during the course of which he had had affairs and sexual relationships alongside his several marriages. His career had ended due to substance abuse and now he lived 'alone in the world'.

At some point he had encountered a narrow evangelical form of Christianity and, although he rarely went to church (he couldn't function well in public worship), he had allowed this theological worldview to be the lens through which he interpreted all that had happened to him. So it was that 'his sins had found him out', he was 'reaping what he had sown' and receiving his 'just deserts'; and such phrases had become for him a form of body and soul armour that both protected him from the 'worldly temptations' he now feared ('No, I won't have a meat sandwich; plain cheese is good enough for me') and 'kept him safe' within the cosmic order. He knew his place – he was a 'convicted sinner' of the worst sort, and that's how he seemed to want to remain.

Peter apparently accepted his situation. How could he complain? He had brought everything on himself and by 'taking the medicine now' he was merely anticipating the eternal punishment he would receive in the afterlife. What was more, it was clear to him that it was 'God's will for him to suffer', because he would, from time to time, experience homoerotic feelings and, since these were 'clearly condemned in scripture', they must surely be an indication of God's 'just' determination to perpetuate his pain and affliction.

If there were to be any resolution of Peter's situation it was clearly going to take a long time. Over about two years we met informally once or twice a week. I did an awful lot of listening, smiling and affirming him as an individual and periodically would suggest gently that I knew a counsellor who might help. He always shook his head. Mostly he would, as though trapped, repeat episodes of his story, but from time to time he would appear with a guitar or pencil sketches; he had a talent for both, though he refused to acknowledge it. Evidently he was open to a relationship with me and eventually he asked what I thought about his situation. At this point he held eye contact with me, something he had rarely done.

I made the decision to disclose that I was a 'minister' (his preferred term). I did this in the hope that – alongside the acceptance I had tried to show him – it might enable him to recognize something of the unconditionality of God's love, reflected in a representative of the church. It did allow him to initiate an ongoing and productive conversation about the many complexities of his theological worldview: from his side, about the nature of God, the status of certain scriptural passages, the meaning of suffering, the reality of the afterlife; from my side, about the radically inclusive message of Jesus, the reality of forgiveness, the unconditional, gratuitous nature of God's recreative love and the nature of embodied human personhood.

In terms of outcomes, he asked in due course to make a formal confession (an atypical request for a Protestant) and then to receive communion. While I was reluctant – not being convinced that the former wouldn't just perpetuate the guilt and avoid the deeper-seated issues – I eventually agreed. Although I tried very hard to convince him that what is confessed is then 'truly forgiven' and, though he might well always remember particular events, they were no longer able to injure him (and that, to use his language, 'scripture guaranteed this'), it soon became clear that, while he recognized the validity of what we had done and that it was 'of God', he could not feel forgiven as long as the ongoing issue of his shame about his bisexuality remained entangled with his narrow interpretation of scripture and so failed to be addressed positively in terms of contemporary understandings of personhood and sexuality.

Even later, when he had come to recognize that there was a variety of legitimate theological understandings and that approaches to scripture and sexuality differed markedly from church to church, Peter remained unable to engage with the business of his own acceptability to himself and thus the integration of his identity and being.

At this point I again attempted to refer him to counselling, even offered to take him there and wait, but he continued to decline. When I moved to manage a mental health charity I tried in vain to get him to visit. Years later I encountered him in a crowded public space. He recognized me immediately, made eye contact, paused for a second and then fled. I still pray for him.

## Case study: 'Lisa'

Lisa was about 24 years old and had recently arrived to do graduate study. A fairly new Christian, she had selected a local church and was beginning to settle there. She was in a long-standing relationship with a younger guy who remained at her previous university. Both were keen amateur sailors and would use this as an excuse to meet up regularly. On one such occasion Lisa was unable to accompany him; tragically, her boyfriend was drowned in a freak accident.

She turned for solace to her church and had a long conversation with her pastor during which she asked all the expected questions about God, suffering and ultimate meaning. Lisa reported afterwards that the pastor had said: 'There is only one question that really matters at all, and that is whether your boyfriend was a Christian.' Lisa told him that he was not. 'In that case,' said the pastor, 'the matter is clear. He had made no commitment and was, sadly therefore, sure to be in hell.'

Lisa was crushed. She left the church and felt, understandably, like abandoning her new faith. Yet she still could not quite believe that, unlike the pastor, 'God could be so crass'. She knew her boyfriend had been good and loving and had begun to imagine a possible future with him. Her course tutor had referred her to counselling but, after an initial appointment, she was told that she wasn't suitable for counselling 'since her issues were theological'. I could see why this conclusion was drawn, but it merely fuelled her sense of anger and rejection. Not unsurprisingly, therefore, during her first few visits to me Lisa simply wept uncontrollably; after that came the anger.

However, during the first six months of our year of meetings Lisa and I 'set sail' – a consciously chosen metaphor – to a variety of countries with different theological worldviews. At first I set the course and we visited places with fairly stereotypical 'black-and-white' theologies (Lisa was a new Christian and this journey was much about exploring the parameters of a faith she barely knew), where she was able to ask some fundamental questions that related to both her presenting dilemma – 'so hell is all nonsense then?' – and to her own ongoing need for spiritual sustenance – 'I never imagined you could think that. It's cool!' Eventually, Lisa was very much in control of where we went. She explored all manner of situations and began to appreciate that people choose to live with particular beliefs and theologies and that her former pastor, even though his manner was tactless and damaging, had also been acting out of his chosen theological convictions.

After about six months she agreed to return to a counsellor; there were unresolved issues of grief and self-image and questions about future relationships that were best dealt with in that context. She had also, by this time, found a much more suitable church where she was welcomed and happy. We continued to meet, but from this point our relationship was about building up confidence in her faith life and giving her the theological and scriptural tools she would need for a resilient spirituality. Occasionally she would mention that 'the counselling thing is going well'.

At the end of the academic year she decided to continue her studies elsewhere: 'not just because I want to put the past behind me, but because it's time to set sail in a new direction.' She kept in touch for a while by email, but then let go. She's now sailing solo; or hopefully not!

## Case study: 'Ali'

Ali was a postgraduate from a second-generation Muslim family from northern Europe. He came to see me after hearing me talk at an interfaith event. He told me that he had always tried to be a good Muslim and even planned to go on pilgrimage to Mecca as soon as his studies were over. After this he spent quite some time questioning me about my understanding of Islam. Then suddenly, quite out of the blue, he disclosed that he was gay. He kept eye contact with me throughout this time, apparently keen to gauge my reaction.

I deliberately remained silent for 30 seconds or more to let the disclosure sink in for both of us. I then asked how he had come to this conclusion and he described how, in his early years at university, he had felt attracted to other male students, to 'their form and beauty', and that these feelings had intensified over the following couple of years, although he had never dared act on them. He had often gone to bars with a few of the men he admired, though generally without consuming alcohol. Now that he was away from home he had become aware both of a desire to 'go further' with a particular individual he had met and, at the same time, of the conflict between his faith and the feelings he felt each time he visited a mosque.

We spent many hours over the next few sessions revisiting the tension he experienced between, on the one hand, what Islam has to say about homosexuality and, on the other hand, the very intense feelings and desires he had, focused around this one individual and other male students in general.

He was quite clear that he could not speak to anyone in his mosque, 'obviously not the imam', or any of the students he regularly met there. He said that there was 'no space and no possibility to air this subject' and that his 'only option was to cease being a Muslim'. He asked about the possibility of becoming a Christian, since this would be a 'least worse option than coming out as a Muslim'.

We talked about the option of counselling, but he felt that a secular counsellor would probably have little real knowledge of Islam, or even 'only stereotypical views about Muslims'. We also discussed at length about what Islam meant to him and he replied that it was, for him, 'the most perfect way of living according to God's plan' and that 'happiness was in submitting to the will of God'. I asked how, if God had created him, God could have made him gay. He had no reply. There was, to his mind, simply no reconciliation between the two parts of himself and no theological leeway for any Muslim to articulate positively the possibility of being both gay and Muslim, even when the difference between faith and cultural context was taken into account.

At this point I told him I knew of a support organization run by gay Muslims for people like him. Yet even when he had made contact with this group and discovered a welcome from people undergoing the same experience as himself, and had come to see that he was by no means alone, he still failed to conceive of a way of reconciling the two halves of his identity. He continues to maintain a semblance of public normality only through painful self-denial.

## Implications for practice

The lived experience of individuals in faith communities is shaped, consciously or not, by theological frameworks of belief and continually rubs up against them. When difficulties arise, psychological or spiritual integration and healing – 'wholeness' in Christian terms, but also *shalom* and *salaam* – is achieved either by jettisoning the belief system altogether (which many do) or by the even more insidious resort of denying that the problem exists (a common response among faith leaders) or else after a process of re-examining and re-imaging deep-seated and dominant theological assumptions about reality, values and identity.

Pastoral care and counselling within the faith-based traditions, or secular counselling that is open to the spiritual practices and beliefs of clients, must be aware of the above tension and be willing to engage with this therapeutic process of re-imaging theological worldviews and doctrinal frameworks.

Moreover, the faith communities themselves need to learn to see their pastoral practice and their belief systems – whether these are understood to be of divine or human provenance – not as 'neutral matrices', but in terms of the impact they have, for good or ill, on the embodied lives of the individuals and groups they seek to serve.

There needs to be a creative dialogue between secular counselling and practitioners of faith-based pastoral care. Both have much to learn from each other in terms of working effectively with the *whole person* and not air-brushing out – deliberately or not – aspects of clients' experience.

Practitioners of secular counselling techniques need to accept that assumptions and worldviews based on religious/spiritual or theological/doctrinal frameworks are not necessarily any more likely to be pathological, illogical or damaging than any other worldviews. While individual practitioners may have a passing or working knowledge of a client's faith stance, much as they might of different counselling schools, there is an important case to be made for greater use of referrals to, and appropriate interactions with, enlightened faith-based practitioners.

For their part, faith-based practitioners need to be challenged into a critical dialogue with their own traditions of pastoral care and with the theological and doctrinal assumptions and values that underpin them. Anyone who is committed to discovering and celebrating the relevance of their faith to the challenges of contemporary life will need to take seriously the fundamental and irreversible insights of postmodern, feminist and other liberationist critiques.

## Ethics and supervision issues

This is a hugely problematic area for practitioners of faith-based pastoral care, since the majority, having had little if any counselling training, are unlikely to have supervision either. While it is true that many British, American and European clergy of most traditions – as well as other faith leaders – often have extensive experience of 'counselling-type situations', it is equally typical for this experience never to have been consistently formalized through recognized and accredited schemes or membership of professional bodies. Instead, clergy may classically have taken a series of short, generic counselling courses or courses geared to specific areas of work or interest. There are, of course, exceptions to this generalization.

While some attention is given, at initial selection and during ministerial formation, to the general suitability and training of individuals as pastoral care agents and 'listening ears', there is typically little or no further resourcing, so that too often the religious professional in their pastoral work is left simply to 'get the feeling' that presenting pastoral issues represent something 'not quite right' with an individual, without any clinical knowledge to draw on or knowledge of referral routes or appropriate boundaries. (This is one of the main reasons why faith-based practitioners historically have never charged any fee for their services.)

Somewhat more common is for clergy and lay Christians to offer pastoral care as spiritual directors, 'soul friends' and prayer 'guides' and 'companions'. Although some churches are now putting resources into the selection and training of suitable individuals, the resurgence of interest in this ancient pastoral practice is still something of a novelty. It is utterly remarkable that, for generations, there has been so little interest in the churches in prayer and meditation as tools for spiritual development and flourishing. Here again, however, supervision is the exception for those involved in this ministry.

What professional appraisal there is (and this is only now emerging as a reality in some churches, synagogues and mosques) almost never considers the quality of 'ministerial' pastoral practice in any effective detail, more concerned as it is with the management and professional development of practitioners. For good or ill, ministers, rabbis, imams and others are trusted free agents – until someone complains – and the evident ethical dilemmas here remain unchallenged.

## Guidelines for practitioners

What has emerged from research and critical reflection over the last two or three decades, whatever the religion, is that pastoral practice needs to be the starting point for theological reflection and not vice versa. For too long faith-based pastoral care has begun by assuming particular theological assumptions to be universally true and normative and then attempting to make people's lives fit the belief system. This is not the case now and can never be so again. To do so is tantamount to abuse.

Consequently, there needs to be a wholesale re-examination of the theological and doctrinal underpinning of faith-based pastoral practice, particularly – in Christian terms – of the real meaning of ideas about incarnation and resurrection, about atonement, integration and human development, and especially concerning human personhood, identity and notions of divinity and perfection. Above all, there needs to be a determined effort to reclaim the forgotten gospel of human nurture and flourishing.

For their part, secular counsellors must be encouraged to work with both the spiritual and religious frameworks and worldviews of clients and also with enlightened faith-based practitioners. The possibilities and opportunities for joint working and the creative use of the overlaps and interfaces are far too interesting and transformative to be ignored. Secular counselling and faith-based pastoral practice are two expressions of a common desire for the attainment of full humanity and the achievement of individual wholeness in community.

## Conclusion

Whatever the religion, faith-based pastoral care uses the various resources of its faith – holy scripture, traditions of prayer and meditation, liturgical, dietary and ethical practices – for the benefit of its members and adherents. While it is often content with a less overtly structured and managed *modus operandi* – to the annoyance of trained secular counsellors – it has, nonetheless, an honourable history of care giving that has shaped institutions and nations and, indeed, the counselling profession itself.

This does not mean that we should be satisfied with an uncritical engagement with the doctrinal or ethical assumptions and 'givens' of the faith traditions; or indeed of the secular counselling traditions. Times are changing, the world is a different place and both professions need to engage with each other in order to better serve humanity. There needs to be a commitment to exploring the many interfaces and overlaps, to creating informed, mutual and creative referral mechanisms, and to identifying and capitalizing on the possibilities for joint working. God, common sense or the irrepressible human spirit and imagination – call it what you will – demands that much of us all.

### Discussion points

1. What, in your view, are the interfaces and overlaps and the possibilities for joint working between secular counselling and faith-based pastoral care?
2. What mechanisms, training or other means can you identify that would bring about a closer collaboration?
3. What are the obstacles to achieving this? Why might it be better to keep the traditions entirely separate?
4. How might the insights, values and practices of secular counselling help faith-based practice to focus on unconditional positive regard and fulfilment as the goal of its pastoral care for individuals and communities?

# 4
# Integrating Prayer in Counselling

*Peter Madsen Gubi*

## Introduction

This chapter explores the place of prayer in counselling. It describes the research methodology used in a qualitative study looking at the use of prayer in mainstream counselling, and it discusses the findings as a contribution to an ongoing discussion about best practice when prayer is integrated into counselling and psychotherapy.

## Background

Although the interface between religion and counselling seems to be a complicated one (Williams 2003), research shows that prayer influences mainstream counselling. For example, 59 per cent of BACP-accredited counsellors use prayer to support their work with clients and 12 per cent of BACP-accredited counsellors have prayed with clients (Gubi 2004). Shafranske and Malony (1990), in a mail survey of 1000 clinical psychologists in the US, found that 24 per cent reported praying privately for their clients. Lange (1983a, b) carried out a survey of the 1284 members of the Christian Association for Psychological Studies. Based on a return of 335 questionnaires, Lange discovered that 53.1 per cent of therapists felt that prayer was an important agent in therapy, 53.4 per cent strongly felt that therapeutic outcome was affected by prayer, 93.4 per cent felt that audible prayer should be allowed in therapy, and 79.4 per cent felt that therapists should pray regularly for their clients.

Bullis (2001) presents empirical data that is based on counselling practitioners' reports of professional ethics and personal comfort with the use of religious or spiritual interventions in practice. From that he finds that 83.5 per cent feel that praying for their clients is ethically appropriate, and 70.5 per cent feel comfortable in praying privately for their clients. He also found that 37.1 per cent felt that it was ethically appropriate to pray with a client in the session, but that only 24.5 per cent felt comfortable in doing so. The use of prayer in counselling is clearly happening, so it is important that there is an informed debate about the acceptability and value of prayer as a spiritual intervention, and that the limitation and value of such practice is critically evaluated to determine what it means in practice to work with a client's spirituality (Foskett and Lynch 2001).

## Overview of my research and the main findings

In the context of this research landscape, this chapter describes the insights that were gained from a qualitative study of counsellors who integrate prayer into their mainstream counselling practice (Gubi 2003). These insights are summarized as 'considerations for good practice' in the integration of prayer and counselling.

In the research, 19 mainstream counsellors (14 BACP-accredited counsellors and 5 CMCS-approved – Churches Ministerial Counselling Service – counsellors) were identified as using overt and covert prayer in their mainstream counselling work (Gubi 2003). They were interviewed using the thematic prompts in Table 4.1.

The purpose of the research was to discover how prayer influences the work of mainstream counsellors who integrate prayer into their practice, and to ascertain if prayer can be used ethically in counselling, and, if so, what the implications might be. The interviews were transcribed and the interview data were analysed using interpretative phenomenological analysis (Smith 1996; Smith et al. 1999). Four main themes emerged. These were 'Defining prayer and understanding process (philosophical level)', 'Covert prayer', 'Overt prayer' and 'Ethical issues and supervision'. Each of the main themes had corresponding subthemes. This chapter presents an overview of the relationship between these emerging themes and subthemes, and an overview of the insights that were gained from the analysis.

The interview data revealed three levels at which prayer influences the practice of mainstream counsellors: a philosophical level; a covert level; and an overt level. At all three levels prayer needs to be underpinned by an ethical awareness and a careful, reflexive consideration of the issues.

At the *philosophical* level, all counselling can be regarded as prayer. Prayer pervades the atmosphere and environment in which the counsellor and client are in communion at a spiritual level. Prayer is an

*Table 4.1*   Thematic prompts

1. How would you define prayer?
2. What were the circumstances that led to you praying overtly with a client in your counselling work? (Are there any case examples you could provide? How do you know when and if to pray?)
3. How was prayer used in each case?
4. Was prayer 'effective' in each case? (How? What 'outcome' was achieved?)
5. Does using prayer change the counselling relationship in any way?
6. How do you justify/understand (philosophically, psychologically, and perhaps theologically when relevant) the use of prayer in the counselling process?
7. Were you able to explore the occasion(s) in which prayer was used overtly in the counselling session(s) freely in supervision? If yes, what enabled you to? If no, what prevented you?
8. Do you have a special way of praying overtly with clients when you work as a counsellor?
9. In what other ways does prayer influence your counselling work?
10. Do you have any misgivings, doubts or reservations about using prayer in counselling?

attitude that is inherent in the counsellor's way of being, providing a context for silence, the quality of attention and the sense of being a part of something bigger to which the counselling work can be entrusted. Prayer provides an existential perspective or frame of reference that makes the counselling work more meaningful at a spiritual level. This is motivational for the counsellor and provides a way of understanding the process of their work. Counselling is 'prayer in action' (Canda 1990).

At the *covert* level, prayer is a valuable, integral and necessary part of the counsellor's supportive practice. It is a personal and private practice in which the counsellor uses prayer:

- to ground and attune herself in preparation for the counselling work, enabling a deeper level of presence, stillness, balance and concentration;
- to place the work in the care of a higher being, enabling connection with the 'here and now' and containment;
- to add an extra healing dimension to the therapeutic work through the use of intercessory prayer on behalf of the client, which also enables the spiritual aspect of the work to be kept in focus;
- to still the mind, aiding peace, calm, meaning, purpose and direction at times of stuckness, panic and anxiety. This helps the counsellor to

stay with the 'not knowing' and the 'aloneness', enabling the connection with the client to be maintained and enhanced;
• to stay with the intense feelings of helplessness, hopeless and despair;
• as part of a spiritual discipline that enables the counsellor to acknowledge her own spirituality, prevent burnout and maintain balance in
her life through fostering a forum in which self-reflection, self-respect
and self-care are intrinsic.

The counsellor may also be upheld by the client's prayer at this level, provided that such practice is not explicitly encouraged by the counsellor,
who instead accepts it in the 'spirit' in which it is offered by the client,
even though at an unconscious level it may indicate issues of attachment
and insecurity. The ethical use of prayer at the covert level is determined
by the intent of the counsellor, in that praying for the client utilizes a
spiritual resource on behalf of the client. This can strengthen the relationship between counsellor and client because it taps into the forces that
become 'powerfully operative in the transcendent encounter' (Thorne
1994, 1998, 2002). If the client knows that the counsellor does this, it can
add to their sense of being cared for, and can reduce the sense of abandonment and separation that the client may feel between sessions.

However, it is important to avoid an unhealthy preoccupation with a
client in prayer (Thorne 1998: 98–99). Magaletta and Brawer (1998) indicate that it is preferable to gain the client's consent, but it may be unethical
to withhold such a practice if the counsellor believes in the effectiveness
of praying for clients away from their presence (Gubi 2001). This has to
be balanced against the perceived reaction of the client if they knew that
intercessory prayer was being enacted on their behalf without their permission. When the counsellor prays on the client's behalf, it is ethically
less problematic to use the 'Thy will be done' approach (Magaletta and
Brawer 1998). The interview data suggest that this approach to prayer
gives the work a more meaningful perspective by reminding the counsellor that the process is part of something bigger than what takes place in
the counselling room and is largely undetermined, full of 'unknowing'
and out of the counsellor's control. The practice also serves to remind the
counsellor that her accountability is also to something greater, as well as
to the client. This can prevent complacency.

At the *overt* level, prayer can be used tentatively with a client who is
open to the process of prayer. However, the use of prayer needs to be
carefully considered. The interview data highlighted the use of prayer
as most likely to occur at the beginning of a session; at the end of a
session; at the termination of a counselling relationship; at times of

client desperation; through the use of silence; through the use of ritual (and in some cases through the use of praying in tongues and the laying on of hands, although this is exceptionally rare practice); through transpersonal imaging; and as a way of communicating appropriate values to the client that are compatible with intrinsic counselling values.

## Implications for practice

Each of the three levels described above has to be *equally underpinned* by an ethical awareness based on the values of fidelity, autonomy, beneficence, non-maleficence, justice and self-respect, which form the ethical framework for good practice (BACP 2002). Throughout the interview data and discussion, various themes have emerged that can provide some guidance in the use of prayer in counselling. These considerations for good practice are underpinned by:

- an awareness of potential ethical issues;
- an awareness of how prayer can be integrated ethically;
- an awareness of the quality and characteristics of the prayer being used;
- a considered awareness of issues of tension and difficulty for the counsellor.

### Developing an awareness of potential ethical issues

The first consideration for good practice is the development of an awareness of potential ethical issues. It is clear from the literature (e.g. Magaletta and Brawer 1998) that the use of prayer is contentious and potentially fraught with difficulty (see Table 4.2).

An awareness of, and insight into, these difficulties is important in preventing the counsellor from colluding with defences and resistance. However, the ethical difficulties, although cautionary, are not prohibitive if prayer is integrated appropriately into practice. A good counsellor knows of potential risks when entering into a therapeutic relationship, but an awareness of the potential risks enables her to facilitate more appropriately without withholding the therapeutic opportunity.

While the ethical difficulties may seem insurmountable at a theoretical level, the interview data reveal that mainstream counsellors whose work includes prayer have carefully reflected on the issues and have reached a place of understanding of the issues where they have found

*Table 4.2*   Summary of ethical difficulties of using prayer in counselling

| Counsellor's process | Client's process |
| --- | --- |
| • Fear of appropriateness of personal disclosure | • Fear of authentic self before God may inhibit counselling |
| • How authentic can the counsellor really be? | • Prayer can be used to deny or distort truth |
| • Potential blurred boundary issues | • Prayer can be used to avoid painful issues |
| • How will prayer impact on the client? | • Prayer can be used to manipulate the counsellor and God |
| • Potential power and mutuality differential | • Prayer can be used to avoid listening to self |
| • Will prayer benefit or burden the client? | • Prayer can be used to avoid challenging self |
| • Fear of collusion with inauthentic prayer | • Prayer can be used to avoid taking responsibility |
| • Prayer can inhibit the challenging of the client | • Compliance with counsellor's expectation |
| • Diversion of attention away from client to God | • Transference issues |
| • Counter-transference issues | • Conflictual issues with God may inhibit counselling if prayer is used |
| • Issues of competency – inadequate training | • Prayer can be used as a defence against insight and self-understanding |
| • Is adequate supervision available? | • Prayer can foster inappropriate intimacy |
| • Possible issues of compliance with client's requests and words | • Prayer may inhibit disclosure |
| • Reliance on God v reliance on self-determination | • The client may fear judgement if prayer is used by the counsellor, and be inhibited |
| • Prayer unrecognized by insurance companies | • Prayer can be used as a way of avoiding possible change |
| • Insufficient research to justify use | • Prayer can be used as wish fulfilment rather than as transcendental acceptance |
| • Prayer not just a counselling technique | • Prayer can compromise client beliefs |
| • Danger of regarding prayer as panacea for all ills | • Prayer can be used to create a spiritual one-upmanship on the counsellor |
| • Praying for particular outcomes inappropriate | • Prayer can be used as indirect communication with counsellor |
| • Danger of imposing counsellor's values, beliefs and prayer practice on client | • Prayer can foster spiritual inadequacy in the clients |
| • Possible violation of work-setting boundaries | • Prayer can be used to foster states of magical superstition, victimhood and helplessness |
| • Need to work within client's religious framework which counsellor may not subscribe to | |
| • Integrity of counsellor may be at risk | |
| • Difficulty of knowing how to introduce prayer into the session | |

*(Continued)*

*Table 4.2* Continued

| Counsellor's process | Client's process |
|---|---|
| • Prayer can detract from immediacy of client experiencing<br>• Prayer can be indirect communication with the client<br>• Prayer can reveal hopes and expectations for client<br>• Prayer can be a place to dump issues without exploration<br>• Difficult to psychologically explore an act of reverence and mystery – different language<br>• Prayer can create an unhealthy oedipal triangle | • Prayer can be presented as a 'quick fix', leaving the client unable to explore ongoing pain<br>• Prayer can dilute the counselling process<br>• Prayer can be used to bypass the complexities of the counselling process<br>• Prayer can be frightening or repellent if the client is associated with strict religious or abusive upbringing<br>• A client who prays regularly, may be reluctant for the counsellor to use prayer if she feels that her prayer should have been enough or if she has been told that she is resisting God's grace by others |

Collated from the following sources: Gubi 1999, 2001, 2002, 2004; Rose 1993, 1996, 1999, 2002; Magaletta and Brawer 1998; Richards and Bergin 1997; McMinn 1996; Tan 1996; Ten Eyck 1993; Webster 1992.

the use of prayer to be less implicated with ethical dilemmas than the literature suggests (see Table 4.3). It could be argued that mainstream counsellors whose work includes prayer have fewer concerns because they are less reflexive and aware in their approach to their work. Yet as a researcher, in most cases I had no sense of their complacency. Instead, I experienced a sense that the interviewees had reflected carefully and ethically on their work and, on the occasions that prayer was used, it felt therapeutically appropriate to them to use prayer.

### How prayer is integrated ethically

The second consideration for good practice is an awareness of how prayer can be pragmatically but ethically integrated. The literature suggests that the counsellor should conduct a formal assessment of the client's spiritual history (Richards and Bergin 1997; Magaletta and Brawer 1998; West 1998a, 2000a). This enables the counsellor to communicate an acceptance of the client's spirituality and gain a better sense of the client's world and spiritual practice. It was clear from the interview data that some counsellors do formalize the use of prayer as

*Table 4.3*  Summary of ethical concerns from the qualitative interview data

| **Summary of ethical concerns from counsellors who integrate prayer into their practice** |
|---|
| • Prayer can change the way the counsellor is regarded |
| • Prayer (particularly transpersonal imaging) may be dangerous to use with a client who is having difficulty assimilating reality (issues of psychopathology) |
| • Danger of imposing the counsellor's faith on the client |
| • Prayer can be an avoidance and a defence |
| • Prayer can be difficult to challenge and explore |
| • Prayer method may not be matched to the client |
| • Cultural pressure to pray which may not take account of the client's needs |
| • Prayer may be mechanistic and routine |
| • Prayer may not be part of the client's agenda |
| • Prayer can enhance the counsellor's power |
| • It may not be culturally acceptable to explore prayer in supervision |

a possible intervention, and are open in their disclosure about their spirituality.

However, many counselling approaches (particularly humanistic approaches) do not conduct 'formal assessments' at the contracting stage of the relationship. The interview data reveal that in such cases, counsellors use pre-contact information or a symbolic environment (often discreet religious symbols in the room or on jewellery) to communicate acceptance of spirituality. Clients who are in touch with their own spirituality can often become aware of the counsellor's openness to spirituality through the counsellor's presence, way of being and unconscious communication.

Instead of a formalized procedure, the interview data suggest that the integration of prayer seems to rely more on a sensitive awareness of the client's needs and an intuitive sensing of the appropriateness of the situation and the client. It is likely that the counsellor has informally gained a sense of her client's coping strategies and spirituality as the relationship has unfolded, so the integration of prayer is more often informed by the quality of attunement and connection between counsellor and client. It is therefore more likely to be a relational and intuitive process based on an awareness of the appropriateness of prayer for the client. Prayer must not be mechanistic and routine (except perhaps in the provision of silence at the beginning of the session) or attributed to external sources (for example the Holy Spirit), except where such attribution actually stems from discernment that comes from the counsellor's conscious awareness.

## The quality and characteristics of prayer

The third consideration for good practice is an awareness of the quality and characteristics of prayer. The interview data suggest that the prayer must have a quality of naturalness about it, with the notion of prayer being introduced with the tentative quality of 'feeling your way' that emerges out of a sense of respect for the client (for example, 'Some people have found this helpful and I wonder if you feel it would be appropriate...'). The prayer has to feel relevant to the context and the 'moment' of what is being shared, and must not interrupt the agenda or take the client away from experiencing the 'felt sense' of the moment. Prayer has to respect the client's autonomy and attention needs to be paid to potential issues of deference and compliance (Rennie 1994a).

In checking out issues of deference and compliance, it is important to gain the client's consent, although to gain formal written consent, as Magaletta and Brawer (1998) suggest, might detract from the intimacy of the moment and lead to an intellectualization of the phenomenon in which the simplicity and power of the experience are lost. It is important that the client is able to refuse prayer, and it seems important that the counsellor is reflexive about her clients never refusing prayer to ascertain honestly if her method of introducing prayer can enable a client to refuse. If prayer occurs with the counsellor's eyes closed, the counsellor may more fully engage with the prayer experience itself, but she may miss having a sense of the client's way of being as they pray.

The interview data suggest that the use of silence at the beginning of a session is the most appropriate form of prayer at this stage, as it enables the client to gain stillness and a focus for the work. It provides a spiritual space which facilitates the client in focusing on their 'point of pain' and on the essence of their deepest self (authenticity) which allows the unconscious to speak. The prayerful space also acknowledges the spiritual context of the work in a subtle way.

> They're sensing that I'm there for them, and the silence is not a cutting-off, it's actually a discovering for us both, where we're going to go. And certainly it feels like opening out – you can feel a settling down. And it helps them rather than sort of say how difficult it was to park, they will then come up with what it is they want to make use of their time.

Praying with words may inhibit the expression of certain emotions. Lengthy prayer and routine, mechanistic prayer are not appropriate. Any verbal prayer needs to be focused on the client's needs and be a simple acknowledgement of what the client wants to bring. Praying at times of client desperation may take the client away from experiencing the aloneness and the fear of the experience. However, after that has first been experienced and explored, prayer at these times may be beneficial at a time when the client's autonomy has been diminished. Meditative prayer may also be appropriate at times when the client is experiencing panic, as such prayer carries anxiety-reducing traits (Shapiro 1980; Helminiak 1982; McDonald 1999). The use of ritual to aid completion, resolution, a letting go and a committal can also be an appropriate place for prayer to be integrated in counselling.

> I had a client... she had a very sad obstetric history, and she'd lost six children, and we worked through this for a few sessions, and when we came to what felt, to be, towards the end, she'd actually brought baby clothes that she'd knitted for these children, and had kept for many, many years. It must have been probably about fifteen years after and she brought these clothes, and she lit a candle for each of these children, and she named them, and then we just committed them to God, with the names, into his keeping... Impossible to recall the exact words, but something like saying to God, acknowledging that these were His children and naming them and committing each of them by name to God for his keeping, and to allow the client, by name, to be able to let them go into His care... I would say that from that time she was much more at peace about this... she was in a far more peaceful frame of mind, a happier frame of mind, when we completed the work... It really felt as if it had been completed, and I think that was the last time the children were mentioned...

However, it is important that the client does not expect instant healing from the ritual, but is able to continue to work on the issues as and when they recur. It is also important that the counsellor checks out that the client does not feel that the counsellor would be disappointed if healing or closure did not occur. This can enhance the client's authenticity. The interview data also reveal that practices such as the 'laying on of hands' and 'speaking in tongues' are rare. Nevertheless, they do occur and are existentially powerful to those who encounter them. It is important that this type of ritual is not routine or mechanistic, and that the counsellor reflects carefully on her need to introduce such practices. Again, the practice needs to have a sense of naturalness about it for both counsellor and client. It also needs to emerge from a discernment of the 'felt sense' of the moment.

Silence that fosters a connectedness to the sacred (Ulanov and Ulanov 1982; Pargament 1997) is a less controversial, but nevertheless overt use of prayer.

> I think the silence gives people an opportunity, and because I believe in Grace... I do think that if I/they can find a way in which to stop for a moment, and become willing, it's that saying 'yes' again, even if it's at a not completely conscious level, that that allows something else to happen, and that's the bit that's beyond us, really... It kind of opens a door somewhere... I don't know – it is the touch of God. I mean, I do believe – a part of me, I have to say it that way, there is a part of me that believes that the grand being, God, whatever words I use, is active in some sense, not simply a large process of which we are all a part. There's another part of me that believes that, but there is a part of me that believes that there are moments when I know it in my own life – the finger of God touches you, and the experience of that is sometimes a conscious experience, a knowledge of being graced, of being blessed, and sometimes not.

While the literature suggests that prayer has the potential to disempower the client, the interview data argue that prayer also has the potential to empower the client. This can be seen in the client taking responsibility for the praying, in the way that the content of prayer changes over time, and in the ability of the client to ask for prayer. All of these can be regarded as signs of developing autonomy. Some of the common uses of prayer in counselling were at the end of a session or the termination of a counselling relationship. Using prayer at these times is less intrusive to the therapeutic process of the session. This use of prayer to convey messages of hope and affirmation reinforces the therapeutic work in which the client has responsibility for healing, change and/or acceptance. Prayer for intervention which introduces connotations of magic (for example instant healing and miracles), victimhood and helplessness is not appropriate and was not evident in the interview data. The use of prayer to 'dump and run' (Gubi 2001) was also not evident in the interview data. Using prayer to end the counselling relationship can act as a way of consolidating the therapeutic gain (Dobbins 2000), enabling closure and termination of the work at both a practical and a spiritual level.

## Issues of tension and difficulty for the counsellor

The fourth consideration for good practice is an awareness of the possible areas of tension and difficulty for the counsellor. Several such areas were evident in the interview data. Whether prayer can be used to communicate with the client emerged as a contentious issue. The literature suggests that prayer should not be used to impose or communicate the counsellor's values to the client (Rose 1993, 1996, 1999, 2002; Webster 1992; McMinn 1996; Magaletta and Brawer 1998), because the client may be unable to challenge what is being prayed, and the use of prayer in this way is open to manipulation and abuse.

These concerns were reflected in the interview data. However, other interview data suggest that certain values that are compatible with the counselling values (for example the client is a person of worth and of value) may be appropriately imparted and sanctified through prayer.

> So we place all this in the hands of God knowing that on your own you feel really weak and vulnerable, even though there are lots of indications of your tremendous growth and seriously working on yourself, trying to integrate your past and become a more wholesome and worthwhile person, although in many of our lives you are already that. So we finish the session by saying thank you God, for Johnny. Amen.

Prayer may also be a useful medium through which the client is more able to hear the counsellor's insight and awareness of the client and of her process. Rather than being an indirect communication with the client, which may be regarded as the antithesis of counselling (Gubi 2001), prayer can be regarded as a direct communication with the client if God is at the centre of the client. Some counsellors were reluctant to enable their client to explore their motivation for, and act of, praying. However, if prayer is to be integrated into mainstream counselling practice, it must not be treated any differently from any other intervention in counselling. Exploration of whatever happens is an implicit part of therapy and prayer is no different.

The interview data revealed that some counsellors explore the client's need to pray before the prayer. Others wait and let the exploration happen in a natural and unobtrusive way. Others explored the client's process after the prayer. Out of respect for the client, it was important to travel alongside the client through the prayer (even if the content did not feel comfortable for the counsellor), and then to unpick the process therapeutically, or challenge the client appropriately by sensitively, congruently, but tentatively sharing the counsellor's insights and awareness of the client in further therapeutic exploration. If prayer is to be used as a therapeutic intervention, it must not assume a 'sacredness' that excludes it from the way other counselling interventions are worked with, even though some (for example McMinn 1996) consider that prayer is different from other interventions.

Self-disclosure of the counsellor's spirituality was also identified as an area of potential tension. Disclosure of the counsellor's spirituality can enable a more profound connection for clients who want to explore spiritual issues, because exploring spiritual material is often problematic for clients (West 2000a, 2002a). However, the sharing of spiritual beliefs may lead to an unhelpful transference phenomenon (Hinksman 1999) or inappropriately influence the counselling agenda. The interview data suggest that even when counsellors make their faith explicit to their client, the use of prayer is still not frequent in counselling.

## Supervision issues

The interview data reveal that bringing issues of prayer to supervision is highly problematic and suggest that this is because many counsellors do not feel free to explore their practice of prayer due to fear of not being understood; fear of being judged; fear of losing respect and credibility; fear of being thought of as transgressing; fear of exposure by the supervisor; lack of trust in how the supervisor will treat the disclosure; fear of condemnation and dismissal of something that is important and precious to the counsellor. The interview data revealed incidents of the supervisor being 'shocked' at the revelation, and of how supervisors from particular modalities seem to be less open to what their supervisee brings and can instil 'fear' in their supervisee. This leaves supervisees finding creative ways of separating out certain aspects of their work to explore among several supervisors or avoiding exploring some parts of their practice with anyone, neither of which is ethically satisfactory and both of which can carry potential dangers for the client (West 2002b; Gubi 2007).

## Conclusion

A central thesis that has emerged from this research is that prayer is no more problematic than other counselling interventions, nor should it be treated any differently from any other therapeutic intervention within the context of counselling and psychotherapy. Prayer needs to be approached with a knowledge and awareness of the possible ethical difficulties, and be integrated in a manner that is respecting of, and enhancing of, the client's autonomy and in a way that fosters the client's wellbeing. There is an assumption in counselling that 'secular' interventions are acceptable and that spiritual interventions are less acceptable. Yet all counselling interventions are to some degree problematic and need the same degree of careful ethical consideration.

No intervention must be regarded as a panacea for all ills, even though it is possible to gain that sense of a panacea about prayer from some writers (for example Ten Eyck 1993). To regard prayer in this way can be disrespecting of the client and is existentially ignorant. If prayer can be empowering, as the interview data suggest it can be, then arguably it is unethical to withhold it (Gubi 2002) if the client has a healthy spirituality and prayer is an important part of their spirituality (Richards and Bergin 1997). If the counsellor also shares that spirituality and is cautious in her approach and in her awareness of her client, then the process should be open to any intervention (or 'mode of relating') that can enhance the client's growth (depending on how 'growth' is psychologically and spiritually defined) and that can enable the therapeutic alliance to deepen relationally (Mearns and Cooper 2005).

The purpose of the research was not to advocate the use of prayer, but it is important for mainstream counselling to become open to the use of spiritual interventions, like prayer, which can be utilized for the benefit of the client. The integration of prayer is intrinsically pragmatic and has to be characterized by openness and acceptance of what is meaningful to the other (Gubi 2008). These qualities are not always evident in counselling and supervision and need further examination at a personal level, as well as advancement at a cultural level in relation to working with the spiritual dimension of counselling.

## Discussion points

1. How do you feel about others using prayer in a therapeutic context?
2. If a new client asked you to pray with her at the end of your first session, what feelings and thoughts would be likely to be triggered in you and what might your response be?
3. Would it make any difference to you if it was the client who did the praying rather than you?
4. How would you feel and act if the client's prayer indicated a belief/value system that you didn't subscribe to or you felt uncomfortable with?
5. If you are a supervisor, how open are you to your supervisee praying with her clients?

# 5
# Compassion in Psychotherapy

*Barbara Vivino and Barbara Thompson*

## Introduction

This chapter presents findings from our qualitative research into compassion in psychotherapy. We consider what compassion is and how it applies to psychotherapy before describing the research. We discuss our findings in the light of the literature, followed by examples from practice. We then put forward a theory of compassion alongside some guidelines for therapeutic practice. Ethical and supervisory issues are considered, as are issues of culture and diversity. Some discussion points are offered by way of a conclusion.

## Background

The mere presence of certain people seems to evoke transformation in another. This occurs, among other places, between clients and therapists in psychotherapy. Characteristics of that transformative presence are not fully understood, but anecdotally have included aspects such as compassion, joy, and love. Although the therapeutic relationship has been shown to be one of the most significant factors related to psychotherapy outcome (Norcross 2002), the person of the therapist is often ignored by researchers and the impact of therapist characteristics like compassion and a spiritual perspective on the healing process are not fully understood. We, the authors, consider compassion to be universal and already to be embedded, albeit covertly in most cases, in the psychotherapy process and the therapeutic relationship. We wanted to understand more fully the nature of therapist compassion and thus conducted a qualitative study of therapist compassion (Vivino et al. 2009), the findings of which we have used to describe more fully how therapist compassion facilitates client growth in psychotherapy.

*Merriam-Webster's Collegiate Dictionary* (2003: 276) defined compassion as 'a sympathetic consciousness of others' distress together with a desire to alleviate it'. Similarly, Gilbert (2005) described compassion as being open to the suffering of self and others in a non-judgmental way with a desire to relieve suffering. Definitions of compassionate love suggest that it incorporates a response to the suffering of another as well as actions that encourage the flourishing of another (Underwood 2002), both of which seem to be intrinsic characteristics of the psychotherapy relationship.

The development of compassion is advocated by most religions, including Christianity, Judaism, Islam, Hinduism, Buddhism and Jainism. Eastern traditions have for centuries viewed compassion as having the potential to heal our minds and bodies and it is held to be a central component of Buddhist psychology (Welwood 1999). The Sanskrit word for compassion, *karuna*, means experiencing a trembling or quivering of the heart in response to another being's pain (Salzberg 1995). The Tibetan word *tsewa* refers to a state of mind or way of being where a person extends how they relate to themselves towards others as well. For the Dalai Lama (1999, 2001), compassion is the wish that all beings be free of their suffering.

Recently, there have been attempts at integrating eastern theory and mind training practices with western forms of psychotherapy (Watson et al. 1999; Young-Eisendrath and Muramoto 2002). Furthermore, several models of therapy, such as dialectical behavior therapy (Linehan 1992), mindfulness-based cognitive therapy for depression (Segal et al. 2002) and compassionate mind training (Gilbert and Irons 2005), refer to compassion as an important component of therapy.

Despite this growing interest, and the centrality of compassion in Buddhist psychology, psychotherapy researchers have focused predominantly on related concepts such as empathy and attachment and have ignored the concept of compassion. Yet, if compassion is a healing or transformative process as Buddhism suggests, than it should be central to our investigations and we should explore what it is and how it works (Gilbert 2005).

We investigated how therapists conceptualize and use compassion in psychotherapy, how therapists develop compassion within themselves, and how compassion differs across cases. In addition, we wanted to differentiate compassion from empathy, which Rogers (1957: 99) described as a therapist's ability 'to sense a client's private world as if it were your own'. Unlike compassion, empathy has been discussed extensively in the psychotherapy literature, particularly in the examination of the therapy relationship (Duan and Hill 1996). Considered by humanistic theorists to be a necessary and sufficient condition for psychological change (Rogers 1957) and by psychoanalytic theorists to be part of the psychoanalytic cure (Kohut 1977), empathy has been a key concept in understanding why and how therapy works, and has been linked with better therapy outcome (Burns and Nolen-Hoeksema 1992). Although compassion and empathy seem intuitively similar, little is known about the similarities or differences between the two.

Because compassion has not been explored empirically in psychotherapy, we used a qualitative research approach to study it, specifically consensual qualitative research (CQR; Hill et al. 1997, 2005). CQR utilizes a research team approach to categorize and reach consensus on the deeper meaning of interview data. We interviewed 14 licensed psychotherapists in private practice who were nominated as compassionate by others in their professional community.

## Findings from the research

Therapists typically defined compassion as being *connected to suffering*. As an example, one therapist said:

> It's simply for me the openness to be present to another's difficulties and suffering... the willingness to be there and open oneself to receiving and connecting with the person that is in the midst of or perhaps even lost in their, what you call it, suffering.

Thus, compassion seemed to be elicited when therapists connected with the clients' suffering and were able to understand and identify with this suffering. This felt resonance between client and therapist seemed to serve as a compassionate bridge to help the therapist understand the client.

Therapists also typically defined compassion as involving the *promotion of change*. According to one therapist:

> Compassion in psychotherapy is using that kind of understanding in a helpful way to help promote some kind of helpful change in the client's life.

This action component of compassion was described by one participant as 'a sword that cuts through slothful ignorance', referring to the Buddhist idea that an important component of compassion is the

.e of uncompromising battle in the face of ignorance or that it
ɔ through' illusions. Thus, compassion goes beyond the western
ɔtion of empathy and implies the necessity of taking action, such that
clients do not stay stuck in their suffering. Therapists also described taking action by going beyond traditional boundaries when necessary, for
example going to a client's home when the client was in crisis.

Therapists specifically stated that they thought compassion was different from empathy. Typically, they suggested that it is *broader and
deeper than empathy*. One therapist said:

> I think of empathy as a capacity to really stand in somebody else's
> shoes and know what it feels like to be, to be with what that person
> is with. But I think compassion takes it a step further in that for me
> compassion really entails an active quality, there is a dynamic nature
> to compassion which is more than just the capacity to feel what it's
> like to be somebody else but to actually be really engaged with that
> person in what that place is and to help them move through it, what-
> ever that might look like.

Therapists generally reported that compassion was *demonstrated through
therapist behaviours*. More specifically, they typically reported that compassion was manifested in therapy when the therapist sat with the client's pain, attuned to the client or listened to the client, and was fully
present. According to one therapist:

> How it manifests is probably in large part more something that is felt
> but also it probably looks like attuning with the client, how I might
> be deeply listening to a client and how I might find just the right
> element for that person's experience to hold in myself and to reflect
> back so that the person in an outer way, in a manifest way knows or
> has an experience of whether they feel really met and understood by
> me and cared about by me.

Participants also generally reported that compassion was manifested in
their *inner experience*. Specifically, compassion was typically discussed as
an attitude or way of being, such as feeling loving-kindness, being non-
judgmental and accepting of the client, and being genuine and open.
For example, one therapist indicated:

> A compassionate response sometimes will draw forth an action, a
> soothing. I tear up some, you know, and I think that people see that

I'm really touched by their predicament, their story, whatever. I feel that what this is, this idea of heart-centeredness, that I try to live from my heart center, I try to counsel from my heart center.

Therapists typically perceived that their clients feel heard, understood and cared about when *they (the therapists) were compassionate* (for example, 'I think they experience a sense of being understood, accepted, not acquiesced to, but accepted, hopefully a sense of welcome'). In addition, therapists reported that clients typically experienced symptom relief, such that clients feel healed, opened up and able to go into their pain and deepen their experience (for example, 'I think when compassion is manifest in my work with clients I can see it, I personally can see it in the client in the way that they might soften, the way they might open more, the way emotion might flow, the way the process might continue moving forward, um, yeah like the blocks are slowly removed').

*Issues in therapists' personal lives* (such as physical illness or discomfort) were typically perceived as interfering with compassion. One therapist said:

With my daughter with serious depression, suicide attempts, and drug use, I got very depleted with the constant trauma and grief and powerlessness and my practice needed to shrink... with some patients, I could find myself feeling very annoyed and irritated when their suffering seemed so minor.

Therapists also identified *things occurring within themselves during therapy sessions* as limiting their capacity to be compassionate. For example, they described having strong emotional reactions (that is, countertransference) to some clients:

I had some fear about my own well-being – the fear closes you off and constricts you. It's like I couldn't open up any longer to whatever was going to go on in the room, I didn't want to be there with him, you know, so, I think I would have to say that kind of makes it impossible to be compassionate.

*Client characteristics* also typically limited therapists' ability to be compassionate. In one example, the therapist stated:

I could not work with a child abuser, a male sex perpetrator. I would refer them out because I would really be limited and hindered in my compassion even though I know there's a small child, a wounded child in there somewhere. I would not be able to sit with that person and feel enough compassion to be helpful.

Therapists typically cited *client behaviors within therapy sessions* as limiting their capacity to be compassionate. A typical cluster of behaviours involved resistance, such that the client did not take responsibility for their actions, was uninvolved in the therapy process, was defensive or was stuck and could not progress in therapy (for example, 'If a person is a blamer, and will not take any responsibility for him or herself, I get very irritated').

All participants mentioned *managing their thoughts and feelings within sessions* as a way to return to feeling compassionate. More specifically, a typical strategy was working at understanding the client's underlying issues. In effect, trying to understand what was going on for clients that made them behave as they did allowed therapists to get past their annoyance, anger or negative feelings and experience compassion for the client's pain. For example, one therapist revealed:

> When I have a client that I have some judgment around, that's, you know it's the judgment that's maybe precluding the sense of compassion, then I really might try to dive more deeply into my understanding of what is, how did this organization arise within this client and try to find a wound that the rigidity is formed around, and by finding and connecting with the wound, then I can develop more compassion and just hold that in my perspective that, you know, this is put here for some specific reason and it is my job to find that out.

A second typical strategy was *self-care strategies outside the professional role*, such as therapy, dream work, meditation, taking vacations and not working when sick. For example, one therapist reported:

> Once I become aware that that's the problem then I might do a number of things like sit and meditate for a while. Other kinds of active imagination processes like shamanic journeying [a visualization technique originally utilized by priest-like healers of indigenous people throughout the world] or you know some way to really go within to find the core in myself of what's strong and full alive.

When asked about how they developed into a compassionate therapist, participants typically reported that they thought that *compassion was an innate capacity*. For instance, one therapist said:

> Compassion is not something that can be developed or dictated. If not there, the therapist has no business being a therapist unless s/he is using a therapy that is not predicated on healing or a deep therapeutic relationship. Compassion is inborn and cannot be taught but can be awakened.

They also talked about having done *work on their own* through therapy, self-examination, learning from their own suffering and meditation that enabled them to feel compassion for themselves. According to one therapist:

> Through my own therapy I was able to defrost the frozen part of myself and re-experience my grief and heal. Because my own therapist was particularly warm, I was able to reveal my secret grief, become compassionate and it also made me decide to become a therapist.

In addition, participants typically felt that they became compassionate due to *experiences within their families*, either through having experienced pain in their family of origin, a valuing of compassion by their family or being a parent. One therapist remarked:

> When I was young, my younger sister, who was thirteen months younger than me, became ill when she was about two... and for the next 2 years she got increasingly ill and then she died. And so I was five when she died. And she was really my first love. So my family's inability to deal with sadness and grief, mourning, carved out a huge space in me for suffering. And I spent my early childhood thinking I was going to grow up to be a saint, that's what I wanted to do. Through my own suffering and the desire to heal the suffering around me, I learned compassion, and then it kind of extended to have the sensitivity for the suffering of the world.

In addition, participants typically reported that they developed compassion through the *experience or observation of compassion* from a mentor, teacher, friend, family member or therapist. For example, one said,

'A particularly profound experience was my therapist at 16, who I felt completely noticed by, completely seen and cared about.'

Participants typically developed compassion *from working with clients* or through their spiritual beliefs or experiences. For example:

> Immersion in my work with pedophiles required me to learn compassion because I got to know the men individually and experience their pain and inability to do things differently, to see their wounds and understand where they were coming from.

> My first Buddhist training was experiential with meditation, training began with a focus on working with self to develop a sense of loving kindness to self which I see as the seat of compassion.

Finally, participants typically said that they developed compassion *from their training as a therapist.*

> I was strongly influenced by an existential-humanist supervisor, who could be compassionate but also have boundaries, be firm and clear and yet be heartfelt and caring in a real way.

## Examples from practice

In this section we provide an example of one case in which the therapist felt strong compassion for the client. We quote directly from the therapist:

> With this client, it's pretty easy to feel compassion... There was a time this summer where she had stopped her meds... and the voices were going to, were telling her to kill herself, and very disruptive. And in fact, she had gone out one night and tried to do it, and threw a rope over a tree. She somehow found a rope and had thrown a rope over a tree, and spent actually a couple of hours trying to do this, but fortunately she was too disorganized to actually do it... I think it's easy with her. Everybody likes her, so I don't think there's been a person who hasn't liked her... She's smart, she's funny, in a sense, she's, she's very pleasant to be with, she I think, she comes to counseling, she comes to treatment, she really kind of follows through, she perseveres.

> She's got a great personality... I mean, there's a lot of things she's not open about, and it's also very hard for her to ask for help, but she

comes every week... she's very much able to form a relationship, and I think that that makes it, that makes it easier... I've heard people say that she's brilliant, but the sad thing, the unfortunate thing is that her mental illness is so severe that, that it's really, I mean, it's really, takes all that she can just to kind of be here...

If anything it [compassion] probably has, has grown in the more than I've gotten to know her... It's a pull for her in terms of the voices. She finds them, the stars are talking to her. She's very lyrical when she's in kind of a more of a hypomanic state, more of a manic state, and I mean it's like poetry coming out of her, out of her mouth when she talks about joining the stars. But then the voices start kicking in. And so, of course, joining the stars that she's gonna kill herself to go join the stars... She's kind of gotten angry with me and also we've been able to talk about that... She also, we use humor... She's pretty able to kind of accept some of the things that I've said, and I've been more direct, I'm pretty direct with her. And a lot of times, she'll come back later and ask me something to correct a perception that she had, she's had me thinking one way and I said, No, you know, I wasn't at all thinking that and I'm really glad you asked. So, she's able to check some things out.

## A nascent theory of compassion

Based on these findings, we propose that compassion in psychotherapy is a broad construct that encompasses elements of therapy process, therapist variables and aspects of the person of the therapist that functions to facilitate client change.

Compassion seems to provide a motivational influence for therapists to engage in and navigate therapeutic relationships with clients who are expressing painful emotions or exhibiting difficult behaviour. Similar to Rogers' discussion of the therapist's way of being rather than way of doing, the therapist's compassion for the client creates an environment where the client feels safe enough to deeply explore and experience their suffering. Exposure to the client's suffering may elicit from the therapist a compassionate response, which allows the therapist to look beyond the client's struggles and resonate to the suffering beneath it, and thus helps the therapist understand the client deeply and convey that understanding to the client.

Furthermore, we believe that the therapist's compassion has the potential to facilitate client change by providing the client with a 'corrective emotional experience', which Alexander (Alexander and French 1946; Alexander 1961) defined as re-exposure under positive circumstances to an emotional situation with which one could not cope in childhood. Alexander (1961) believed that the curative powers of psychotherapy were due to the clients' ability to express aggressiveness and vulnerability with the therapist without being punished (as they may have been with parents), and they could also assert themselves without being censured. Although Alexander (1961) suggested that favourable circumstances were necessary for this corrective emotional experience, he did not describe them. Compassion from the therapist may be one of these favourable circumstances.

Similar to mindfulness approaches in therapy (Linehan 1992; Kabat-Zinn 1994), a compassionate stance from a therapist may serve the function of helping clients become non-judgemental observers of their thoughts, feelings and processes. When therapists are able to experience compassion, they appear to experience an acceptance of clients and of themselves. This acceptance may allow the clients to fully express and experience their emotions, thoughts and difficulties, as well as to observe and accept themselves, thus creating space between themselves and their difficult experience. Similar to Freud's (1932) concept of the observing ego, clients' capacity to develop distance between themselves and their experiences frees clients from suffering and illusion and gives them insight and the ability to choose appropriate responses or action.

We do not think that the clients' corrective emotional experience in therapy is limited to repairing damage created in childhood. Instead, we think that through the process of experiencing suffering in the presence of a compassionate therapist, clients experience compassion for themselves and are therefore able to create distance from, observe, accept and then integrate parts of self that they avoided and found shameful and unacceptable. It is not enough for clients simply to expose their suffering to another person for healing to occur. Rather, they must expose their suffering in the presence of a compassionate other, someone who can go beyond intellectual understanding to connecting with the pain and suffering at a deep level. Perhaps the warmth and acceptance that are extended to another in compassion counter feelings of isolation, bringing the sufferer back into relationship with another and with themselves.

The therapist's ability to resonate with the client's experience was described by Kohut (1977) as 'vicarious introspection'. Thus, the therapist's own experience of suffering and working through that suffering allows them to 'get' the client and have compassion for them. This compassion is behaviourally communicated to the client ('I understand your pain'), who then feels understood ('I am not alone in my suffering and can allow myself to experience it') and thus experiences symptom relief ('I can let some of my pain and suffering go'). Through the client's experience of compassion and with the active participation of the therapist in promoting change, the client can move forward either through specific action or internal processes and experience relief from suffering or distress. The therapist's ability to be compassionate allows the therapist to accept the client even when the client is experiencing painful emotions and to work through their countertransference reactions.

The experience of compassion seems to incorporate an acceptance of the client's thoughts, feelings and experiences and an acceptance of the therapist's own thoughts and feelings that seems to allow the therapist to sit with what is occurring without the need to rush to premature solutions. This acceptance seems to provide room for creative solutions to the client's dilemma to emerge from the therapist and the client. Rogers (1957) hypothesized that acceptance brings about change. In this apparent paradox, instead of attempting to change the client, the therapist strives to accept the client and change will follow naturally. Therapists' ability to experience their own suffering and have compassion for themselves seems to help them subsequently to be compassionate with the client or to allow the client to express their suffering in the therapy session.

## Implications and guidelines for practice

Our findings indicated that a therapist's ability to feel compassion may fluctuate between clients. Thus, it seems important for therapists to become aware of and understand more fully when they feel more or less compassion with particular clients. The inability to feel compassion for a particular client may let therapists know that they need to do something (for example seek supervision or consultation to regain the compassion, or terminate with the client without putting the blame on the client). In addition, we believe that the ability to feel and relate compassionately to our clients is a barometer that lets us know when we need to focus on self-care strategies and encourages us to maintain our own practice of spiritual renewal and maintenance (for instance our own therapy, meditation practice, aligning with higher aspects of ourselves and exercise).

While we agree with most of the therapists in our study who felt that the ability to feel compassion was innate, we also believe that it can be awakened or developed more fully. In fact, when we work with our clients in deep ways, our ability to feel compassion grows. This process involves actively cultivating compassion towards others within ourselves.

Practitioners are encouraged to conceptualize compassion as an ability to connect with a client's suffering, but also to see the value of the process of suffering to heal clients and move them to greater growth. Understandably, clients often avoid experiencing their suffering. The therapist, however, can see the client as greater than than their suffering and see beyond that suffering. Thus the therapist can help the client use the suffering in a beneficial and purposeful way to grow and expand, instead of seeing suffering as something 'wrong' and fighting it or blaming themselves (which simply creates more suffering).

It is important for practitioners to have worked through some of their own suffering and have an understanding of the path through suffering. Practitioners who have grown from their own experiences of suffering can feel compassion for clients and model the experience and moving beyond suffering. In this way, compassion incorporates the potential of who the person can become as differentiated from sympathy or empathy, which focuses more on the present pain.

Practitioners are also encouraged to think of compassion as more than just 'being with the client'. It is also the double-edged sword that cuts through illusion. Being compassionate also means challenging our clients to take responsibility, to wake up.

## Ethics and supervision issues

Compassion may be an important foundation for effective counselling, therefore ethically and professionally therapists should strive to develop compassion within themselves. As psychologists, we are ethically bound to be emotionally competent to treat clients. Although 'emotional competence' has not been fully described by ethics boards, compassion could be an important component of this competence.

Conversely, therapists who feel excessive positive countertransference towards a client may lose objectivity and place themselves at higher risk by failing to observe serious pathology. Therefore it is important for a therapist to examine her feelings towards a client to differentiate between compassion, which includes appropriate boundaries and does not involve enmeshment with the client, and excessive positive counter transference.

In supervision, just as in therapy, it seems important for supervisors to feel compassion for their supervisees. Studies on supervision (Ladany

2004) have shown that it is important for the supervisee to feel safe and understood by the supervisor so that they can reveal difficult and potentially shameful material to the supervisor. Thus, supervisor compassion could be an important component of a successful supervising relationship. In addition, since the supervisor models the relationship to the supervisee, a compassionate presence in supervision may facilitate a parallel process with the supervisee and their client.

As supervisors, we have found the concept of compassion to be helpful when advising trainees to look beyond the client's often resistant or annoying interpersonal behaviors to the suffering below. Helping trainees cultivate compassion for themselves is also useful during the early stages of training, when they feel incompetent and overwhelmed by the task of sitting with clients, making and learning from mistakes, and taking in the constructive feedback of supervisors. Supporting a supervisee in learning about their own fluctuations in compassion may also assist them to support and renew themselves on a regular basis.

Helping a supervisee to explore their compassion or lack of compassion for a client may assist in the process of exploring countertransference issues. What gets in the way of feeling compassion for a client may be the clinician's unresolved personal issues elicited from the client. Working towards being compassionate may facilitate a therapist's own work and serve as a guide for supervisors to assist clinicians in working towards being compassionate as well.

In addition, therapists in training often struggle with connecting to a client's pain, 'allowing' clients to experience pain or challenging clients to change. It could be helpful for trainees to know that even experienced, generally compassionate therapists sometimes have difficulty being compassionate. Perhaps training programmes could be developed to teach beginning therapists about compassion, especially to help them awaken compassion within themselves. In addition, developing compassion may help beginning therapists learn and use more advanced therapist skills, such as the ability to challenge clients empathically.

## Diversity or culture

Compassion seems to be universal in nature and cuts across cultural boundaries, as evidenced by its important position in most world religions. However, therapists may find it more difficult to feel compassion for clients of certain cultures or ethnicities. It is important for therapists to be aware of differences in compassion or lack of compassion as an indicator of a need to examine their beliefs and limitations. Connecting to the universality of suffering unites people and helps therapists understand individuals from cultures which might seem very dissimilar to their own.

## Conclusion

The therapists in our study, who had been nominated by others in the professional community as being particularly compassionate, revealed much wisdom about the role of compassion in psychotherapy. Therapists clearly believed that compassion is a healing force in psychotherapy. Compassion may help therapists understand or 'get' a patient on a deeper level; serve a transformative function; allow clients to see themselves from a broader perspective; serve as a corrective emotional experience; and motivate therapists to work with difficult clients.

We have only begun to understand the function of compassion in the psychotherapy process, yet our findings indicate that compassion warrants further investigation and more explicit focus in the training and practice of the transformative aspects of the person of the therapist.

### Discussion points

1. How are compassion, empathy and sympathy different or the same?
2. Is it possible to feel too much compassion for a client?
3. Is it ethical to continue to see a client for whom you do not feel compassion?
4. How does compassion develop? Is compassion learned or innate?
5. What interferes with your ability to be compassionate?

# 6
## Counselling, Spirituality and Culture

*Fevronia Christodoulidi*

## Introduction

In this chapter, I will present some of the process dynamics related to the intersection between counselling, spirituality and culture, as revealed through an exploratory, qualitative and heuristic study of the experiences of seven counselling practitioners of diverse cultural and spiritual backgrounds. I will begin by contextualizing my study, which adopted a focus group method, in the recent literature, before explaining the rationale behind its design and its major questions. I will then discuss the main findings, matters arising and some of the implications for training and supervision. Guidelines for practitioners will also be suggested.

## Background

We live in an increasingly globalized society, where people are facing challenging existential and cultural issues, both at an individual and a collective level, particularly in relation to identity, human relationships and communication, as well as race relations, interpersonal and intercultural (mis)understandings, political and religious differences. There is, hence, an inevitable strive towards rediscovering certain values that may assist in redefining the self of people as travellers, interpreters, translators, guides, settlers or borderland crossers, in search for belonging and meaning making within the self and the world.

Counselling and psychotherapy often become the 'reflecting mirror' or 'container' of such processes. They may be attributed to the need and expectation to assist in relieving or resolving such identity crises and confusions. They may be seen as practices that can facilitate the process of discovering meaning and cultivating harmonious relationships at an inter- and intrapersonal level, but also extend it among wider communities. Cultural and spiritual values are those that are mostly in question within the composition of contemporary multicultural and multifaith societies, where the mixing of histories, ideologies and beliefs presents both challenging and promising dynamics.

Out of a desire that counselling and psychotherapy avoid repeating certain oppressive or discriminating functions, but instead aspire to be a liberating and therapeutic force, my study focused on exploring therapists' conceptualizations of the spiritual and cultural dimension as they interact with each other, the influences of their spiritual and cultural background on their lives and practice, and the therapeutic processes occurring when working with spiritual and cultural issues. I hope that the insights gained will sharpen our understanding of the implications of such issues for effective counselling provision, training and supervision within the therapy arena, as well as the wider effect on the discourse around inclusion and conflict resolution.

## Literature context

In recent years a vast body of literature (for example D'Ardenne and Mahtani 1989; Carter 1995; Lago and Thompson 1996; Laungani 2007; Moodley 2007a) has developed focusing on areas that relate to the cultural dimension of counselling (for a comprehensive review see Palmer 2002). From the US, we have documents that are directly related to the provision and process issues of cross-cultural therapy, such as the 'Guidelines for providers of psychological services to ethnic, linguistic and culturally diverse populations' (APA 1993) and the 'Multicultural Counseling Competencies' by the Professional Standards Committee for the Association for Multicultural Counseling and Development (AMCD; Sue et al. 1992).

In terms of the issues related to the spiritual dimension in therapy, following some pioneers in transpersonal psychology (Maslow, Buber and so on) there has been a growing literature and research during the last couple of decades around spirituality and its relation to and position within counselling (just a few examples are Grof and Grof 1989; Thorne 1991, 1998, 2002; West 1998a, 2000a, 2002a, 2004a; Wilber 2000; Swinton 2001; Ankrah 2002; Richards and Bergin 2005). Doctoral research projects around specific spiritually related topics, such as the use of prayer in counselling, embodied spirituality, psychic energy in counselling or encounters with a spirit guide, have also been accepted and conducted (see for example chapters in this volume by Gubi, Yusef, Gorsedene and Wardle), breaking new ground in both theory and counselling practice and addressing issues that have traditionally been considered as taboos or otherwise pathologized (Jenkins 2006, Chapter 2 this volume).

Pedersen (1997) has suggested that multiculturalism is the 'fourth force' in the counselling profession, while Cortright (1997) has described transpersonal psychology as the 'fourth force' in psychology, currently encompassing the wisdom of the world's religions and spiritual world-views towards the expansion of human consciousness and the fulfil-ment of human, multidimensional potential.

One could argue that those movements in the field of contemporary counselling and psychotherapy may manifest a response to the exis-tential angst in the modern way of living, the rapidly changing com-position of western societies, the migration from the developing world and the integration movement in the therapy professions. Most of the time, the constructs and dynamics of spirituality or culture as related to counselling have been examined separately, with the exception of a very few studies. A remarkable example is the volume by Fukuyama and Sevig, who developed a conceptual framework within which to understand and utilize the two concepts in integration, drawn from the belief that 'spiritual processes can facilitate multicultural understand-ing. Concurrently, the multicultural learning experience can serve as a stimulus for spiritual growth' (1999: 15).

Such a context presents questions around where practitioners in the therapy field stand, within themselves as well as in their professional role, in front of such a picture, something that has driven the perspec-tive of this study.

## Setting the scene: Why explore practitioners' perspectives?

There is a general recognition that 'spirituality remains a difficult issue for counselling and psychotherapy' (West 1998a). Similarly, 'for a long time cultural and racial issues have been viewed as the client's "issues", implying something that therapists are disconnected from or even problematic' (Eleftheriadou 2003). Most scholars have shown a predominant interest in examining issues related to spirituality and culture from the client's perspective. It is often acknowledged that counsellors appear typically not to understand and respond to their clients' spiritual and cultural needs, despite the fact that there has been increased sensitivity around issues of gender, race and ethnicity in counselling (Pedersen 1997: 99). Given that the counselling relationship is co-constructed by both client and counsellor and the counsellor's self-awareness is vital, my interest has been in exploring this issue *from the counsellor's and psychotherapist's perspective instead*. This choice was as a result of acknowledging that the therapist's own beliefs and value system play an important part in the co-created dynamic in the counselling room; hence, it became necessary to provide an interactive space so that such a voice could be expressed.

I proposed to bring such diverse voices together in a sort of 'multi-cultural and multispiritual conference'. In my opinion, the central axis of such paradigm shifts, also requiring an interdisciplinary dialogue, is the ongoing cultivation of the awareness of the parties involved – specifically of therapists – who inevitably bring with them their cultural background, therapeutic modality, spiritual belief, practice context and so on. In the light of such an inquiry, the study was aimed at examining the following questions:

- How do counsellors and psychotherapists from diverse cultural backgrounds perceive the spiritual and cultural dimension within themselves and the therapeutic relationship? How does this affect/inform their practice? (Q1)
- What would be the challenges/problems/opportunities occurring in a consideration of the processes and interactions of the dynamic forces of spirituality, culture and counselling? (Q2)

In the following section, I will summarize the major aspects of the focus group study, before moving on discussing the main findings and their relevance to the purpose of this research.

## Focus group study

It is crucial in any research for the researcher to come to a decision around the most appropriate method of collecting data, having reached a pragmatic acceptance of relevant challenges and dilemmas (West 2001b, 2007). Looking at the questions outlined earlier, two components appeared important. These had to do with the *diversity* of the research sample/participants and the importance of the *process interaction* among the three forces of spirituality, culture and counselling, as well as that of the focus group participants themselves. Given the relatively unexplored territory and controversial nature of this phenomenon, choosing to conduct a focus group session for initial data generation seemed appropriate, as:

> Focus Groups are particularly useful for exploration and discovery while getting an in-depth interpretation of a topic or learning more about groups of people who are often misunderstood. As a qualitative research method, focus groups create a process of sharing and comparing amongst participants to generate data. (Krueger 1994)

Seven participants, of diverse cultural backgrounds and spiritual perspectives, were recruited for a focus group interview (Christodoulidi 2006). The focus group composition is summarized in Table 6.1.

The recording of the focus group session produced a transcript that was approached and analysed from a heuristic methodological perspective (Moustakas 1990, 1994). This is a paradigm that emphasizes the personal involvement of the researcher with the topic and 'uses this involvement to aid the gathering of data and the forms of data analysis chosen' (West 2001b: 128). Heuristic inquiry is a highly reflexive methodological approach, described to be taking place in six, non-linear stages (that is, initial engagement, immersion, incubation, illumination, explication and creative synthesis; Moustakas 1990) as a process of the researcher's engagement with the research focus, drawing from autobiographical triggers and 'living' the phenomenon and the conduct of the research itself in its multiple and full dimensions.

The above description matched my own presence in my research focus, as a person and practitioner who has immigrated into UK culture and has been involved in a number of psychospiritual processes that inevitably influence my values, worldview and counselling working style. Such a perspective is a factor that underpins my levels of reflexivity and dialogue with co-researchers. In the following section, I present some of the insights that were produced through this process.

## Findings from research

The meanings attached to the unfolding of the phenomenon were co-constructed among the participants and the researcher. All voluntarily engaged in the heuristic process, where the attempt was to share the dialogue that would hopefully illuminate the dynamics between the culture of spirituality and counselling, as personally experienced. The focus group members appeared to be moving 'from the individual to the general and back again... from the feeling to the word and back to

Table 6.1 Focus group participants' profiles

| Participant | Ethnic Background | Spiritual Perspective | Training | Practice |
|---|---|---|---|---|
| A (m) | British | Buddhism (influence by) | Hypnotherapy Integrative | NHS |
| B (f) | Irish/African | Elements of New Age, African spirituality etc. | Person-centred | Youth and community work |
| C (m) | Celtic/Irish | Christian Catholic | Multicultural | Spiritual community/ privately |
| D (m) | N/a (Afro-Caribbean background) | N/a (not specific description) | Jungian/systemic Psychodynamic | Self-help PD |
| E (m) | Italian (3rd gen.) | Sufi (convert) | Person-centred | Counsellor training |
| F (f) | British | Christian evangelical | Person-centred | Counselling in church |
| G (f) | Turkish (2nd gen.) | 'secular spirituality' (Muslim heritage) | Transpersonal bodywork | PC training |

Note: The words used for the 'descriptions' are not to label a particular stance of each focus group member, but more to give a more general perspective.

the feeling, from the experience to the concept and back to the experience' (Craig 1978: 57).

At first glance, the data revealed the following broad themes in the narrative accounts of co-researchers:

- Participant's (counsellor's) own personal story
- Exploring the meaning of the term 'spiritual/spirituality'
- Exploring the meaning of the term 'cultural/culture'
- Exploring the links/interactions of spirituality and culture in counselling
- Examples from counselling practice
- Training (whether the issues are addressed or not)
- Supervision (whether the issues are addressed or not)

A dominant finding has been the acknowledgement of a complex debate around *defining* the concepts of 'spirituality' and 'culture'. The group members appeared to need to discover common ground or a shared language around what they were invited to reflect on and find ways of articulating. This was central to the discourse and the analysis revealed a number of different ways of expressing the constructions of meaning around those concepts.

When exploring the meaning of *spirituality*, the discourse was around the forms, characteristics and contexts outlined in Table 6.2.

*Table 6.2* Discourse around spirituality

| Forms (of spirituality) | Characteristics (adjectives) | Context |
| --- | --- | --- |
| Religion | Transpersonal | Church |
| Christian spirituality | Egalitarian | Places of worship |
| Healing (practice of) | Universal | Temple |
| African spirituality | (maybe) Inherited | Retreat centre |
| Spiritual direction | Immanent in all | Counselling |
| Feminine spirituality | Awakening | room |
| Faith (traditions or | Trans-generational | Residential |
| denominations) | | setting |
| Masculine spirituality | | |
| Faith journey | | |
| Embodied spirituality | | |
| Spiritual practice | | |
| Spiritual images | | |
| Mediums | | |
| Meditation | | |

Some of the expressions and phrases that the focus group participants used to describe the *experience* of the 'spiritual' in their lives and in their work with clients are the following:

- being connected with 'presence'
- (being connected to) my spiritual self or psychic self
- being initiated into that path
- 'spiritual emergency'
- being in touch with something greater
- 'embracing all'
- 'greeting that divinity within you'
- being engaged with people in that meaningful struggle
- experiencing inner stillness
- (being) open and accepting
- being energetically open (or awareness of my energetic 'taking' into another person
- (being) deeply connected with God
- reaching a place of deep trust
- experience of oneness
- moment of higher consciousness
- seeing the aura around that person's body
- sensing the people or the energies being present in the room

In terms of the discourse around *culture*, participants described its forms and manifestations as well as the experience of it, as summarized in Table 6.3.

The 'meaning units' described in the above tables were articulated by participants as they perceived them in their own lives, in their multiple personal and professional roles, in relation to their perception of themselves and engagements with others, as beings with cultural and spiritual influences. Such a dialogue revealed that these concepts are multifaceted, often presenting angles that may seem contradictory to each other. Throughout the focus group session, a number of juxtapositions became evident in an attempt, on behalf of the participants, to clarify and make distinctions in relation to concepts/ideas that held particularly significance for them. Some of those were more vividly demonstrated by offering examples from practice. Here I give some of those juxtapositions while quoting directly the focus group members' examples:

- *Spiritual versus religious awareness*: 'religion is perhaps part of spirituality because I have met some people, including clients, who are

*Table 6.3* Discourse around culture

| Forms/manifestations | Experience |
|---|---|
| Cultural self | Outsiders in a culture |
| History | Awareness of 'differences' within |
| Symbols | groups |
| Black-and-white films | Crossing cultural boundaries |
| Meaning of a name | 'Things like culture I try to unbound' |
| Accent (language) | Rejecting culture as a self-definition |
| Poetry, song, story, TV, novel | Being 'half' of my community but also |
| Ancestry | different |
| Secular nation | Mixed race people |
| Cultural image, racial image, cultural | (Being) oppressed and discriminated |
| mask | against |
| Very black (woman), incredibly dark | Race as a narrative |
| skin | Black-and-white position |
| Ethnicity | Sense of 'at home-ness' |
| (Race) connected to class, gender, | Myriad of cultural realities |
| culture | Sameness v difference |
| A mixture that can't be named | Power dynamics |
| Cultural identity | (The culture of) action, production, |
| Cultural sensitivity | doing v being |
| Cultural stories | Knowing my history and letting go |
| Racial processes/racism | The counter culture-ness of counsel- |
| (Cultural) influences | ling and therapy |
| Diversity | Two big cultures descending into me |

highly religious and have not an incline of the spiritual mysticism, as I understand it.'

- *Taking spiritual responsibility versus having a spiritual life that includes ritual*: 'but for me, that spiritual path involves that I take responsibility for how I am in my life and how I am with other human beings... but there isn't someone telling me how to be and that for me is a distinction between a religious life that has a way of the way I "should" be in the world and the life that I choose which is "taking some responsibility" in the way I do that.'

- *Culture versus race*: 'culture was used as a mask to actually hide the racial processes that were happening... because the issues around race are tied up with dynamics of power that are difficult to approach without raising hidden, uncomfortable agendas.'

- *Sameness versus difference (culturally and/or spiritually speaking)*: 'I often find it harder to work with people when we come from a similar cultural background or faith because too much is taken for granted, we tend to assume that we are on the same page although we might be on a totally different wavelength.'

- *Embracing the whole self versus rejecting an aspect of the self*: 'We seem to fragment ourselves or our clients by trying to fit into a box or label about which groups we belong to or which worldviews we live by, spiritual, cultural or other, ending up not embracing the whole of the person.'
- *Counselling/therapy versus indigenous or traditional healing*: 'Different cultures perceive healing or what we call in the West "therapy" in different ways.'
- *A culture of 'doing' versus a culture of 'being'*: 'I include practices of meditation in my counselling work which is about stillness... such a contrast to our culture that focuses on constantly doing and achieving.'

Additionally there were issues like the links between 'transpersonal' and 'person-centred' values as a theme, as well as whether or not counselling language and terminology are used on behalf of participants, as part of the discourse analysis. The 'culture' of therapy itself seems to be intertwined with its interaction with uses of culture and expressions or meanings of the spiritual. Many contradictions appeared to be related to the contrast between individual and collective understandings, interpretations and values, depending on each participant's cultural and spiritual.

What I was left with when reflecting on the data was that the process of interaction amongst spirituality, culture and counselling was not clearly put into words, as if the links between them are extremely subtle or resisted or somehow inaccessible. My intuitive interpretation of that observation is that it may be the challenging dynamics of power that are provoking such responses (or lack of them) and further research would potentially reveal some of that 'hidden' agenda. As one co-researcher highlighted, 'it sounds to me like we are trying to define the indefinably really', while another group member vividly remarked, 'I do wonder whether it's like splitting a hair almost'.

## Matters arising

The literature review conducted throughout the study, together with conversations with co-researchers, colleagues and the process of data analysis, suggests something that Fukuyama and Sevig confirm when they state, 'recent counselling literature seems to segment multiculturalism and spirituality' (1999: 15). It is acknowledged that counsellors are not always in the position to fully empathize with or understand the cultural aspects of their clients' religious and spiritual context, despite the fact that there has been increased sensitivity around issues of gender, race and ethnicity in counselling (Pedersen 1997: 99).

However, an inevitable shift has occurred due to changes in the philosophical and theoretical climate in science, philosophy and psychology during recent decades. This has provoked several worthwhile attempts to explore different value systems and worldviews, including the spiritual dimension and needs within specific cultures. The acknowledgement that counselling and spirituality are inevitably bound up with understandings of culture has motivated authors to explore spiritual dimensions and perspectives within specific cultures dominated by one or more of the world's religions. There is literature referring to universal versus culture-specific approaches to multicultural counselling (Fukuyama 1990; Locke 1990), which include universal and culture-specific expressions of spirituality. There is also a thought-provoking discussion around what forms of help people tend to seek, according to their cultural influences, related to traditional healing practices alongside formal therapy (Moodley and West 2005; Chapter 9 in this volume).

The following points are a brief overview of the major issues arising from this study:

- There is a debate around clear definitions and finding appropriate language for spirituality and the experience of the spiritual, particularly in differentiation to religion and faith. A similar discourse unfolded around the meaning of culture, race, racism, diversity and such debatable concepts.
- Although, according to the literature and personal experiences from my practice, spirituality is culturally bound and those forces seem linked together, it appears that, with a few exceptions, the counsellors and research participants cannot talk about these two together but discuss them separately.
- Significant attention is given to the dynamics around 'sameness' and 'difference', with all the assumptions and prejudices brought to the surface in each stance.
- Participants appear to draw attention to the importance of practitioners' cultivation of self-awareness and exploration of spiritual and cultural heritage/identity.
- The issues of spirituality and culture seem to be either excluded or seen as separate in counselling training and supervision, or are

often not integrated in training curricula or comfortably addressed in counselling supervision. Similarly, some participants encountered difficulties in working with such issues in personal therapy.

It seems that spirituality and multiculturalism tend to be compartmentalized, resulting in missing the deep potential that could be reached if those two integrated. Fukuyama and Sevig (1999) dedicate a whole chapter to describing how 'spiritual values and multicultural values are closely linked and inform the respective processes of spiritual evolvement and multicultural learning'. They examine the interface of spiritual and multicultural competencies and propose an integrative model that 'builds bridges' between the two 'forces in motion', based on bringing integral values and mindsets together in a synergistic and symbiotic way to assist in personal awareness, development and increased effectiveness in counselling.

I believe that striving towards a model of integration would open up possibilities of increased and informed awareness, improvement of relationship dynamics, mediation and conflict resolution. This would require an active and intentional dialogue with each other, maybe an interdisciplinary one that would enrich the resources available. The tensions revealed in such a 'trial' dialogue in the scale of this study may be leading suggestions for further research, for example collecting such data by moderating focus groups or interviews in other cultures, not particularly in western ones, or put clients and counsellors in dialogue about what may potentially be silenced. Trainers and counselling supervisors, as well as the research community, could be facilitators of such a courageous dialogue. However, this would require that an attitude combining rigour, humility and mutual respect of a variety of perspectives is allowed and cultivated. Some of the implications for counselling training and supervision are discussed in the next section.

## Implications for training and supervision

The focus group participants were encouraged to reflect on how these issues of spirituality and culture were addressed during their training or in a supervisory relationship.

It was obvious that a sense of frustration was expressed on behalf of the participants in relation to the identified need for cultural and spiritual issues to be more integrated within counselling training, supervision and practice. A paper written by Rowan (2001) provides a useful framework and guidance points for what could be called 'transpersonal supervision' to be effective and valuable to counsellors with a spiritually informed approach to therapy. Similarly, Lago (1996), among others, suggests workable guidelines for supervisors of therapists following a 'transcultural' approach to their practice. As for training, traditional counselling courses tend to encourage the study of therapeutic process, inner awareness, theoretical perspective and enhancement of skills, but do not concentrate much on societal issues (Lago 1996) and research suggests that the difficulty lies more in promoting the acquisition of specific skills rather than in improving their knowledge (D'Andrea et al. 1991).

With reference to the inclusion or exclusion of those issues in counselling training, apart from the participant who had a purely transpersonal training route where this was at the core of the curriculum, others mentioned experiences of spirituality being 'laid alongside counselling' rather than genuinely integrated and seen as 'acceptable and professional' enough or being seen separately, in contrast to systemic training which embraced issues of culture. Another participant clarified that these were addressed more under the umbrella of 'diversity issues' during his training. Those attitudes were explored in a pilot study conducted by Valda Swinton (2007), who suggests that there is now increasing interest in exploring spirituality in counselling training and claims that she is not 'aware of a better place than in the training forum for trainees to be given the opportunity to talk about their spiritual assumptions as they would talk about any other assumptions they may hold' (2007: 19). This leads us to think that the cultural assumptions are also to be included in this kind of talk. However, if this is not in fact happening, does this not suggest that counselling trainers also need 'training' or such awareness and sensitivity themselves?

Within the flow of the focus group discussion, the participants responded to the question of whether the issues of spirituality and culture are welcomed in their supervisory relationships in different ways. For example, one participant had mixed experiences of occasions where they were welcomed and others in which they were not, in which case he was reluctant to make a supervision contract with the colleague that denied this type of work. Another group member talked about having the need for two supervisors, where one would address the issues that were not met by the other.

The difficulties and complexities arising around the willingness or capacity of counselling supervisors to embrace and incorporate issues of spirituality (and maybe less so, but also present around cross-cultural dynamics in therapy) are, promisingly, discussed in recent literature (West

2000b; Williams 2003; Ladany 2004; Jenkins 2006). It has been argued that there is a 'natural home' for spirituality within the multicultural literature on counsellor training and professional development (Fukuyama and Sevig 1997; Bart 1998), since the two incorporate values that imply a 'symbiotic relationship' (Fukuyama and Sevig 1999) which may be invisible at first sight or too challenging. The ethical responsibility towards any counselling-related and research activity that also relates to the nature of working with those issues is addressed in the following section.

## Ethical issues and international dimensions

Given that the participants who took part in this study were qualified and practising therapists themselves, having been engaged in personal therapy as well as regular supervision and having discussed and pre-agreed with them the relevant ethical responsibilities towards conducting research (De Vaus 2002; Bond 2004), any risks in relation to their participation appeared to be limited. However, in the context of discussing the particular topic of inquiry, Ganje-Fling and McCarthy (1990) suggest that is it useful to consider the following as potential risks when spirituality and culture are to be integrated in counselling and psychotherapy. These are:

- *Premature spiritual interventions*: a safe relationship needs to be established given that society in general presents difficulties around discussing such issues openly; this applies to discussing culture as well.
- *Blurring of boundaries*: who is the most appropriate person to explore such issues with? Is it necessarily a counsellor or a therapist?
- *Countertransference*: where does the counsellor stand in relation to these matters? Are their values and beliefs too similar or too dissimilar to the client's? Any tendency to proselytise should be carefully monitored.
- *Referral to religious professionals*: awareness of limits of competence and appropriate decision making around the best source of help.
- *Lack of training*: relevant training, supervision or interdisciplinary research may be required.

Such ethical issues have different degrees of severity depending on the work setting and context in which counselling takes place. What is the philosophy of a given service, either individual or organizational/institutional? Is the service itself mono-cultural in structure and diversity of professionals and do they make space for learning from each other?

Alongside such ethical questions, it would be useful for the reader to consider certain limitations of the focus group study described earlier, in order to view the questions that may arise in their own context. Keep in mind that this was small-scale research, based on focus group data of participants who have predominantly grown up in the UK for most of their lives. UK culture is quite diverse and multicultural, with a number of ethnic groups, faiths and worldviews cohabiting. Those present a number of tensions and controversies as well as opportunities for mutual learning, whenever equal opportunities, freedom of speech and humanitarian values as well as policies are applied. One question arising is what would emerge if such a dialogue took place in a different part of the world. What would happen if therapists across the globe were invited in a kind of multinational forum to reflect on the intersection of spirituality, culture and counselling? Would such a discussion be possible or would the debate around finding a common language of understanding appear more intense? What sort of dynamics of power would potentially emerge?

Bearing such questions in mind, a closer look at recommended guidelines for practitioners follows.

## Guidelines for practitioners

This appears to be a topic that has no easy answers, but it seems crucial that more questions are raised and kept in awareness for continuous reflection. In striving to remain congruent in the therapy room and to pay attention and respect to the widely recognized importance of the therapeutic relationship or alliance for positive therapeutic outcomes, rather than emphasizing therapeutic techniques or interventions (Rogers 1961; Lambert and Bergin 1994), it seems necessary to raise the importance of cultivating openness as well as humility when addressing the subtle intersection of counselling, spirituality and multicultural awareness from a psychological perspective. Fear, taboo and lack of awareness about such complex, sensitive and often debated issues among counsellors, counselling supervisors and trainers often instead leads to their exclusion from the counselling process, which as a result creates barriers and limits to effective communication and the outcome of therapy.

Inevitably, trying to sensitize the therapeutic community towards cultural sensitivity includes the need to pay attention to the spiritual beliefs, cultural perceptions and experiences of those seeking therapy, as well as of the practitioners themselves.

It is necessary to remember that integrating or adopting a culturally and spiritually sensitive approach in therapy, based on recognition of the importance to counsellors of being self-aware and aware of the clients' cultural and spiritual worldviews, does not mean that therapists are expected to know worldwide perspectives on spirituality or worldwide cultural heritages and norms. Such a stance would be a utopia given that within cultural groups or spiritual experiences and beliefs there will certainly be myriad varying strands of individual experience and interpretation.

The above is closely linked to the issue of practitioners developing their own self-awareness, the cornerstone of most therapeutic approaches, although it often appears to be insufficiently worked through, especially around the issues of cultural identity and spiritual perspective. Rowan (1989) has taken the strong argument of maintaining that good therapists should have their own spiritual discipline. This is also supported by West (2000a), who claims that trainees should at least be exposed to information on and the processes of major faiths, spiritual development and related topics. Similarly, Carter (1995: 228), drawing from his studies on therapeutic dyads and relationship type studies, asserts that his findings 'strongly indicate the importance of training a therapist to explore the meaning and significance of their own race and to understand how race influences perceptions of self and the client'.

It is suggested that counsellors and psychotherapists seek opportunities for cultivating the following:

- Spiritual and cultural identity: counselors should be aware of their own spiritual stance and elements that form their cultural identity, at a personal level. A deconstruction of the symbolism, myths and nuances in these two areas that may be either culture specific or archetypally universal may be seen as a fundamental starting point, although not an easy task or process.
- Spiritual competencies: counsellors should be able to describe to their client or supervisee religious, spiritual and transpersonal expressions from culturally diverse perspectives (depending on the given spiritual and/or cultural background).
- Multicultural competencies: counsellors should understand their clients' worldviews in terms of several cultural factors, which may encompass spirituality.
- Empathy: this appears to be the quality that 'opens the doors' to developing the highly tentative skills that are required for counselling work. Moustakas links that to 'intersubjectivity' and says that 'the method through which the Other becomes accessible to me is that of empathy, a thereness-for-me of others' (1994: 37).
- Consciousness-raising: a suggestion to demystify the links between spirituality and culture could be that counselling trainers and supervisors

work collaboratively around such issues, whenever possible, or at least find opportunities for exchanging ideas in peer or study groups, given that supervision includes an educative dimension and training similarly incorporates a supervisory role, although boundaries are to be kept distinct.

An important reminder is that developing such competences and attitudes is a continual learning process rather than a goal-oriented achievement. All the above can be explored through self-dialogue, personal therapy, peer discussion, critical and reflexive reading of a variety of literature, personal development activities and raising the matter in training and supervision contexts. I also believe that it is important to gain insight by engaging with life and 'everydayness' as a holistic opportunity for cultural and spiritual awakening via travel, keeping a diary, engaging with art, literature, drama, languages and cross-cultural encounters. There is so much we can learn from each other in such a variety of contexts, when interacting with an open heart and an inquiring mind.

## Conclusion

This piece of research has drawn our attention to an area that appear to present significant and interesting challenges. On the one hand, the construct of culture may be perceived as invisible in itself until made visible through contrast (Sussman 2000; Grabosky 2005); on the other hand, spiritual perspective, experience or faith is a highly taboo territory within the counselling profession (West 2000a; Jenkins 2006). In light of the historical origins and development of the counselling and psychotherapy profession in Euro-American or western cultures (Sue and Sue 1999), together with the acknowledgement that such a discipline has a dominant 'culture' of its own, it seems that what often appears to be the monocultural perspective of the helping professions often leads practitioners to cultural or spiritual insensitivity, silencing or resistance.

In more practical terms, it is important to be able to observe oneself and others in such a way that what is invisible or resisted can become more visible. A cross-cultural context teaches us a lot about our own culture (Storti 2001). This may lead to a greater understanding of who people are in their natural context and also why any differences of belief, appearance, status and so on may be experienced as disturbing. Why are we so attached to what is known, to what is familiar, when actually what is known may only be assumed due to the fear of opening up to a broader and higher level of existence that is beyond any single characteristic?

My personal answer would be that there can be no respectful dialogue without meeting the image and presence of the 'other' within one's own self. It comes through each one of us and the whole of humanity opening up to the acknowledgement that each lives within the other. Such a perspective is illustrated in the following words, which I saw inscribed on a temple wall when visiting an *ashram* (spiritual community) in India:

> The whole world is one single tree;
> The different countries are its branches;
> Its root is God;
> Human beings are the flowers;
> Happiness is the fruit;
> Self-realization is the sweet juice therein.
> —Baba

I view this piece of research as fundamentally useful for the therapeutic community as a whole (counsellors, mental health practitioners, counselling supervisors, counselling trainers) and, as a result, for their clients/service users' wellbeing. Positioned within a broader picture, since increasingly counselling skills and perspectives are used within the territory of resolving conflict (West 2003), further research on this topic may suggest significant insights that may contribute to the development of harmonious global dialogue.

## Discussion points

1. What is your cultural heritage? Are you aware of the various characteristics that form your identity and how those influence your life and work (ethnicity, race, gender, age, religion, ability, socioeconomic status)?
2. Do you think you have sufficient awareness and skills that are appropriate for the clients' needs, both in the spiritual/religious domain and the multicultural context?
3. What are some implications of the issues discussed in this chapter in terms of how you practise counselling and psychotherapy? Do you talk about those with your supervisor? Is your supervisor open to exploring those issues?

# 7
# Embodied Spirituality

*Dori F. Yusef*

## Introduction

In this chapter I present the story of my research into embodied spirituality. The main aim of this study was to examine the journey of spiritual embodiment, tracking the phenomenon of the body, outlined in the brain, emotions, visions, histories, illness, experiences of alternate realities and connections between the self and other. This research was carried out through a deep and ongoing process of heuristic self-reflection (Moustakas 1990, 1994) to surface my own understandings of the phenomenon being researched and by research conversations with nine body-based practitioners.

My presentation of the research is subjective in style and uses stanzas created by me and from participants' transcripts. These are poetic: they heighten mometic resonance with the text and enliven the reality of the experiences. This is in the spirit of A/r/t/ography (Irwin and De Cosson 2004), which was a major influence on my research approach and advocates an arts-based and creative approach to lived inquiry. (For a further discussion of my methodology, see Yusef 2008.)

Initially, this chapter may appear somewhat different from the other chapters in this volume, but the breadth and depth of my research study reflect common themes of healing, transcultural issues, presence, resonance, alternate realities, ethical considerations and spirituality. My focus here is on my lived inquiry and on conversations with body practitioners in which the counsellors' role in healing and spirituality emerge.

In terms of the structure of this chapter, I introduce my personal premise for my research study; questions I tussled with; findings that illuminated the research; concluding illuminations and the implications for practice.

## Inner awareness

> We come spinning out of nothingness
> Scattering stars...
> We are the unconditioned spirit
> That's trapped in conditions for a while
> Like the sun in eclipse... (Rumi in Chopra 1995)

When the counsellor, in a state of some health or coherence, sits with the client, in a state of incoherence, harmony or healing for the client is attained by a process that can be regarded as entrainment. At the cellular level, it would appear that the body is affected, is engaged, is involved. Atoms spin into a physical manifestation 'That's trapped in conditions for a while/ Like the sun in eclipse'. We can be seen as being absorbed in many dimensions, embodying each one. Our appreciation of these dimensions is dependent on our inner awareness and congruence.

My intention, as a psychotherapist, is to 'do no harm'; to achieve this and to facilitate healing, I must have self-awareness and take responsibility for it. This research study ultimately explores the areas of connectivity and relationships with oneself and another, all emanating through these dimensions. Ultimately, the questions of culture, ethnicity and faith transcend both the transpersonal and deeply personal journey of this research.

## Background

This piece of research was a personal journey catapulted into life by the death of my mother in February 2001. The urge to search for the essence of existence and meaning became an existential imperative at that point and I was dissatisfied until I had plunged deeply into an oceanic experience of grief. Wondering at the universe and creation with a sense of awed numbness and amazement, I felt there was only one way I could satisfy my hunger for answers; that is, by an intensely precipitous immersion into a transformative journey.

My 'being' in this world carries with it enormous responsibility. Who I am as an individual and my intentionality have an effect on another human being; my very existence is interrelated with the other. As I sit with someone in psychotherapy and in a relationship, I can affect their experience of being in this world – just as they affect mine. Furthermore, if within this experience I possess knowledge and understanding, then my responsibility to the other is greater and so I must develop my self-awareness and spirituality.

My research is also an exploration of embodiment and the experience of alternate realities. The body provides gateways to these places that are as universal as the body itself. Davies et al. (2004: 36) remind us, 'We do not have bodies, we are our bodies and the thoughts and feelings we have, emanate from the entire body and not specific organs'.

There is the possibility of experiencing a profound sense of the interrelatedness of all bodies, whether physical or otherwise and with consciousness throughout the universe. I feel that this transcends any cultural issues and engages with presence. Likewise, connectivity and relationships are essential to us and at the core of all consciousness.

Our consciousness could be termed 'spirit' and I use the metaphor of the golden thread of the labyrinth myth which can unify us all. This is the Greek myth in which Theseus, the hero, is given a ball of golden thread to take into the labyrinth with him on his mission to kill the Minotaur. By unwinding the golden thread as he finds his way through the labyrinth, Theseus is able to find his way out again after killing the Minotaur.

The ball of golden thread was given to me symbolically by my ancestors – of whom my mother was the most significant to me. The thread is symbolic of a consciousness permeated with love, the most enduring connection of all. So I become Theseus, going into the labyrinth of my research study with only this golden thread to help me to retrace my steps and present my findings.

## Findings

I was in a place of silent illumination
Coming up
From the well of darkness into the river of light... (Yusef 2008: 169)

The data emerge from conversations with other body-related practitioners and from my story, which is the record of my auto-ethnographic journey. In doing so I offer 'a rich example of some of the ways disjuncture, fragmentation and juxtaposition' can influence how we make sense of the data (Markham 2005: 815).

To present 'findings' is a challenging and unclear process. For me it required an engagement that is physical, emotional and spiritual. This allows the intuitive and unexpected to emerge in a creative and synthesized way, as described by Bochner and Ellis in their review of performative research: 'The performance explored ways of articulating research "find-ings" through the medium of artistic expression' (2003: 508). For me, the use of the body is to embody the research questions and the data.

The process of in-dwelling in the research data leading to illumination is a common feature of a heuristic approach to research, as delineated by Moustakas (1990, 1994). So I describe my 'findings' as illuminations that bring to the surface lights of understanding. Illumination lights up the darkness, making visible the invisible – a trickle of understanding becomes a river of illumination, 'where the exact contents of the water are never the same' and the observer's subjective experience depends on 'what part of the river they have seen'. The more perspectives a researcher employs, the more 'dimensions and consequences of a text will be illuminated' (Kellner 1995).

These illuminations separate into strands of understanding rather than distinctive analytical findings. They present the body's phenom-enology through various experiences, highlighting the themes that are mentioned above. These illuminations resemble colourful crystals shining light onto our humanness. Each participant's story is a facet; the whole thesis a many-faceted jewel. These strands are headed: jour-neying, the body, out-of-body experience, embryology, working with the body as a practitioner, psychotherapy, neuroscience, subjective experience of illness, healing, embodied spirituality, connectedness, consciousness, shamanism and alchemy, death, the formless into form, the experience of otherness, the cosmos and exceptional human experi-ence. They reveal gateways that exist in our bodies as well as multitu-dinous pathways to connectivity. Each connection is another realm of experience, and so the gateways are the entrances and exits to realms where we connect and disconnect ourselves.

In making meaning I have inevitably been subjective as, using a quali-tative research approach, I can only be. I select from the transcripts per-tinent stanzas to illustrate these strands. They are a mosaic or a collage that have reduced the conversations with body practitioners and my story into strands and patterns. The choices are anonymous, permitted and referenced. I will briefly visit each strand in turn.

## Journeying

I experienced two kinds of journeying during my research project: as a pil-grim, in a group with other pilgrims, typified by the collective experience of the PhD research group to which I belonged; and alone, represented by a journey into the labyrinth of uncertainty, which was my PhD journey. To this lived inquiry I needed to trust the process of the research and my immersion in the research material. This immersion resembles the laby-rinth to me to which Theseus is sent to kill the Minotaur who is threaten-ing his people's freedom: he is trusted to go on behalf of others. My motive is symbolically to 'kill off' all that threatens my freedom and the freedom of others, on a transpersonal level. This freedom could be the freedom to accompany our clients and fellow travellers into their labyrinths.

This has a strong ancestral quality and is transgenerational. My mother hands me the golden thread, symbolic of the bond of love I have for her on one level and the spirit on another. To elect to go on the journey is the choice to immerse myself in the PhD research. The thread is the guide that takes me through.

> The connecting point is this issue of gateway
> shifting in reality.
> Not just to do the shifting,
> turns out to be a journey.
> I travel
> a journey
> through time & space, (Yusef 2008: 173)

## The body

Working with the body enhances the attunement between the practi-tioner and the client. There is potentially a transpersonal element to the depth of presence experienced during such times and an immersion in the other's space, although the individual remains a singular entity. This immersion is greater than what Rogers (1985) calls 'advanced empa-thy' and seems to be a genuine experience of the other's world. Rogers (1985) suggests that empathy involves sensing the client's private world as if it were your own, but without ever losing the 'as if' quality. I am suggesting going further than this, 'as if' you are the other person to a deeper experience of the other person.

The body has a wonderful integrity that manifests messages through what Gendlin (1973) called 'felt sense' and edges of experience (Mindell 1984, discussed below), as if suddenly entering altered states, like spin-ning and nausea, or through dreams. Mindell talks about the 'Dreambody' (1984), where the body will dream up sensations to reveal itself.

*What Does it Mean to be in a Body?*

> Body... body work...
> sensations... emotions

thoughts arising, dreams...
images... desires.

Everything I experience is an experience
of being in my body. Spirituality
is an experience of being in my body. (Yusef 2008: 175)

## Out-of-body experience

The experience of being out of body is as powerful as in-body manifestations. This can occur at both exceptional and ordinary times. It can be spontaneous, dreamlike or experienced as a depth of emotion taking the individual out of their physicality. These emotions can emerge from deep meditative states, attunement with nature or through trauma and shock. I experienced this state during my grieving process; my body shut down and my awareness existed out of my body, in what could be called a liminal space. Practitioners can experience this while also attuning to a client's body, deep emotion and their in-body experiences.

Paradoxically out-of-body experiences
require in-the-body experiences. (Yusef 2008: 177)

## Embryology

The development of the body from conception to death is, I would argue, the most powerful journey that we undertake. The experience in the embryo can be seen as resembling this journey symbolically. Drawing on the notion of the 'speech of the embryo' (Van der Wal 2006) where movement is the 'voice', the firings of the synapses in the brain and later the death of those functions means that something has been passed on and it passes out. This *something* is, I would insist, the embodied spirit that manifests 'trapped in conditions for a while, like the sun in eclipse' (Rumi 1995). Embryology, then, is the earliest record of humanness, relationship and connection. Wordsworth talks about 'fair seed time' for his soul in his *Prelude* (1960 [1805]: Book First); this could describe in poetry the embryo's beginnings and its movements. At this time the connection between mother and embryo is established and the sense of other and self begun.

babies are pretty psychic,
pretty connected to consciousness.
They even know where they come from.
They come from the whole

come into,
the womb, or afterwards. (Yusef 2008: 179)

## Working with the body as a practitioner

From Reich (1961) in the early to mid-twentieth century through Lowen (1958) to Mindell (1990, 1995, 2000, 2004) and others working as practitioners, the body becomes a sacred space to work with. Contact and connectivity are keys to in-depth knowing and insight into the client's and therapist's issues and experience. They reach a liminal space, accessing knowledge where the body speaks its mind and muscles and tissues reveal themselves. Through touch, the body expresses its needs and energy circulates between client and therapist. Movement, voice-work and the interaction between the therapist's and client's bodies form a dance like a 'pas de deux' (Janesick 2001) of body conversation revealing powerful processes, bringing insight and resolution. (In ballet, a *pas de deux* is a duet in which dance steps are performed together.)

My major source of an altered state experience that I work with.
Working with tissues
I can make contact with the tissue,
I'm there in it. (Yusef 2008: 180)

## Psychotherapy

Body psychotherapy has an immediacy that the 'talking therapies' cannot often access. The body can reveal its secrets and hidden traumas, which are usually suppressed and expressed through illness and disease. The therapeutic relationship becomes a sacred vessel for what I call transmission and transformation. The direction and focus of the therapeutic work emerge through the skilled use of touch: muscle, tissue, skin, molecules and cells. The relationship facilitates the interaction and dialogue between the body, self and the therapist. Edges (Mindell 1984) reached in the therapeutic encounter are expressed by the body and can be 'translated' by the therapist. They are the journeys the body makes during illness, stress or trauma or when one sense reaches an edge to slip into another dimension.

As therapists, we need to be self-aware
and receptive to the other;
we become transmitters or channels to wisdom,
bringing awareness to the client's processes.

The session is a gateway and the therapist the
gatekeeper. (Yusef 2008: 185)

## Neuroscience

Neuroscience, an umbrella term including psychology, psychiatry, infant observation, neurobiology, neurochemistry and neuro-immunology, is the study of the nervous system, which exists throughout the body. 'The brain is a very complex network of feedback loops and mutually regulating systems' and they depend on the body's three dimensional structure to become recognized (Carroll 2003–2004, Seminar 1: 1).

The body–brain produces a fascinating, complex and intricate structure that self-organizes. Prigogine (1977, 1980, 1984) describes the phenomenon by which a system's internal structures organize themselves and maintain through self-regulation (Cannon 1915, 1939), known as homeostasis. It is an exquisite milieu of micro-structural processes. These form the backdrop for the functioning of the body's self-regulatory systems:

> the basis unit of analysis is not changes in behaviour, cognition or even affect, but rather... the development of more and more complex psychobiological states that underlie these functions. (Schore 1997: 595)

Body practitioners and neuroscientists have equal respect for the importance of the mind–body interrelationship. One participant studied neuroscience and used it as a screen against the mystical: and yet the mind–body mesh of neurons, synapses and the milieu can itself be seen as mystical!

If every single nerve of my body
reiterated all of this
all of the time
what is the outcome? (Yusef 2008: 188)

## Subjective experience of illness

The experience of illness can be seen as allowing the body to reveal itself at a deeper level, both cellular and emotional. Illness encapsulates the body's system, producing symptoms manifesting at many levels and also in liminal spaces. My personal experience of illness has facilitated journeying into what can be called the 'body-realm' where dreams of ancestors and memories live, where fear resides and where the body demands attention. Illnesses reveal symptoms far deeper than just the illness itself. The tissues of the body can then be understood as the liminal spaces where stories dwell, awaiting discovery and self-disclosure.

> Does my body contrive the illness to tell me
> something? (Yusef 2008: 189)

## Healing

Healing is to make whole and often occurs in some altered state(s) of reality. There seems to be a stronger sense of the spirit when some states are experienced, and this can also increase after great emotional suffering. Spiritual awareness can come through the practitioner's use of bodywork, shamanic journeys or alchemical processes within the relationship. Healing can occur through attunement between therapist and client, the intention of the therapist, the connection between therapist and client and what can be called transcendent warmth. This could also be experienced as resonance with the other. The practitioner's hands at times seem to possess a consciousness that directs the body to self-heal. Coherence, entrainment and harmonizing energies are part of this healing process. Each of these settles the chaos of the illness into order. Coherence is 'electrical'; entrainment mirrors pulsation and energy; harmony combines both.

> Now is that still wisdom in the touch
> that knowing...
> you know this person knows. (Yusef 2008: 192)

## Embodied spirituality

Embodied spirituality, or being incarnated into the physical world, can be viewed as accompanied by meaning, purpose and consciousness of a higher principle, an Unknown. Such a stance endorses meaning and initial apprehension becomes trust in something greater at work. Spirituality can be located within the body, manifested by the body – a temple to the divine principle. I have experienced this research as phenomenological embodiment, and felt the research questions physically. It seems that other people have also experienced alternate realities accessed through and by the body, bringing an appreciation of other embodied states.

> That part of us is the higher self
> or the god within us
> the body is the temple for our God.
> The divinity to shine
> we see it outside of us. (Yusef 2008: 194)

## Connectedness

The sense of connection can be experienced within the body and between bodies. Attunement, connection and memory manifest, I believe, at a quantum and macro-cosmic level. The essence of the body's quantum expression reflects the expanse of the cosmic level. The 'womb of the universe' is inside us as we are inside the vast expanse of space. Connectivity is in our very pores and when we experience pain, others can share the experience. Such connections can be transcendent and profound – the sense of otherness experienced alongside the experience of oneness. Love, unity and connectivity are expressions of attunement, resonance, linking to all creation, nature or with another person. Connection transmits through the body, especially in female cyclical processes and emotional states. It is a gateway to other realms of experience and connections to 'spirit entities'.

> I can touch people – I touch people and I become emotional and sometimes shed tears. (Yusef 2008: 197)

## Consciousness

We can see consciousness as present everywhere and in everything. Awareness of that is perhaps the key to understanding, it can be heightened in body-work and it can be experienced as permeating the whole body. Some practitioners described consciousness in their fingertips, when the client is touched. It can manifest itself through intense moments of emotion, spiritual transcendence and sensation. These states can bring exceptional insights and compassion into the therapy. Altered states bring consciousness into different time zones and the experience usually brings meaning. Consciousness can be projected into other realms of experience and lucidly, in dreams.

> Consciousness must be related to meaning.
> We're in an altered state of consciousness all the time.
> All the time;
> dreams is one example,
> drugs is another. (Yusef 2008: 202)

## Shamanism and alchemy

My experience of the research process has been transformative and emotional. I can view it as a shamanic journey on which I elected to venture, experiencing a deeply alchemical process, where my body span into unknown states. Each stage has revealed other levels, planes of experience and understanding. In alchemy, various components are burned, cooled and synthesized in a flask, to create the symbolic philosopher's stone. The flask for the alchemical process has been my PhD research and my body. The Native American shamans use peyote, a plant to access sacred places and realms symbolic of what alchemists call the 'philosopher's stone'. I would suggest that the body can reach these sacred places without ingesting herbs or drugs; in that sense the body can be seen as the peyote, as a holy sacrament and as a flask.

> Well the Shamanic journey is mostly on your own...
> that part of it, but if you think about
> it it's often the drummers of the tribe that bring you back to this
> world... So the journey too is on your own
> but then having someone welcoming you back is the thing you're
> missing,
> the welcome.
> This culture doesn't have a tradition around
> Shamanism. (Yusef 2008: 204)

## Death

Death is the last frontier and a powerful reminder of the life we lead. The experience of loss and the fear of it can bring powerful alchemical transformation. The boundary between life and death is distinct in one sense and yet indistinct in another. There is a liminal space in between, described in religious and esoteric traditions: a realm experienced by the living who can then contact those disembodied entities. It is a transition from one realm to another. In literature, the concept of death inspires poetry and wonder. Losses in life can transform, bring understanding and bewilderment, causing emotional trauma. The individual swings along the pendulum of grieving despair and peace: 'losses in life may give space to either despair or positive changes and spiritual growth' (Kenyon 1994: 201).

Premature death brings with it more regret and heartache than usual: the anguish of what could have been is experienced. Psychotherapy helps us to reflect on those questions and emotions, especially around the death of loved ones. Hikmet (1979) in his poetry expresses this sense of experiences that have not yet happened.

> See we make this big separation between the dead and the living and
> of course at one level, it's true and on another level the distinction
> might not be so great. (Yusef 2008: 205)

## The formless into form

That which is created out of nothingness into form, like a thought, is transient and powerful. We as embodied beings are such forms. Centuries earlier, Rumi said:

We come spinning out of nothingness, scattering stars like dust,
We are the unconditioned spirit that's trapped in conditions for a
while like the sun in eclipse.

We become form in order to experience the world with our senses. Grumet talks about coming into form to speak, to be seen, touched and to tell our stories so others can see us (1991: 69). Form articulates the self, to witness and be witnessed and to in-form. We can experience the formless in dreams or altered states. It enters through gateways, the body being one, a universal portal to the spirit of the formless. In heightened states, a sense of unity with all forms is experienced.

We are the creator
the act of creating
and the created.
It just shocked me –
it really shocked me. (Yusef 2008: 208)

## The experience of otherness and alternate realities

These can be accessed within therapy through deeply attuned sessions and resonance and other deeply empathic experiences. Attuning with the body brings consciousness to a heightened level of subtlety and a sense of 'otherness'. Changing energies and altered states reveal the subtleties of the transcendent and other entities can be experienced. Sometimes, deceased relatives or loved ones are recognized. Such encounters can occur in natural surroundings when there is emotional expansion, attunement and love and can manifest through bodily functions like menstruation. Despair and joy can invite the extra sensitivity necessary for these experiences, as well as ordinary incidental moments.

As I gaze more and more, 'my soul' and 'my I' become one;
as the gaze goes further the 'soul/eye' splinters into fragments
and mingles with 'otherness' and becomes oddly united in singular
multipleness. It's hard to speak this... (Yusef 2008: 213)

## The cosmos and male and female energy

The macrocosm and the microcosm are energies. All that exists between is also energy. Vieira (2002) describes them as consciousness and argues that the universe itself is conscious. At a quantum level, all energy is the same and matter is just energy organized differently. There is a universal energy field that healers and body practitioners can access, work with and harness. It can come as a surprise to those trained in chiropractic, neuroscience or other formal scientific disciplines to tune into to this powerful energy field. One of the participants spoke about the awe he experienced when this powerful field manifested itself. He was humbled and somewhat afraid.

According to Brennan, there is a field organized with points of geometric and pulsating lights, spirals, lines, clouds and sparks and 'It pulsates and can be sensed by touch, taste, smell and with sound and luminosity perceivable to the higher senses' (Brennan 1988).

Male and female energies are historically based in myth and religion. Symbolic feelings of femaleness and maleness are experienced by sensitivity to their subtleties and forces. The divine feminine and masculine energies possess spiritual aspects, which are worshipped in many esoteric traditions.

> The male has to die in service of the female,
> to enable the magic to occur.
>
> In which universe are we in,
> this one,
> a parallel one?
>
> multiverses?
> Which body am I in at the moment
> the Astral,
> the Etheric
> the Gross. (Yusef 2008: 215–16)

## Exceptional human experience

An exceptional human experience (EHE) is defined as something transformative and including an exceptional content. Near-death experiences, out-of-body experiences, intense grief and heightened awareness in moments of ecstasy are EHEs. They can be psychic, mystical, otherworldly, but I feel they can also simply be extraordinary-ordinary experiences in the moment. These experiences produce insights and revelations that can transform people, sometimes for ever. They serve as catalysts to life events and decisions. Poincaré (1982[1913]) referred to them as catalysts, exceptional to research, extending the parameters of research and enabling the experiencer to view their world differently. Recording one's highlighted subjective life can track the extraordinary experience that is embodiment.

White (in Braud and Anderson 1998) describes the reflexive role of EHEs and their importance in the research process. She sees them as inspirational tools that deepen the research subject: dreams, lucid dreams, hunches, hypnogogia (twilight states of the sleep–wake period), visions, hallucinations, empathy, extra-sensory perception, ESP within interspecies, out-of-body experiences and synchronicity. She suggests that we as researchers should respect these experiences and use them to promote research, enriching the material: 'research would not exploit its subject matter but would empathise with it and as it progresses, make many connections rarely glimpsed before' (in Braud and Anderson 1998: 144).

> I have journeyed into the Unknown...
> And there I met Shock, Numbness and Grief
> They spoke to me
> They told me many things
> The frozen ice of their very words
> Pierced my heart
> Like shards of glass;
> And slashed my soul
> Into a million brilliant points...
> And on my return
> There was No-thing
> And no-one. (Yusef 2008: 220)

## Illuminations

In these concluding illuminations, I include the implications for practice, ethics, supervision issues and personal reflection. I address four major areas, which conclude the research inquiry, from the macrocosm to the microcosm: global, individual, research and psychotherapy and my personal journey. My story was, and is, an expression of a lived experience; the conversations with other body practitioners are the stories of other lived experiences – they interconnect at all levels. The stories merge into *one story* of human embodiment.

## The macrocosm – the global

The universal principles of energy and connectivity bring the relationships of the therapist, client and the global community together. The implications for world politics are momentous. Equality and shared distribution of both wealth and knowledge and connectedness are obvious necessities, described by economist Jeffrey Sachs in the Reith Lectures (2007). When quoting John F. Kennedy from a speech in 1962, Sachs recalls the essence and power of that connectivity and the need to appreciate each other:

> The world is inter-connected in unprecedented ways that require unprecedented strategies for global co-operation... Our problems are manmade – therefore, they can be solved by man. And man can be as big as he wants. No problem of human destiny is beyond human beings. Man's reason and spirit have often solved the seemingly unsolvable – and we believe they can do it again... For in the final analysis, our most basic common link is that we all inhabit this small planet. We all breathe the same air. We all cherish our children's future. And we are all mortal. (2007: Lecture 3)

Interconnectedness is a reality at all levels of human existence, whether it manifests itself at a cellular or macro-universal level, in therapeutic relationships or across all nations. The intention to 'do no harm' at the core of psychotherapy if adopted by all nations and all peoples could truly change the world. The body of the globe could become healthy, thrive and be the gateway to prosperity and creativity.

Lorimer describes an 'ethic of connectedness' required by the global community to create such a world, suggesting that if there is unity of consciousness it must imply an ethic of consciousness also. He develops the idea of interconnectedness from science – biology, physics and psychology – by not isolating them but treating them as 'holons', 'a whole and a part'. Each cell and molecule is necessary for the construction of the body; the body is necessary for the earth, the earth necessary for the solar system and so on. Physicist John A. Wheeler asserts that the universe is not outside us; we are part of it and we participate in its manifestation as well as observe it: 'We are not only observers. We are participators. In some strange sense this is a participatory universe' (Lorimer and Drew 1995: 19).

## The individual – the microcosm

At the individual level, our many-embodied existences combine; Pert (1999) describes these existences in the body. The morphic field, developed by Sheldrake (2000), supports our interconnectedness and none loses its integrity as a manifestation of each 'embodied existence.' This idea of the morphic field, though questioned by some scientists, describes a field where patterns of activity and structures are shared and transmitted in biology and nature. It can be affected and influenced by organisms and can resonate there. As cosmic starlight maintains its intensity for millions of years and aeons of light-years away, so I believe that the light of our bodies can maintain a similar integrity. Human connectivity is arguably underpinned by aeons of history and *infinite memory*, in the form of quantum mechanics (Schwartz 2002). This claim is perhaps controversial, but the implication of connectivity is present throughout nature and expressed from macrocosmic space to microcosmic waves (the remnants of sound from the Big Bang at the origin of the universe) and quantum waves or particles (the tiniest light-photon particle in an atom). How can we not affect the client who sits before us with their pain and suffering, willing us to 'help them?' How can we be unaffected by that pain, suffering and trust? Ideally, we are 'becoming' together and can meet the world in connection.

According to Vieira (1996), the aim is to evolve into *Serenissimus*, the perfectly evolved Homo sapiens who exists in a high dimension and whose intentions are always cosmo-ethical or altruistic; those described as the moral and ethical responsibilities we have to all species, the Earth and the cosmos. The Serenissimus can only develop within a trusting relationship. We need each other to connect to ourselves and to the universe we inhabit, whether that habitation is physical, mental or spiritual. It is pure love, an interconnection of a force that survives death, perhaps continuing to be as vibrant there as anywhere in the material world. We are creators and co-creators of this magnificence and majesty, but none of this would be meaningful without the feedback we receive from others or the universe receives from us, its offspring. We must ethically respond to the feedback as well as ethically give it.

Reverence for all life is an aspect of ethical connectedness. Albert Schweitzer described it and so did esoteric traditions:

> Just as white light consists of coloured rays, so reverence for life contains all the components of ethics: love, kindliness, sympathy, empathy, peacefulness, power to forgive. (Lorimer and Drew 1995: 24)

> Everything that from eternity has happened in heaven and earth, that life of God and all the deeds of time simply are the struggles for

Spirit to know itself, to find itself, be free for itself, and finally unite itself; it is alienated and divided, but only so as to be able thus to find itself and return to itself... As existing in an individual form, this liberation is called 'I'; as developed to its totality, it is free Spirit; as it is love; and as enjoyment, it is Blessedness. (Hegel 1974)

## The research – the psychotherapist

Perhaps we are striving to evolve and be 'the person of tomorrow', as Rogers predicted (1995: 350–52). He sees this person possessing the characteristics of openness, authenticity and scepticism regarding science and technology that is used to conquer the world, desire for wholeness, wish for intimacy, process, the certainty of change, caring, attitude towards nature, anti-institutional, authority from within, unimportance of material things and a yearning for the spiritual. He believes, as I do, that such persons should be comfortable in a world that consists of vibrating energy, without solidity, in a process of change, with minds which, in a larger sense, are both aware of and creating the new reality. 'They will be able to make the paradigm shift' (ibid.: 352). Both research and psychotherapy should contribute to this evolution: research that matters and is useful to approach the profound issues in our lives that are relevant to us today.

Engagement in transcultural issues, politics, ethical issues and the deeper aspects of meaning and purpose are relevant in research inquiry. How research is undertaken, its methodology, and how research findings are presented are both very important. I support and value artist-based research that demands rigour and immersion that are personally demanding. Richardson, in developing criteria for her ethnographic work, frames issues of 'substantive contribution, aesthetic merit, reflexivity, impact and... reality' in qualitative inquiry (2000: 251–5). Like Mullen (2003: 170), who supports the community of researcher/artists, she suggests an approach that empowers and engages with the public. These criteria stem from experiential research combined with emergent results and many-faceted possibilities and 'are reflected in the research method they demonstrate, experience, embody and ponder' (Richardson 2000: 255).

The psychotherapeutic responsibility is, I believe, to extend practice by extending the self as the practitioner, to explore the profound issues of the human predicament. Practitioners require an appreciation of the body, mind and spirit as holistic and a holon, the whole and its part. This includes the many gateways of human experience and their appreciation. The BACP (2002) requires us ethically to 'do no harm' and to treat the client, participant and researcher with trust, fidelity and integrity and in relationship. We need to take responsibility to know ourselves in order to become fully present with our clients and participants. In this way, the therapist's congruence will not contaminate the therapeutic relationship but bring insight and understanding.

Colin Feltham suggests that we use psychotherapy and counselling research that counts and therapy that matters. At a conference at York St John University in 2005, he asked what counts and to whom. He recommends that we address the definition of the therapeutic relationship and the numerous important issues in practice and life – to delve deeper into the human demise rather than general daily issues. The question of connectivity and collaboration is vital – 'Why are there no avenues to research, collaborating with other fields?' – and important issues 'can also be politically addressed' and social systems changed.

Supervisors who are willing to explore, pioneer and evolve themselves are the only ones who can adequately supervise these in-depth interactions; this requires courage.

### The personal – the golden thread

I have reached the end of this particular journey and, like the pilgrim, have found a certain peace in this destination, but it is only a full stop in a long paragraph in this chapter of my story. Travelling through this territory has been hazardous and dangerous at times, but also exciting and serene. The serenity came from the depth of connectivity, felt during the dangerous and exciting experiences: the sense of spirit, both in entities around me and in fellow travellers. I feel a connection with my ancestors before me and sense continuity ahead of me in the very core and microcosm of my body. Each molecule, cell and atom is a gateway to other embodied realms.

Who I am is not bound in time and space, but is eternal. It is linked to those who have come before and those who will come after.

> To me it's external to what I think of as me.
> It's not constructed by me.
> It exists
> as it has always existed
> before I existed
> will exist after I cease to exist. (Yusef 2008: 380)

What has been written came at times spontaneously and intuitively, but with it came unexpected insights and revelations, from an unknown and uncharted territory.

## Conclusion

Finally, in a conference in Bangalore in 2008 focusing on transcultural diversity, psychotherapy and spirituality, I ended my presentation with the following quote:

> When travelling from Persia to Konya, Veled, Rumi's father is asked: 'Whence and whither thou goest?' to which he replied, 'Who are we to question God's Will. We come from a place with no form and it is to this place that we return.' (Önder 1993: 8)

I said to my conference audience:

> Who am I to come to you with these thoughts? To a land immersed in spirituality and the sacred. This is my interpretation only; it is not the truth. However, beyond Indian-ness, beyond Anglo-Saxon-ness, beyond any other -ness, we are pure spirit. We are all the same. We come from a sphere without form and it is to this sphere that we will return. We are all connected.

Remnants of a dying star
Spinning into eternity
From whence we come
To whence we go
Stardust to stardust
Concentric rings
Radiating light
Into the Night
The Eternal Night
I am there. (Yusef 2008: 240)

This journey of spiritual embodiment has explored the phenomenon of the body through various states, revealing themes of healing, transcultural issues, presence, resonance, alternate realities, ethical considerations and spirituality. The final reflections conclude four important results for the world, the individual, research and personally. Overall, the message lies in the connectivity and interrelatedness of all beings and our responsibility to each other.

### Discussion points

1. What is the role of creativity in facilitating empowerment, personal development, spiritual awareness and healing?
2. How important do you think body awareness is in the process of therapy?
3. How far does the responsibility of the therapist extend in the therapeutic relationship and to transformation and change?
4. To what extent do culture and the world political framework affect the therapeutic relationship?

# Part Two
# Therapy and Healing

# 8
# When Counselling Becomes Healing

*William West*

## Introduction

In this chapter I will explore the varieties of healing that can happen within the therapeutic encounter, drawing on my own experiences and research and those of other therapists. I will consider how to deal with and make sense of such experiences. Finally, I will focus on ethical issues and how to maintain appropriate boundaries and best use of supervision.

The healing that occurs at the heart of effective therapy remains something of a mystery. This seems appropriate to me. We can research and explore the ingredients of what makes for the best possible therapy and begin to understand the central role of the therapeutic alliance and the part played by specific and non-specific factors. Nonetheless, why do some clients get profoundly healed and some only partially so, some for all time, some just for the moment and some not at all? It seems intrinsically part of the human condition that human healing remains enigmatic.

## My experiences

When I first began to practise as a body-work therapist (West 1994a, b) I worked strictly within the Reichian framework offered by my trainer. After about 18 months I began to use some techniques from the related approach of bioenergetics (Lowen 1958), which proved to be helpful to my clients but of which my trainer did not approve. The spell was broken. I began, especially working with therapy groups, to draw on a range of humanistic approaches to which I had previously been exposed and which I felt would be beneficial to the clients involved.

I was encouraged in this development by my supervisor at the time, who was himself of a humanistic orientation.

This process went even further when I found myself working with a young man with a chronic and painful health condition. It made sense to me to encourage him to keep a diary that recorded his emotional state, his state of tiredness and how painful his condition was on a rated scale. This enabled us to explore patterns in his illness and triggers for increased levels of pain. So I was now drawing, in effect, on cognitive behavioural therapy in the interests of this client. This was even though I was, at that time, intellectually opposed to CBT.

So my maturing practice as a therapist became increasingly eclectic or integrative within a broadly humanistic framework. I am aware of the debate around the use of the terms 'eclectic' and 'integrative' (see for instance Palmer and Woolfe 2000). Such a practice development from pure school to eclectic or integrative is not uncommon (Hollanders 2000a, b). Indeed, it is my view that humanistic therapists are naturally drawn to integrative or eclectic practice (West 2000c).

However, it was more of a challenge to me when I became a spiritual healer. I trained as a spiritual healer within a very different tradition to a therapy one, with its own differing ethical code of practice but without a requirement for supervision, though I did choose to seek some super-vision. Spiritual healing can be defined as:

> a natural energy therapy. It complements conventional medicine by treating the whole person – mind, body and spirit. Spiritual Healers act as a conduit for healing energy, often described as 'love and light' which relaxes the body, releases tensions and stimulates self-healing. The benefits of healing can be felt on many levels, not just the physical, and the effects can be profound. (NFSH 2008)

Spiritual healing can have dramatic effects, including how it is imme-diately experienced by clients. However, many clients report very little beyond a sense of peace and relaxation, perhaps some tingling sensa-tion and a feeling of heat from the healer's hands. Healing does not necessarily mean a physical cure. However, through spiritual healing clients are often able to come to terms with, and be more accepting of, their illness. From such an attitude some physical improvement might occur. Many spiritual healers offer their services for free.

At first I had separate groups of clients for both my therapy and spiritual healing work. Then one day a therapy client asked about my spiritual healing work and whether he could have some. This was clearly a supervision issue, but my therapy supervisor declared himself not competent to advise me on this. Although I did decide to offer this client spiritual healing, especially at the end of therapy sessions, questions remained. These included:

- How did the therapeutic alliance change when healing was used?
- Should I make sense of my work within a therapy framework, a healing framework or some new combination of both?
- When the ethical or practice frameworks disagreed, which should I obey?

My PhD study into integrating counselling, psychotherapy and spiritual healing (West 1995) was one very useful way of exploring these questions. Although I hoped that I would find some answers to my questions in a way that satisfied me, I did not. However, exploring the various answers that the therapists who participated in my research had achieved I found tremendously helpful.

## What is healing?

For the purpose of my doctoral studies I developed a catch-all description of healing:

the use of one or more of the following: intuition; presence; inspiration; psychic; shamanism; altered states; (spiritual) healing methods; subtle energy work; mediumship channelling; use of spirit guides; and transpersonal work. (West 1997: 291)

In my interviews for my doctoral research, I found that there were three broad and distinct usages of the word 'healing':

- as a blanket term for the outcome of any caring activity by a care worker, be they medical (e.g. doctor, nurse) or social (e.g. social worker, probation officer, counsellor);
- as a word to describe intentional activity by someone aligning themselves as a healer, which may or may not involve energy exchange;
- as a way of describing unintentional experience which appears similar to the previous point and which can occur within the work of counsellors and psychotherapists. This idea is well described by Rogers' concept of 'presence' (Rogers 1980), Thorne's concept of 'tenderness' or Buber's (1970) 'I/Thou' relationship.

In this research, I found a number of therapists were either experiencing or using spiritual healing in their work and I interviewed 30 of them. There were sometimes problems arising in their supervision (discussed below). Towards the end of my doctoral study I surveyed my 30 interviewees and 27 replied. Of these 27:

- 23 had felt that healing energies were present in their work.
- 20 did hands-on healing on occasions.
- 10 did aura work.
- 8 worked with spirit guides.
- 6 saw auras.
- 6 acted as channels for healing energies or communications.

Unfortunately, it is not clear from my survey how many respondents did any of the above within a 'therapy' session and also how often. Some of my respondents (9) were clearly seeing people separately for spiritual healing or therapy, and others (18) were only practising as therapists.

## Unintentional healing in therapy

One of the people I interviewed spoke about their experience of healing moments as a therapist:

> When a certain level of resonance is achieved something comes in. It's a bit like if you wanted to describe the mechanics or the dynamics behind the phrase 'when two or more are gathered in my name'. If you take that phrase and the implication of that – when two people are in resonance, where there is a common purpose and there is something of a common field, and there is harmony there – I do think that there is often at that moment something else, something of the 'other' comes in at that point. That is my experience, that suddenly there is more than just two people in the room.
>
> Now, whether that's Grace, whether that's insight, whether that's healing, whether that's God – it depends on your language – it's certainly, I feel, a qualitative difference, and I see that in the client. And at some point after that moment, I will probably draw their attention to it, because I think it's important to acknowledge...
>
> I'll take the credit that through my skill, we have got to that place; now that's where I will take credit. I haven't healed them, that's not my energy, 'cos I'm on the receiving end. Something in them has been triggered, they go out glowing, sometimes I feel drained... But

when you are talking about the Grace coming in, we both get something from it. (West 1995: 289–90)

There is a lot to be unpicked from this narrative and it puts me in mind of Brian Thorne's (1991) discussion of 'renderness' or Rogers (1980) discussing 'presence'. My interviewee is talking in energy terms (as do both Thorne and Rogers), with resonance as a metaphor for a deepening of the interconnectedness between him and clients. In the special healing moment 'something of the "other" comes in'. Rogers talks of 'profound healing energies being present', Buber (1970) in terms of a change from an I/It encounter to an I/Thou encounter. My respondent, like Brian Thorne, is keen that the client is invited to acknowledge what has happened. Notice how he takes credit for his facilitation skills but not for the special moment – 'I haven't healed them, it's not my energy' – and that he has benefited from the energies also. It is also apparent that Christian words are underlying his story: two or three are gathered, which Christ is reported in the Bible as saying, and the use of the word 'Grace'.

On reflection, the above description of healing should not be called unintentional. The therapist is allowing the possibility of such healing experiences to happen, he is using his skills to enable the experience to develop, but he is not actually doing the healing, he is not doing hands-on healing or aura work – 'I haven't healed them'. However, most spiritual healers would also say that they are channelling healing energies rather than using their own energies directly.

In an attempt to make sense of my respondents' discussions of (spiritual) healing, I was moved to write at the time:

I think there's a very real problem of language... that we've a number of different words we can use to try and capture an experience that's beyond words. Are we talking about God? Are we talking about the Higher Self? Or the connection between the Higher Selves (of client and therapist)? Or the energy field that's created between two people when they tune in together? How much of this energy is from outside, and how much of it from those two people, or what's created between them?... I think these things are pretty impossible to answer, indeed they may be unanswerable. However, I think it's great to talk about. I don't think we have to sort of foreclose on the dialogue just to reach a conclusion. (West 1995: 304)

Today I cannot improve on these words or further clarify matters. However, this whole vexed territory remains to my mind an important part of modern-day therapy. If you wish, it is about the mystical side of therapeutic work, of human life.

As another example of an 'unintentional' spiritual healing experience, we can consider Greg Nolan's (2008) research into meaning moments within supervision. He reports a research interview with a therapist who talked of a client's story about their spiritual experiences. Greg asked his respondent to sit with the phenomenon and explain what it actually felt like. His respondent was moved to tears and said:

> the words that come up are 'touched by grace' and I think that's how they felt too… I've never articulated that before (*sniffing back and laughing through the tears – grabs a tissue*). I don't think my supervisor at that time could have heard it actually… (Nolan 2008: 174)

Greg then asked her what she meant by 'grace' and she related it to Rogers' core conditions, especially acceptance, since 'that's the bit that links back to my [religious beliefs]'. Greg then wonders if that was beyond Buber's I/Thou. She agrees:

> Yeah! Yeah definitely! Yeah (*sniff*) we met in an other world (*laughs, sniff, laughs*) we met in the world of infinity and… beyond person-alities… (*sniff*) and I will always treasure that (*struggling with tears of emotion and deep feeling – crying openly*) … (*sniff*). And I suspect that they will too. (Nolan 2008: 174–5)

What I find interesting about this dialogue is how, with Greg's skilful facilitation, the therapist is so moved in revisiting the experience of hearing the client's spiritual experience. It seems that the research inter-view takes on a healing aspect of its own. I also notice that the therapist says, 'I don't think my supervisor at the time could have heard me.' This probably explains something of the power of Greg's acceptance of her experience of her need to be heard in the same respectful way that she was able to hear her client's.

## Ethics

There are, of course, ethical questions that arise around the active use of spiritual healing techniques in therapy. These clearly include the following:

• Contracting and informed consent for the techniques. I believe that the whole issue of informed consent in therapy needs to be re-examined (West 2002b). How can we expect clients to consent to therapy if they have never previously experienced it and how can we possibly explain what it will be like? The client arriving for their first session is likely to be in a somewhat troubled state, making *informed* consent an absurdity. The idea of revisiting consent on a regular basis is another matter.

- Impact on therapeutic boundaries (see below).
- How the therapeutic relationship is altered, which includes the differences in role between being a therapist and being seen as a healer. This will have an impact on issues of transference, countertransference and therapist congruence. This all requires very careful exploration and thinking about, especially any sense that the two roles might be seen or experienced as being conflicted.
- Whether it is appropriate to withhold spiritual healing when the therapist believes it might well benefit the client. If we know of techniques that would benefit our clients and never consider using them, then this itself is an ethical issue.

These issues are also touched on by Peter Gubi in the context of the use of prayer in therapy in Chapter 4 in this book (further discussed in Gubi 2001, 2002, 2003). Such questions are all appropriate matters for supervision.

## Boundaries

Each school of therapy has its own version of appropriate boundaries. Each therapist may have their own fine-tuned version of such boundaries, and I can imagine boundaries being a little different with different clients or with the same client on differing occasions.

Introducing any innovative technique or merely allowing the therapeutic encounter to take new forms requires, I believe, that the therapist reflects on the boundary and consent issues involved. This impact needs to be considered for more than merely its ethical dimension. Questions that arise include:

- How the technique might change the therapeutic relationship, albeit in some subtle way.
- Its impact on the therapeutic alliance, including congruence, transference and countertransference.
- How the therapeutic boundaries are changed by the use of this technique or encounter.

- How the therapist talks about the innovation, the contract and the consent involved.
- What unease the therapist might have and what to do with such unease.
- What might be the possible negative effects of the innovation.
- Whether the therapist needs supervision before introducing the innovation.
- What questions need to be discussed in supervision regarding such an innovation.
- How the therapist conceptually fits the innovation into their model(s) of the therapeutic encounter.

## Supervision

Every significant event in therapeutic practice warrants supervision. This might well be impractical, but each event or collection of events of the same kind needs supervision. Innovative practices such as spiritual healing by active use of techniques or by allowing a healing atmosphere to develop require careful consideration in supervision. This needs to be discussed, even if it results in problems within the supervisory relationship. All supervisory relationships have their limits, including their life spans. It is far better to terminate a supervisory relationship than to maintain silence about innovative practices. Innovative practices require careful supervision for the sake of both therapist and, especially, client. Good supervisors, like good therapists, can be hard to find but never impossible!

Some likely supervision difficulties can arise for the therapist around talking about spiritual healing and spiritual healing encounters:

- Feeling judged.
- Feeling that such experiences will be seen as unprofessional or unhelpful to the clients involved.
- Feeling that merely telling the supervisor will be experienced as unhelpful.

Of the 30 therapists I interviewed in my doctoral research study into therapy and healing, 8 had experienced some difficulty in getting appropriate supervision. One of them was moved to say, 'I am going through supervisors as they generally consider I am helping people to become schizoid' (West 1995: 327). This was not my take on her practice when

I interviewed her. It points to how challenging it can be to supervise therapists whose practice does involve spirituality and healing.

Another, very seasoned therapist spoke of her difficulties in using an eclectic approach:

> You go to supervision and you talk about your client and you say you're mixing things and you're bringing in a bit of this and a bit of that, and then the supervisor gets upset. But you have to make your choice. I hope I am choosing for the benefit of the client and for the benefit of myself now, not for the benefit of the supervisor. (West 1995: 329)

It is likely that if the supervisory relationship is already experienced as less than perfect, such fears might well prove to be true. Also someone experienced as a very good supervisor might well still have their own countertransference or prejudiced response to hearing about spiritual healing. As one of my research respondents put it:

> It seems that the supervision relationship has to be healthy, has to be therapeutic, has to be healing, and just because it's called supervision doesn't mean it's going to be experienced that way. (West 1995: 336)

## Taboo

> I'm very careful whom I talk to about it [spirituality] even my supervisor. (respondent in West 1995: 331)

There seems to be something of a taboo or at least only partial acceptance of spiritual and healing moments that occur in therapy. Supervisors who rightly act as gatekeepers for the practice of talking therapy seem at times to be confusing issues of therapist competence and appropriate practice with what we might call innovative or advanced practice on another level.

Clarkson (2002: 39) reminds us that we need to 'differentiate between the psychologising of spiritual hunger and the spiritualisation of psychological problems', while John Rowan (1993) accuses Jung of psychologizing the spiritual. Both statements should cause us to reflect on what therapy is about, what it is good for and where its limits lie.

Both therapy and religion offer us implicit, and sometimes explicit, views of the good life, both offer us methods of achieving a better life and both help us face suffering. However, neither is a good substitute for the other. In my view, when they can work together the best benefit is achieved. One way of understanding how they fit together is via Ken Wilber's spectrum of consciousness model (Wilber 1980, 2001), which I have explored elsewhere in more detail (West 2000a, 2004a; see also Rowan 1993, 2005).

Wilber (1980) argues that the highest human development is achieved through spirituality and that both western therapy and eastern and western spiritual practices can help. He maintains that the models of human development common in the western therapy world ignore the higher and more overtly spiritual levels of human development. He insists that western therapy helps us best to progress through the lower levels, but that the higher levels need spiritual practices. While this model is intriguing and controversial, it does allow to move on from a 'one-size-fits-all' position and think about what approaches best help our clients at their present state of development and crisis.

Good therapists, I believe, should welcome the role of healthy spirituality in a client's move towards wellbeing. Spirituality, like sexuality, can become addictive, can take on a shadow side (Vaughan 1991), can become a way of avoiding and masking other problems. Plainly, not all spiritual and religious practices are good for all people for all time. Humans mess up, so humans inventions like organized religion mess up too, as do therapists.

There is, though, a boundary to be recognized. Good therapists can work with their client's spirituality and with spiritual healing moments in the therapeutic encounter. However, a therapist is not a spiritual guide, director, companion or teacher. These roles do often overlap those of a therapist, but they are different and should not be practised by the same person with the same client.

Brian Thorne (2002) approaches this same territory from a somewhat differing perspective. He insists on acknowledging the spiritual element in the person-centred approach to therapy by referring to its 'mystical power' and suggests that the person-centred therapist be considered as a secular priest. I find this an attractive notion, since it implies that the person-centred therapist can, and indeed should, be competent to work with spirituality and spiritual issues arising for, and with, their clients and indeed in their own lives.

However, I am aware that a number of person-centred therapists struggle with the word 'spirituality' and what it means. To them it can link to, and become entwined with, organized religion. Before you know it the baby is thrown out with the bathwater and one is hearing all too familiar stories of painful experiences around religion in the therapist's childhood. There is such a need for healing here. There is also a training need.

Until the therapy world as a whole learns to respect and move on from outdated notions of religion, and until the world of religion drops its outdated homophobia which only reinforces therapists' prejudices, then the danger remains that therapy itself becomes a substitute for religion, leading to what Robinson (1997) refers to as the 'ontological collapse' of spirituality into psychology.

## Conclusion

Any innovative practice in therapy can feel uncomfortable and raise ethical and other issues requiring careful consideration, including supervision. Nonetheless, the healing experiences discussed in this and subsequent chapters are usually seen as especially helpful to the clients involved. It would be a real shame if therapists limited their effectiveness through fear of the consequences of being open to such experiences. It does take courage as a therapist to be present to clients' suffering. It takes extra courage to be innovative, but the clients involved deserve this, and therapists deserve the support from supervisors and others to do this work. Further issues relating to such practice will be explored in Chapter 14.

### Discussion points

1. What is your understanding of healing moments within the therapeutic encounter?
2. Do you consider such moments as spiritual? If so, why? If not, why?
3. For therapists or clients: consider the description of healing offered in this chapter. Which of the words apply to your therapeutic experience?
4. Do you feel able to share as fully as you would like all aspects of your practice with your supervisor?

# 9
# Traditional Healing in the Course of Counselling and Psychotherapy

*Roy Moodley and Olga Oulanova*

## Introduction

In this chapter we explore the issue of clients seeking traditional healing while undertaking counselling and psychotherapy. We begin by exploring the role of traditional healing and healers in health and wellness. Second, we look at the possibility of the two healing modalities sitting side by side; and then discuss the reasons for clients wanting to engage in these two healing domains: traditional healing and counselling. Next, we consider the research on clients who access traditional healing and healers to contextualize the processes and practices in the West. Using the case vignette of Shiva (Moodley 1998a), we discuss the complexities of such relationships and the ethical implications for this kind of dual intervention.

## Background

Traditional healing or 'folk counselling' (Tseng and Hsu 1979), alternative and complementary healing practices have played a key role in the health and mental health of many cultures since the dawn of history. However, in more recent times we are seeing a tremendous growth of these practices or some variation of them in Europe and North America (see Rack 1982; Lee et al. 1992; Lee and Armstrong 1995; Moodley and West 2005; Lake and Spiegel 2007).

Some examples of these traditional healing practices are the following:

- *Ayurveda* (Hankey 2005) is a healing system of India, dating back to 1700 BC, as described in the classical texts of Susruta and Caraka (200 BC–400 BC). With its emphasis on mind, body and spirit as a single unity, it offers herbal treatments to bring about a holistic harmony of the person (Kumar et al. 2005).

- *Bhuta Vidya* (Rao 1986) dates back to 500 BC, as recorded in India's philosophical and religious literature, including the Rig-Veda (Royal knowledge), the Upanishads and the Bhagavad Gita, as well as in the tradition of yoga. The Atharava Veda, one of the Vedas, refers to devils and spirits as causes of illness and prescribes cures for them. The general belief that the cause of mental maladies lay in the supernatural reinforced the need to seek remedies in religious and magical techniques (Moodley and West 2005).
- *Sahaja* (Neki 1975) therapy signifies the 'innate nature' that a person is born with. It is close to humanistic psychology and emphasizes the social and environmental aspects of a person's wellbeing (Kumar et al. 2005).
- *Shamanism* (Eliade 1964; Tseng and McDermott 1975; Kakar 1982) – the word Shaman comes from a Northern Siberian tribe, the Tungus. Shamanic practitioners are known by different names in different parts of the world. A Muslim healer is called a *Pir* or *Sayana*, and a Hindu healer may be known as *Baba, Ojha* or *Tantric* healer. Shamans regard themselves as conduits between the supernatural and the patient and conduct therapy through the processes of 'possession' and 'exorcism' (Kumar et al. 2005).
- *Siddha* (Kumar et al. 2005) is a system of healing, dating back to 5000 BC, which originated in southern India. Similar to Ayurveda, treatment is directed to restoring the balance and equilibrium of the three humours (*vattam, pittam* and *kapham*). Treatment is individualized to meet each patient's needs (Kumar et al. 2005).
- *Spiritism* (Hohmann et al. 1990) is based on a belief in reincarnation and the use of mediums, who mediate healing through a process which stresses the concept of spiritual 'fluids' around the body (Hohmann et al. 1990).
- More contemporary versions of traditional healing practices include Sufi healing (Christi 1991), Morita therapy (Tseng and Hsu 1979; Chen, 2003), Naikan therapy (Tseng and Hsu 1979), Shiatsu (Jarmey and Mojay 1991), Zen Shiatsu (Poulin and West 2005) and Qigong (Lake 2002; Chen 2003), to name but a few.

A comparative study on alternative healing and healers found that middle-class Americans practise beliefs and techniques that include naturopathy, homoeopathy, acupuncture, yogic healing, psychic and faith healing, and the new age therapies (see Heber et al. 1989; Kessler et al. 2001; Poulin and West 2005). According to Field (1990: 275), the 'diversity of alternative medicine and spiritual healing methods are usually associated with neo-religious cults or charismatic religious movements'.

However, descriptive accounts and survey studies examining the use of traditional healing (for example Sayed 2002; Berg 2003; Moodley and West 2005) and interviews with traditional healers and patients (Vontress 1999; Monteiro 2004; Sima and West 2005; Solomon and Wane 2005; Moodley 2006) seem to suggest that contemporary uses of these practices have been grounded in particular cultural, social and political contexts, for example colonization, western colonial literary texts, resistances to cultural dominance and a desire to regain pre-colonial health-care practices. It also seems that clients from across the diversity spectrum (race, gender, class, sexual orientation, disability, age and religion) access traditional healing. The most obvious groups, but not limited to these, are the indigenous and immigrant groups who seek traditional healers mainly from their own cultural and ethnic communities, but also from other cultural groups who happen to live among them.

In addition, there appears to be research into 'voodoo' and other traditional healing practices funded by the Department of Health in the UK, at the Maudsley Hospital (*The Guardian*, 16 February 1999: 16), and the Social Science and Humanities Council of Canada (SSHRC) has funded research into the role of traditional healers in counselling and health promotion that is taking place in Toronto (see Moodley 2007b). Through these and other studies we are beginning to get a strong sense of the critical role that traditional healers and healing practices are playing in the health and mental health care in the West.

Clearly, it seems that more and more people are entering the realm of the 'Other' to find physical, emotional and spiritual healing; and it seems that they do this alongside conventional treatments. For example, they may see a western physician for a particular physical or mental ailment while taking alternative medicines, such as acupuncture, homoeopathy, yogic healing and herbalism. Some people visit religious places of worship for 'spirit-filled' healing (see Garzon 2005), others consult traditional healers, such as Latin American voodoo doctors, Aboriginal medicine men and medicine women, Hougans from Haiti, Hakims from Pakistan, and Viads from India, while at the same time they consult western doctors. It is also possible to find in counselling and psychotherapy a middle-class ethnic minority client wearing a 'blessed amulet' from the family Hakim or Obeah man or woman (Caribbean healers). Thus the client is in touch, so to speak, with the healing components of two different traditions of healing at the same time. For these clients this particular practice may be based on their understanding of a multicultural self in which the psyche accommodates the two healing modalities.

## The role of traditional healing in health and wellness

A review of the research that has explored knowledge of and attitudes towards traditional healing suggests that these culturally specific healing practices occupy an integral place in the lives of many diverse communities. For example, survey studies with indigenous populations suggest that cultural healing practices continue to play a critical role in the health care and wellbeing of Aboriginal communities (Hurdle 2002; Canales 2004; Vicary and Bishop 2005). In the North American context, Canales (2004) found that for many Aboriginal women traditional practices formed a central part of their self-care and wellbeing (see also Beals et al. 2006). Similarly, Wyrostock and Paulson (2000) surveyed urban Canadian Aboriginal students' attitudes towards traditional healing practices and found a strong interest and active participation in traditional healing among a large majority of respondents.

These findings are especially interesting given that this was a sample of Aboriginal individuals residing in an urban centre where information on and the services of traditional healers may be difficult to access. Recognizing that traditional healing practices persist and continue to provide support to indigenous peoples, Canadian Aboriginal communities have made tremendous strides in integrating traditional knowledge and healing practices into their health-care interventions (see McCormick 2000; Poonwassie and Charter 2001; McCabe 2007). Several Canadian Aboriginal groups have developed unique approaches to wellness which are largely based on the holistic worldview inherent in Aboriginal cultures, as well as on indigenous values and specific cultural practices (Poonwassie and Charter 2001).

A similar pattern of revival in the use of indigenous healing methods and an increasing recognition of their value can be observed outside North America. For example, in describing social work interventions with native Hawaiians, Hurdle (2002) states that traditional practices continue to occupy an integral role in lives of Hawaiian indigenous communities, because they are grounded in their particular cultural and traditional framework of healing. Among Australian Aboriginal peoples, Vicary and Bishop (2005) found that traditional ways of healing were generally preferred over western ones in addressing mental health concerns. It seems that having had their indigenous knowledge and cultural healing practices disavowed and denied to them as a result of colonialism, indigenous communities have in various ways been retrieving many of their healing practices that went underground, so to speak (Moodley and West 2005).

We also see the growth of traditional healing practices happening on the African continent. For example, in post-apartheid South Africa traditional healing and healers are now playing a central role in the national health-care system (see Edwards 1986; Donald and Hlongwane 1989; Kahn and Kelly 2001; Berg 2003; Bojuwoye 2005). Indeed, this seems to be the case across the globe, where interest is growing in 'folk counselling' traditions: in the Caribbean (see Jorge 1995; Marshall 2005), in South America (González Chévez 2005; Comas-Diaz 2006), in South Asia (Kumar et al. 2005) and in the Middle East (Al-Krenawi 1999; Al-Krenawi and Graham 1999).

In Brazil, for example, Hohmann et al. (1990) state that traditional practices have flourished and at present greatly complement a deficient mental health-care system. In the Rio–São Paulo area alone, for instance, there are more than 75 spiritist psychiatric hospitals that integrate medical and spiritist techniques (Moodley and West 2005). For traditional healing and its healers to reach this level of power in the infrastructure of society, the process is trusted and its healers are respected, since they have a profound understanding of the complex and intricate ways in which their society organizes itself. Indeed, this understanding has become possible as a result of the developmental way in which indigenous healing methods have evolved, and especially its potential to resist and survive colonialism, globalization and post-modern advances in the technology of western health-care practices.

## Concurrent use of traditional healing and western therapies

The inclusion of traditional methods alongside conventional therapies is an age-old phenomenon, but has recently been taken up by a wide range of people across cultures, genders and social classes. The sustained interest in and utilization of traditional healing practices by ethnic minorities as well as dominant cultural groups represents a noteworthy phenomenon. It signifies a resistance to the whole notion of individualism, psychopathology, unconscious phenomena, DSM-IV and other Eurocentric ways of body–mind division of the human being. Indeed, what accounts for the continued appeal of traditional healing to diverse populations is the possibility of not only interrogating the Cartesian body–mind splitting, but the fact that the diversity and multicultural practices of health and mental health care get acknowledged and validated as legitimate methods of treatment. In turn, the immigrant and indigenous communities who are the chief recipients of traditional healing, with these practices forming an integral part of their culture, are themselves acknowledged and accepted as part of society. Clearly, this has a ripple effect: it decreases intercultural and ethnic tensions, promotes a positive self-concept and self-esteem, and makes for a more conducive environment within which a diverse and multicultural society can be created and continue to develop.

It also seems critical for clients who hold different worldviews to make choices about seeking a dual relationship. In this section we examine the perceptions and stereotypes about the other's worldviews, and the assumptions about health and illness representative of minority communities. Such an exploration will enable us to uncover the difficulties which are often encountered when thinking about the role and value of traditional healing and healers in our society; more specifically, it will help us understand the client's need to have a dual relationship – to undertake conventional counselling and psychotherapy as well as consult with a traditional healer.

This pattern of simultaneously using traditional and conventional, or western, health care can be understood by exploring perceptions of such dual relationships in other parts of the world. According to Littlewood (1990), for patients in most 'Third World' societies there is no question of accessing two or more treatments. It is done as a matter of course, even for the smallest of illnesses. In many communities there is a choice to seek help from a traditional healer, or use conventional medicine, or both. This may be due to the fact that as some studies suggest, ethnic minorities, people of colour and immigrants use a different conceptual framework to represent and present their illness and discomfort (see Asuni 1986; Buhrmann 1986; Fernando 1988). One single therapy approach may not solve the problem, so clients access healers who are multimodal, *viz.*, traditional healers. For example, Buhrmann (1986) in her work with Zulu traditional healers observed that clients do not divide their 'illness' into different categories of somatic, psychological and psychosomatic; that they do not split themselves into good and bad parts, but express their distress as 'when part of me is ill, the whole of me is ill, irrespective of what the illness is' (Buhrmann 1986: 26). It seems that a 'close correlation exists between a patient's cultural beliefs about his/her illness and between his/her understanding of the treatment of such distress' (Moodley 2000: 163).

The availability of the different kinds of cure will complete the frames of reference of illness conceptualization and representation by the patient. In other words, clients will be able, if given the opportunity of receiving different cures (for example, talking therapy and traditional healing), systematically to organize the expression of their problem into the discourse of the healer, thus 'presenting their subjective distress to each therapist appropriately... competing and contradictory cures can be held alongside or in tandem with each other without necessarily creating conflict in the patient' (Moodley 2000: 164). As Lilian Gonzales Chevez (2005) says, following Kleinman's (1980) thoughts, traditional healing systems contribute and are reconstituted in the context of a cultural system that elaborates its cognitive strategies.

Research suggests that a significant proportion of ethnic minority clients resort to traditional healing practices in their daily living for a number of reasons. For example, South Asians often seek the support of a traditional healer not only in times of crisis or psychological difficulty, but for the purposes of marriage, birth of a child, moving house, accepting a new job offer and so on (see Dein and Sembhi 2001; Hilton et al. 2001; Nathan 2005; Rao 2006). Hilton et al.'s (2001) interviews with South Asian immigrant women in Canada found that many value and frequently use South Asian healing practices in their daily lives. Although some considered simultaneous use of traditional and western health practices to be contradictory, a significant number reported utilizing these two approaches concurrently.

Research also shows that people access their own cultural traditions of healing, as well as those that are offered by mainstream services (see Donald and Hlongwane 1989; Dein and Sembhi 2001; Vicary and Bishop 2005). For example, Dein and Sembhi (2001) presented illustrative case studies of patients who had consulted Muslim spiritual healers and Ayurvedic practitioners while receiving mainstream psychiatric care. It appears that this help-seeking behaviour was largely influenced by patients' beliefs about health and illness. In general, these patients felt that while mainstream health care attended to symptoms, it is traditional healing that addressed the underlying cause of the disease. From Dein and Sembhi's research findings it appears relatively common for some South Asian individuals residing in Great Britain simultaneously to resort to mainstream psychiatric services and access traditional and culturally specific forms of healing (see also Ineichen 1990; Kumar et al. 2005).

Reflecting on the use of traditional healing in South Africa, Donald and Hlongwane (1989) also offer case study accounts describing how mainstream counselling interventions and traditional healing practices were sought out conjointly in a school setting. Interestingly, reviewing the outcome of one case, the authors argue that intervention from either counselling or traditional healing alone would not have been as successful as the concurrent use of the two approaches. The case studies presented in these research endeavours seem to suggest that in very diverse communities (that is, a South Asian immigrant community in Great Britain and a black community in South Africa) individuals simultaneously seek out traditional healing practices and conventional health care.

Similar patterns of traditional healing utilization have been reported in other cultures and communities, for example Islamic healing in Paris (Nathan 2005); Jewish healing in New York (Praglin 2005); traditional and cultural healing in Tanzania (Sima and West 2005); African-centred healing in the US (Graham 1996); and Mexican traditional healing (Gonzales Chevez 2005). In Argentina, 'especially in the south, psychotherapists work alongside traditional healers, respecting the cultural beliefs of the indigenous healers' (Gomez 2007: 714), while in Brunei, 'most psychotherapy is provided by traditional healers (*bomoh*)' (Kumaraswamy 2007: 738). Yet another example of this pattern of the concurrent use of traditional healing and mainstream mental health care is offered by Moodley (1998a, 1999a). He discusses two case vignettes where clients use traditional healing while undertaking counselling and psychotherapy. One of these is discussed later in this chapter.

## Why do clients in therapy consult traditional healers?

For some clients, particularly visible minority clients, traditional healing has been the primary source of healing before they become familiar with the process of counselling. In fact, for many of these clients counselling and psychotherapy are alternative and complementary practice, and therefore engaging with them is done with a certain kind of scepticism and anxiety. In the same way, westerners used to think about Chinese traditional medicine and South Asian Ayurveda, meditation and yoga, but now have no difficulty in seeking out acupuncture, yogic therapy, Ayurveda and meditation and wellness clinics. On the other hand, the same cannot be said for ethnic minority clients who undertake counselling and psychotherapy: many drop out after the first session, a number leave prematurely and many express poor outcomes (see Moodley 1999a for discussion). Many reasons have been proposed by multicultural therapists for such client behaviour. These include a mistrust of counselling and psychotherapy practitioners, client–therapist differences, misunderstanding clients' illness representations and presentations, stereotyping clients, culture-insensitive methods and physical and psychological barriers erected by service providers, to name but a few (Kareem and Littlewood 1992; Bhugra and Bhui 1998; Moodley 1999a, b, 2000; Moodley and Palmer 2006).

Given these enormous hurdles, it stands to reason that ethnic minority clients will engage with what Ataudo refers to as 'the contact medicine' that identifies with 'cultural fuels', such as belief systems, customs, ancestor consultation, ancestor worship, community and cultural values (1985, cited in Moodley 2005). Indeed, when counselling and psychotherapy interventions appear to be patronizing and racist, clients will retreat to this 'other' place to recover their humanity (Moodley, 1998a). Or even if they do not have any negative experiences in counselling, they may choose also to consult a traditional healer for what counselling and psychotherapy cannot offer them – perhaps, a spiritual space.

If the reason is not inherently metaphysical, then clients still have the right to make choices about seeking other types of alternative forms of therapy, and one that is not monoculturally western. For ethnic minority clients there could be a desire to seek a culture-bound healing practice that is grounded in particular theories of health, illness and cure seeking (see Kleinman 1980; Good and Good 1982; Moodley 2000, 2006). According to Good and Good, 'the meaning of illness for an individual is grounded in... the network of meanings an illness has in a particular culture... and the care patterns that shape the experience of the illness and the social reactions to the sufferer' (1982: 148). Thus for the clients who consult traditional healers alongside counselling and psychotherapy, the reasons may be complex, and cannot be put down to just a dissatisfaction with, or a resistance to, western counselling and psychotherapy.

In examining the western and traditional outlooks on mental health, it appears that there are underlying differences between the two. In traditional healing there is a holistic conceptualization of health wherein spiritual, physical, emotional and mental wellness is regarded as inseparable, while in western mental health, the focus is often exclusively on the mental and emotional components (see Duran 1990; Ross 1992; Garrett and Carroll 2000). Thus when clients seek the help of a traditional healer they are in a position to address their spiritual, physical, emotional or mental wellbeing in one consultation or with the same healer, whereas in the western model a client would seek the support of different therapists for each of the various aspects of themselves (Morse et al. 1991). For example, for spiritual issues one may speak to a priest, for ailments of the body a physician, for emotional concerns a counsellor, and for mental needs a psychiatrist. This is in stark contrast to the holistic conceptualization of wellbeing characteristic of traditional healing.

Furthermore, while western health care understands illness as located in and limited to the body or the mind of the person and consequently focuses on the individual client, traditional healing commonly conceptualizes disease more broadly, recognizing disturbances in the outside environment as playing a part in the affliction (Friedman 1998). In the traditional healing outlook, disease is thought of as disharmony either within the person, or between the individual and the community, or the individual and the universe (Bojuwoye 2005; Ross 1992). Therefore, in its approach to helping, traditional healing emphasizes relatedness and the significance of relationships. Traditional healing aims to restore harmony and balance within the spiritual, physical, emotional and mental aspects of the individual, as well as between the individual and the community (Duran 1990; McCormick 1996; Garrett and Carroll 2000; Bojuwoye 2005; Poonwassie and Charter 2005).

While the above discussion of the discrepancies between the conventional and traditional conceptualizations of health, illness and healing is merely a brief overview, some significant differences between the western and traditional understandings of mental health become evident. It is therefore reasonable that on those occasions when counselling proves inadequate to address the entirety of their needs, clients may indeed consult a traditional healer. Taking a more holistic approach, the traditional healer may in turn be able to address some aspects of the client's mental health to which conventional psychology, psychiatry or psychotherapy has failed to attend.

As discussed earlier and as the literature suggests, vast numbers of individuals see mental health professionals and traditional healers concurrently (see also Novins et al. 2004). So how does this discrepancy in worldviews and approach to health and healing play out when a western-trained counsellor or psychotherapist engages with a client who also consults a traditional healer? What are some of the challenges that a counsellor may encounter in this situation? What sorts of ethical dilemmas arise for the mental health professional? Grounded in the clinical experience of the first author and supported by findings from the counselling and psychotherapy literature, an exploration of these central questions will form the remainder of this chapter.

## The case of Shiva

Elsewhere, Moodley (1998a, 1999a) has written about clients who consult traditional healers while in psychotherapy. It seems that through the traditional healer, clients are able to identify cultural metaphors, symbols and archetypes that are outside the parameters of western psychotherapy. In this section, we re-examine one of Moodley's case vignettes (Moodley 1998a), the story of Shiva, a patient who, while in psychotherapy with Moodley, also consulted a traditional healer. But first, here is a brief description of that therapy. Shiva was a South Asian man, living in England, fluent in English and Punjabi, and teaching English as a second language at a local adult education centre. He self-'diagnosed' his situation as one of 'depression'. Moodley, on the other hand, felt that Shiva was grappling with some deep-seated material concerning family and transgenerational issues, among them immigration, racism, cultural dislocation and socioeconomic status.

Shiva was in therapy for over a year. During this period, a composite picture emerged of his life and the issues that concerned him. Shiva was able to articulate his thoughts and ideas in very complex and imaginative ways on topics such as existentialism, socialism and Hindu philosophy. On a number of these occasions, Moodley would comment and reflect on the relationship between Shiva and himself, wondering if there was something of the Oedipus position. In the context of where the therapy occurred (in an academic institution), Moodley also reflected on the reality of doing therapy in an institute with its own colonial history and notions of academic and patriarchal power, and how this was played out through the performances of masculinity, power and aggression in the therapeutic relationship.

While Shiva was in therapy, his spouse instituted divorce proceedings, at which point he dropped out of therapy only to return many months later, saying that he had apparently seen a Vaid (traditional Hindu healer) a few times who had conducted some rituals and read his 'charts' (Vaidya is a traditional Hindu healing technique using Ayurvedic medicine). This event became the topic of discussion for the whole therapy session. Shiva said that he needed to 'sort out a few things' in 'Indian time' and 'Indian space'. He felt that his visits to the traditional healer were beneficial to his spiritual life and his *dharma* (life cycle or life journey). Interestingly, for many weeks after this disclosure, the conversation tended always to include the experiences with the traditional healer.

In the concluding remarks of the case vignette, Moodley (1998a) reflected that working with Shiva offered a new dimension to the whole process of therapy. There is no doubt that counselling and psychotherapy have many limitations, particularly in the context of clients who express complex aspects of their multiple cultural and ethnic identities, as in the case of Shiva; especially since his conversations were marked with numerous and multifaceted metaphors, symbols and archetypal images of his Indianness and his Britishness. Bringing this to consciousness during counselling was not quite straightforward for the therapist, who used traditional psychoanalytic theories as holdfasts by which every psychopathology may be explained.

We wondered whether Shiva's visit to the traditional healer was a result of a specific cultural 'lack' in western counselling or whether the experience of western therapy created a deeper awareness within him so that he could go beyond the metaphors and symbols that western counselling and psychotherapy invited him into, but was unable to take them any further. So therapy may be able to go to the point of cultural sensitivity but be unable to go beyond multiculturalism. Or could it be that multiculturalism itself is inherently limited and limiting, and therefore needs (re)placing in psychotherapy (see Moodley 2007a)? Could the client have experienced an awakening of his spiritual self through therapy, counselling and psychotherapy having taken him there but being unable currently to process it with him?

According to Holmes (1985: 248), 'as treatment progresses a patient's metaphors change level or deepen, giving a richer and more varied set of possible responses, resonances and relationships'. In his therapy, Shiva needed an(other) site, an(other) ritual, an(other) place where these new symbols and metaphors were released and set free in a more culturally focused idiom; namely, the Hindu philosophy of *svadharma*. *Svadharma*, or life task or life goals, is the ground plan of a person's life. For a detailed discussion on *dharma*, *desa* (the culture in which a person is born), *kala* (the period of historical time in which the person lives) and *srama* (the effort required of the person at different stages of life), see Kakar (1982: 37).

Reflecting on psychological metaphors, whether or not they are culture and ethnicity specific, can be very illuminating for both the therapist and the patient. However, this area is often problematized as a result of the changing nature of metaphors and the sociopolitical and historical contexts within which metaphors are constructed. It seems clear that when psychotherapists enter the inner world of patients who are dissimilar to them in respect of culture, ethnicity, race, gender, class, caste, sexual orientation, disability or religion, consideration must be given to the variety of meanings clients may construct.

## Ethical issues and their implications for therapy

As we have discussed thus far, a significant number of ethnic minority clients consult traditional healers at the same time as they see counsellors and psychotherapists. While accessing different therapists in this way may not pose a problem for the client, such dual relationships can present counsellors and psychotherapists with considerable ethical dilemmas. Although professional guidelines and codes of ethics directing counselling practice have begun to recognize the immense diversity among clients' cultural backgrounds and are striving to address ethical concerns which may emerge in this context, these documents do not always provide sufficient guidelines when it comes to supporting these dual relationships.

Moreover, while we are accustomed to the client–therapist–supervisor relationship, particularly in terms of parallel process, we still have not figured out another process that will explain the client–traditional healer–therapist relationship. Indeed, conventional psychotherapy raises boundary issues concerning any form of dual relationship. However, clients have been engaged in one form or another with alternative or complementary healing that is not seen as a 'talking cure'. There is no difficulty in accepting or questioning a client's choice of having acupuncture and psychotherapy in the same week, indeed the same day. So why would it be difficult for a client to see a traditional healer alongside a therapist? Since the psychotherapist's domain is the mind and psyche, a similar claim can also be attributed to traditional healing practices, and boundary issues then become an ethical concern for counselling and psychotherapy. A client cannot serve two 'masters'. However, within a relational model of counselling this may not constitute a threat, since each dyad is a unique self-generating clinical relationship within which the client's psychological distress is shaped, interpreted and ultimately produces its own specific version of healing (see discussion by Good and Good 1982).

Another example of an ethical dilemma that may arise could be around the idea of collaboration with a traditional healer. Although collaboration between western professionals and traditional healers is encouraged, even at the tentative level of referring clients to alternative healing practices or traditional healers (see Duran 1990; McCormick 1996; Restoule 1997; Sima and West 2005; Solomon and Wane 2005), this situation can pose serious ethical dilemmas for the counsellor and psychotherapist.

One such quandary can be explored by considering a case that may present itself when working with immigrant or indigenous clients, who often, as discussed earlier, tend to see traditional healers. Since counselling and psychotherapy treatments are dependent on sound 'empirical' evidence as a necessary rationale for any intervention, referrals or collaboration with traditional healing and healers becomes very difficult. The Code of Ethics of the Canadian Psychological Association reflects this view by endorsing 'interventions that... have reasonable theoretical or empirically-supported efficacy' (CPA 2001: Standard II.21). This principle proves problematic in working with an Aboriginal client who may benefit from a referral to a traditional healer, or who may wish to explore the meaning of their traditional healing in therapy.

In her discussion of ethical issues in multicultural counselling, Pettifor (2001: 30) argues that '[the] belief in scientific empiricism and empirically supported interventions has the potential to exclude the use of culturally appropriate humanistic and spiritual healing experiences'. Indeed, while little empirical research has been carried out to establish evidence for the therapeutic benefits of indigenous healing practices, qualitative accounts suggest their critical role in restoring an individual's mental wellbeing and their ability to enhance western counselling (see Juntunen and Morin 2004; Hunter et al. 2006).

The most favourable treatment alternative could indeed include referral to, and subsequent collaboration with, a traditional healer. Yet this may present a counsellor or psychotherapist who holds a firm belief in sound empirical evidence with an ethical dilemma. How does one explore a client's experiences in traditional healing when one believes these ways of helping to be invalid? And importantly, does one refer a client for traditional healing despite the lack of empirical evidence? What would collaboration with a traditional healer look like if one does not believe that traditional interventions are therapeutic enough?

Interestingly, the Code of Ethics of the Canadian Psychological Association addresses this kind of dilemma by recommending 'consulting with, or including in service delivery, persons relevant to the culture or belief systems of those served... and recommending professionals other than psychologists when appropriate' (CPA 2001: Standard II.21). This is indeed an important guideline to consider when providing services to clients who are seeking, or are considering seeking, traditional healing. While professional ethical codes of practice do at times provide satisfactory recommendations for working with clients who concurrently consult traditional healers, and certain ethical dilemmas may hence be resolved by adhering to these guidelines, counsellors and psychotherapists must however continuously engage with the moral and ethical dimensions of working with a diverse range of clients.

## Conclusion

We are aware as therapists, at least anecdotally, that many minority clients often travel to their 'home' countries to seek help from a traditional healer at times of serious illness, and also when western psychology and medicine have failed. For these patients it seems that the cultural idioms and metaphors, and the cultural archetypes embedded in their unconscious, can only be accessed within a particular psychic space and time. It is as if the healing process is bound by culture, history and memory. As Kirmayer (2003: 249) says:

> In multicultural societies, sufferer and healer may live in different worlds and may not share the same notions of the roles of patient and healer, the appropriate place and time for healing, the meanings of symbolic acts, and the expected outcome.

Might it be that the problem as we discussed earlier is with the concept of multiculturalism as it is practised in the West? It sets up the failure in the first place. Perhaps if communities were less apartheid-like in the way they live in the West – separate, different, minoritized and often marginalized – the sufferer and healer may find an appropriate place and time to make sense of the symbolic aspects of their lives as they live in the same world.

Since the symbiotic relationship between a particular culture and its history makes up the ingredients of the healing ritual, it seems that integrating some of the traditional healing practices into counselling and psychotherapy (and vice versa) may be the future direction to achieve a positive health and mental health practice. This change has already begun, for example:

> influenced by Western approaches, contemporary Chinese forms of counseling and therapy have evolved into new hybridized forms that take into account Chinese cultural beliefs, philosophical traditions, and help-seeking practices. (Chang et al. 2005: 114)

And in North America the use of mindfulness meditation in CBT (cognitive behaviour therapy), yoga, shiatsu and reiki in therapy generally are clearly demonstrating that this is the way forward. So in the final analysis, clients can choose to enter and stay in counselling and psychotherapy because it is also a place that provides a psychic (re)treat for 'the other'.

## Discussion points

1. What do you think are the challenges for clients when they access both traditional healing and therapy?
2. What are the challenges for therapists when their clients access both traditional healing and therapy?
3. Is referral desirable between therapists and traditional healers?
4. What would facilitate cooperation between therapists and traditional healers?
5. How do therapy and traditional healing fit within a multicultural society?

# 10
## Assessing a Counsellor's Use of a Seemingly Spiritual Gift

*Christa Gorsedene*

## Introduction

This chapter asks how a counsellor, faced with the possibility that they have found, or been granted, a source of help in their work from an intelligent spiritual source, might proceed to check the seeming source, and whether cooperation with it is for good or ill. In other words, if some special gift seemed to be knocking at one's door, how might one try to avoid the possible twin pitfalls of either giving the seeming gift too much credence or prominence, or perhaps wasting the gift through hesitancy or scepticism.

Many an author has written about how, when counselling is undertaken with the best efforts at care and respectful honesty by a therapist who also tries to fit themself for the task through the struggles of personal development, they may experience moments when something extra and beneficial emerges from or joins forces with the counsellor–client relationship (Rogers 1980). This may variously be, or be conceptualized as, for instance, 'simply' human relational depth (Mearns and Cooper 2005), involvement of higher selves (Whitmore 2000), the transpersonal (Rowan 1993) or assistance from a beyond-the-earthly spiritual dimension (Wardle, Chapter 11 in this volume). This chapter aims to draw the reader along the story thread of my own increasing experiences of 'something extra'. The accessible tale and its offshoots are offered as both worked example and vehicle for thought, encompassing organic – and sometimes faltering – practioner development, client-work potential and conundrums, and wondering about the nature and value of things.

*If* one can countenance the idea that transpersonal or spiritual help may occur in counselling, and *if* one also concedes that the transpersonal encompasses great diversity (Wilber 2001) and/or that the spiritual partakes of *inexhaustible mystery* (Ferrer 2002), I posit that *then* the idea that the intelligent spirit might grant a variety of help in counselling – and even help of which one has not heard before – is not unreasonable.

## Personal background

Many experiences in recent years have given me the chance to consider this question 'from the inside', from a starting point of agnosticism married with a penchant for logic. However, I quite properly want to be given away, not only for the usual reason of showing the reader the 'lens' of myself through which they are seeing my research, but also because I find that sketching out my story frankly, in common language, enables people to grasp what I am about better than academic abstractions, opening a way to clearer consideration of diverse kinds afterwards.

Assuring my reader that such a degree of use of self is consistent with my heuristic methodology (to be expanded later), I shall now – by kind permission and slightly amended – quote from my tale as I wrote it for *Thresholds* (spring 2007), both content and style revealing myself. I have four reasons for doing so:

- The quoted story boldly discloses the researcher's 'lens'.
- Unhedged by abstractions, I hope it will put the reader vividly in the picture.
- It offers the reader an opportunity to note their own flow of responses, boosting relevant self-awareness.
- The stark telling actually *is* part of checking the alleged phenomenon, laying it open to the widest scrutiny not only by people in academically critical mode but also to similarly stark and stimulating vernacular riposte and debate.

### Agnostic counsellor and spirit guide: Can such an unlikely team ever help?

Surprise and delight, doubt, challenge and exhilaration have been writ large in my life since my spirit guide first declared himself to me – an agnostic! – in 2001.

I had recently finished my professional training as a person-centred counsellor. My co-students had been a brilliant, full-blooded bunch, which was just as well, since during my diploma years I experienced shock after shock as 'impossible' yet helpful coincidences happened to me at an ever-increasing rate. Without their listening – acceptant but robust – I doubt I could have survived those years of straddling my old just-material-plane and my tentative new something-more world views. Cognitive dissonance or what!

I really felt I had found the vocation to fulfil me when I passed my diploma, if only I could find a job. Little did I know that a path and a task were about to come and take me by the scruff of the neck! Visiting a Scottish cathedral I experienced a synchronicity (I knew the concept by then) right beside the tomb of its patron saint Mungo, directly followed by a huge wave of a marvellous feeling I had never felt or dreamt of before. Words do fail, but 'wave of love, overwhelming yet kind' goes in the right direction.

It was on the same trip that I also chanced on my first encounter with a pendulum dowser, whereas I had already learnt from a diploma tutor the value of exploring life and self with images of human situations or types, such as a good pictorial tarot deck provides. Over the following months a process unfolded whereby the dowsing, the pictures and Mungo cooperated ever more organically in helping me navigate life's problems. It was a process in which I was both fascinated willing student, and bemused questioning observer of myself and 'it all'.

To cut a very long story very short, in 2003 I started a PhD expressly to put this phenomenon up for scrutiny – with the approval of team-mate Mungo, of course. I had already dared, heart in mouth, to disclose it to a friend here and an acquaintance there, and it had seemed also to assist them in personal development or dealings with life – but would this hold under the gaze of the wider, more stringent academic world?

Disclosing my relationship and modus operandum with Mungo to a new person involves trepidation and daring for me. People react so variously and unpredictably depending on their pasts, their faiths, their concepts and so on. For instance one New Age enthusiast was keen to have a go at engaging with guide and cards only to back right off when someone else in the room reconceptualized it by saying 'that's occult'. Likewise Christians may cool towards me on the basis of the biblical verse about not conjuring spirits whilst others say 'this could be God working through Mungo, yes please'. The list of responses and pigeon-holings goes on, but put you in the picture I must.

The other person (or occasionally people), whether PhD participant(s) or otherwise, meet with me and we decide either that we want to choose our issue to explore, or that we prefer to let Mungo flag something up. When it comes to feel right in our conversation, we 'open the line' to Mungo who dowses to me a picture card or sequence thereof for us. The cards are neither predictive nor answers on a plate from 'on high'. The idea is rather that they are Mungo's contribution to the meeting, inviting our responses and whatever conversation (informed by person-centred values) therefore ensues, perhaps leading again to more pictures from Mungo and so on until a right-feeling end-for-now arrives. It is a richer, more responsive process than just adding pictures into a two-earthly-people meeting, but responsibility for discernment stays firmly 'down here'.

I have engaged with 36 participants in my PhD, 8 of them even having each met me for a series of 4 taped Mungo-sessions (now thematically analysed). A large proportion of the participants experience a 'Lightening of the Heart', whether of just one or both of two broad categories, namely the 'PHEW!' and 'WOW!' types.

Let me give a couple of examples of the 'PHEW!' type. I call one the 'constellation of concerns'. Suppose an array of pictures comes where each one represents a trouble in the participant's life. The participant may feel relief that their companion can see just how hemmed in they are, or they may even feel cared for and understood by whatever it was that so arranged the cards. Then there is the '3-party dynamics' type. For example, whereas over the years I have got used to speaking my mind to Mungo with comments like 'whatever are you driving at here' etc., participants may bring in their deferences towards (seeming) authority figures or their tendency to shyness around a pair (Mungo and me) already familiar with each other or whatever, and once such dynamics have been spotted they can be questioned and worked with. If the PHEW! type is about enhanced looking into concerns, there is an expansiveness to the WOW! type. For instance, occasional EHEs (extraordinary human experiences) have happened, always as yet pitched to a level that is vista-widening yet not unnerving to the participant. For example, an agnostic experienced a meaningful sentence 'coming into her like an arrow' in a way that was completely new for her: 'It was clear, it stayed, it rings true, it gives strength, it's like a mantra that came'. On the other hand a religious believer suddenly said in one of our sessions 'I'm feeling almost, and this is very strange for me, a powerful presence around... I can't explain it... But

I am at ease with it'. Each of them thus experienced something new in a timely, supported and impactful way, and their worlds of what they experientially knew to be possible were enlarged.

...and so were mine! So am I still an agnostic? Well, yes and no. My experiences with Mungo have turned me into a believer in something vast and intricate beyond the world of our current senses and science, and that at least part of it can creatively work with us at least part of the time towards increased love-with-truth. But far from putting a lid of certainty about 'everything' on it for me, the experiences have lifted lids galore. In the words of a saying long since beloved by both my 'inner scientist' and my spirit, and which fits my questioning quest like a glove, 'the greater the island of knowledge, the longer the shoreline of wonder'. For me, Q.E.D!

## General background

Returning now to a more academic level, the heuristics of Moustakas (1990) offered a methodological backbone suited to the passionate desire of my research, namely to study the phenomenon as it already was, neither distorting nor fracturing it but rather giving space for deeper and/or expanded experience should it arise. Moustakas' system seeks to plumb some aspect of human experience by means of several defined phases, including the researcher's immersion of herself in that aspect at length, with a willingness to 'be put through it' (Scott 2008). Findings from such research are therefore deeply personal, yet that very quality often touches and/or elucidates universal chords or others' depths. In resonant vein, the research account I shall give here risks seeming so 'one-off' as to be irrelevant to others, yet I promise that I will put forward a tentative, potentially general claim at the end.

Moustakas' heuristic methodology, though disciplined, is well suited to exploratory (as distinct from verificational) research, where one starts out still largely ignorant about quite what one thinks one is dealing with and how one may come to know more – that is, with ontological and epistemological uncertainty – and this was the beauty of it for me. As my research progressed it entered unexpected areas to such a degree that the greater part of situating it within other literature had to be done later. It would be incongruent with its de facto organic quality (Clements et al. 1998) to give background literature *en bloc*; in actuality it had – and still has – to be flexibly responsive and growthful.

## Findings from research

I intended my own heuristic immersion to be merely through participant sessions with the supposed Mungo, but in fact 'it itself insisted'
that the research be undissected from my wider life. For some years
prior to the PhD I had been experiencing synchronicities and fortuitous
timings as helping in my life's concerns (Jung 1973), while the dowsing out to myself and others of highly relevant card images in Mungo
sessions could be construed as synchronistic (Von Franz 1980). In a
kind of reversal of this, once I had recruited my pilot participant in a
normal manner and we had experienced some coincidences (her word)
not only within sessions but also between them and our two lives, synchronicity also seemed to start flagging potential participants to me,
and the encounters proved wonderfully rich if I followed these flags.
Furthermore, as I struggled with the care of very ill loved ones in my
life, those flagged participants themselves or ideas from our encounters
turned out strangely often to be the very persons or notions that could
help me in caring, there at precisely the times I needed them.

All in all, it was difficult to avoid the impression that something beyond
myself and my participants was joining in with intelligence, helpfulness
and a tendency towards interconnection. This would be neither surprise
nor problem to many a believer; given that they were not troubled by the
forms of this seeming agency, of course. But for me with my steadiest foot
still in the agnostic-sceptic camp, it was, just as before the PhD research
but now writ larger, stunning: both wonderfully yet also ground-shakingly
so. These developments meant that I was no longer researching only
cooperation with a putative spirit guide. To now deny synchronicity a
large role or, for instance, not to consider what various belief systems have
to say on how 'it all' (however named) could act in mysterious ways for
care and love would be to ignore the elephants in the room.

Thus my quest to quality-check a seeming spirit guide through research
encounters has resulted not merely in the expected main bulk of findings, namely participants' experiences of and responses to their Mungo
sessions and my own reactions thereto, but also this second bulk of unexpected 'elephants' on my heuristic path. I have in fact met several more
'elephants' and exemplify just one more here as a token. Often I have
pondered something only to stumble immediately afterwards on a writer
echoing (or rather, pre-echoing) or answering me, and I heuristically note
myself to have felt 'in tune' and supported by this, irrespective of how
(ir)rational that may seem. For example, within this very chapter, having
written my *'if, if, then'* phrase, I found myself wanting reassurance that

it really was a recognized form. My very next reading, of a book chanced on in a charity shop, included comment on the *if... and if...; then...* syllogism in *The Limits of Science* (Medawar 1984).

Such assistance of study by synchronicity has been commented on by many (White 1998). My aim in exemplifying the post hoc confirmatory version that I often experience was to be able now to state, with clear examples to hand, a heuristic observation of myself: the coming of so many 'elephants' along with my spirit guide research has an impact on how I feel and think. I notice that I, a sample human being, feel a sort of conviction meter (for want of a better expression) nudging across from doubt to belief-till-shown-wrong within even my agnostic-sceptic breast in the face of this 'elephant herd', and furthermore, that since Mungo 'marches with this herd' I feel more won over towards credence in him (whatever 'he' might really be) and his power and inclination for good.

That credence could not stand, however, were the other research findings from participant sessions nondescript or, even worse, indicating harmfulness. In actuality my encounters with 36 research participants amazed me with the sheer range and diversity of both the events that occurred and the participants' attitudes to Mungo, me and the cards. There were no simple spectra, say from disbelief to convicted faith, but rather a vast terrain of complex, nuanced 'takes', ways of relating to it all, effects of so doing and indeed stories of their own prior encounters with spirits. In effect, this gave me an overarching lesson – which I realize I could see either as an amazing chance, or as 'designed' with impressive skill and breadth – to expect not merely differences in how people meet spirits but individualities that never cease to surprise, from the striking idiosyncrasy to the subtle twist which changes lots more.

I have as yet been unable to set my results against those of very similar research, having not yet found among writings on spirit guides any which work significantly through the use of tangible objects. Compare Mungo's and my use of picture cards, about which I as quasi-channel do *not* have 'just knowing' of what is meant, to (from Grof and Grof 1989) '[spirit guides'] messages are usually received in the form of direct thought transfer or through other extrasensory means'. Occasionally communication can take the form of verbal messages. Light has rather been shone onto the phenomenon from different angles by the frequent penetrating questions and observations of participants themselves, as in Chris's case and her comments on my not-knowing.

During our session Mungo sent a card to 'Chris' and me which neither of us could make sense of in our context. I asked for clarification, in answer to which the pendulum swung in a way that puzzled me. I then put questions to him *out loud* (rather than only in my head), so that his and my groping towards clear communication was above board, witnessed as well as possible by Chris. Her eventual feedback read:

> Your relationship with Mungo is inclusive, that is, I felt involved rather than shut out from something exclusive to you. Your communication with him was aloud and open. This was vital for me... I perceived him as having a broader perspective on things (especially when some of his answers had you stumped initially).

## Ethical considerations

Just as Chris implicitly raised issues of transparency and power, so did feedback from several participants illuminate other possible dangers. For instance, 'Anna' commented, 'sometimes I felt there was a bit of an imbalance between Christa and Mungo – that she deferred to him'. This led me to muse on how the health of the relationship between Mungo and me matters, since this work can affect people profoundly, not only through the content of sessions but also, and perhaps even more so, by the fact that it happens at all. A person's worldview may be shaken by experiences beyond their prior ken, as 'Susannah' pithily put it:

> you can't just walk away from this like you walk away from the dentist and say 'I believe in dentists'... if you [think] there really is a real spiritual voice there on the other side, can you just ignore this knowledge for the rest of your life, or do you have to start thinking about... your whole relationship to spirituality?

Pivotal change can happen for believers too. 'Shelagh' tells how after being diagnosed with multiple sclerosis (MS) years ago, she prayed but felt it was

> into the void... I turned away from spirituality thinking there was no solace or comfort in trying to reach 'spirit'... [But in our session] the first picture card... showed me my life as it is now. It was so true it hurt. The accuracy was overwhelming. It invoked a tearful emotional response from me and wonderment that it hit the nail on the head... The [session's] experience has left me feeling... my 'spiritual tap' turned on... this will help me to deal with family problems.

I do not wish to jeopardize or taint such work with 'muddiness' between Mungo and me.

Striving for cleaness and clearness is of the essence in counselling the very vulnerable. For instance, how to discern between offering benevolent spirit involvement and only encouraging detrimental or delusional ill-ness is a serious question, and yet risking such help may be the only thing that can work. My participant 'May' had suffered years of mental illness, triggered by her fear that her daughter's sudden death had been due to unhappiness. Our first Mungo session resulted in May deciding to do intensive further work with a hypnotherapist. Though gruel-ling, it brought her into contact with her daughter's spirit, and peace. Reflecting later on our session she said:

> That had a really big effect. I was suicidal. Nothing had worked. I was running out of friends I could talk about this with. It was a spiritual issue, and talking with you gave me a spiritual space. And it reminded me of the spiritual dimension, which I'd lost contact with. It put me back in touch with my own higher self and therefore that power and trust.

For my part I own that I dared to take that risk because an exceptionally striking synchronicity had flagged May to me followed by pendulum confirmation to 'go there' by Mungo, and I had by then experientially learned to trust this pair of 'referrals' (given my own mindfulness that was always still in play).

However, mindfulness notwithstanding, one is dealing with power, and the question I raise here is: If a counsellor comes to experience (seeming) spirit contact, might they be justified in turning away from that were it unsettling for themselves, and/or might they through blank-ing out the risk leave some of those they meet in the lurch? Counselling does value wholeness, from integration within the person to recogniz-ing their situatedness within their entire world. My participant 'Carol' had been frightened by a poltergeist-like spirit encounter and hurt by others' dismissiveness, and had grown wary:

> It's like coming out. I will only come out if I feel it's safe, that they won't just laugh at or diminish me. These experiences are incredibly powerful. Life-changing. I've looked at the universe in a different way ever since. I knew I could talk about it to you because of your Mungo-connection, and it has been a relief.

Similarly, *if* one has reason to believe one is being helped in counselling-type work by an intelligent spirit with a wider view and/or agency, *then* is it good to honour that intelligence by following (discerningly) outside-the-box suggestions from it, or should one stay within approved parameters? I offer a participant story as grist to the mill. I was due to drive over an hour to 'Sarah' when she phoned to cancel, being so depressed that she couldn't face anything so needful of thought. Mungo then told me privately to ask if I could visit her anyway, but simply in order to tell her the story of a recent sequence of Mungo events, and she agreed. If I expected anything, it was that maybe the story would hold some meaning helpful to her. It turned out, though, that she simply found the story undemanding yet interesting and calming, such that after it she volunteered that she would like a session after all. She later reported that the whole meeting had shifted her 'mental wellness from about 20% to about 70%, a real noticeable lift', to a state where she herself could push herself on. (In the interests of heuristic transparency, I must own that afterwards I delighted in the cunning ploy which enabled it all to happen.)

Of course, key or deep changes happen in other counselling too. What is special here is that a new or fresh connection to an entire 'quarter' of a person's self may be involved (spirit alongside body, heart and mind; witness May above); and that the cards etc. 'sent' by Mungo often steer the other person and me to the crux more quickly; witness Shelagh. Such power could easily be too much or too soon, but in practice Mungo has matched his interventions well to a diversity of people. Nowadays I look for good pitching as one 'litmus test' for quality, and indeed congruently report that I savour it after the event.

There are many other ethical concerns around this 'edgy' research and unusual form of encounter, but I leave it at that, hoping that the above has sufficed as a token not only of the issues but also of how the actual research itself is helping their disclosure and airing.

## Supervision

Others have written of the counsellor's need to find a supervisor willing to work with their spiritual aspects lest, otherwise, parts of the counsellor's work remain unethically concealed (West 2000a). Work with a spirit guide (or perhaps other spiritual source) brings a further supervision opportunity, in that besides talking *about* one's teamwork one can *show* oneself in dialogue with one's guide (or relating to one's source). This I have done with both my counselling and academic supervisors (though it took some nerve), and it has brought the benefits of greater scrutiny, exploration and indeed plain understanding from them all.

Logic and care indicate that *if* I may be cooperating with an entity and/or energies from some further spiritual domain, *then* it behoves me to consider that contact therewith might present dangers unknown to me, and conversely that the domain might offer some protection and/or 'supervision'. Both 'Benedict' and 'Carol' quoted to me from *Hamlet* the line 'There are more things in heaven and earth, Horatio, than are dreamt of in your philosophy'. Quite! Hearing prior spirit encounter stories from participants has been an education for me – again, whose breadth and seeming skill impress me – about what a diverse and sometimes nasty spirit dimension there is, or at least might be. How do I (or any counsellor) opening work with Mungo (or any spiritual source) know whether this time it really is him or at least a force for good? My considered ethical strategy is to start any dowsing by saying loudly, clearly and mindfully *Love and Truth*, and then absolutely to insist on the pendulum swinging a certain way before I go on. I cannot know if that shuts the door to harmful energies, but I am doing my best to invite good 'supervision' while also 'cleaning' my intentions and allowing the other person to hear my values in simple terms.

The popularity of spiritual internet sites bespeaks how much desire for spirit connection is out there, only too able to feed gullibility, subservience or corruption. Such power and lure heighten the need for supervision of counselling or research which could be seen as in that arena, and not only for clients' or participants' sakes. There are also the safety needs of the practitioner who dares to operate this way, open to harsh transferences or being pigeonholed with charlatans. My own experience is that the more I have invited criticisms from participants – especially counsellors who could have blown ethical whistles – the less disempowered by fear of what 'they' might say I have become.

## Matters arising

Given the popularity of predictions and mediums, whether New Age, spiritualist or 'tabloid', it bears emphasizing that I experience neither Mungo nor synchronicities to work with me and participants thus, but rather through resonance and pertinence to our selves and situations of the events and/or symbolic images that come. I value the warning shots across my bows of a couple of my participants sliding towards wanting medium-style answers on a plate. By contrast, meeting 'Hilda' (and others) assured me that my participant sample included bracing sceptics. She felt disappointed, saying:

> It just seems to me to be a funny way to have a conversation [using cards etc.]... he hasn't made his presence felt... [nor can I see] some

kind of evidence... to make me think that it [this alleged entity] is there, and I don't have this, not at all.

Clearly, Mungo-style interventions are not for all at all times, although a logical consideration is that *if* one is open to an intelligent spirit source, *then* decisions by that intelligence about when to 'be hot or cold' could influence this alongside the person's own predelictions.

Running for now with the *intelligent spirit* notion, it seemingly chose to 'be hot' to Julian when his relationship with Mungo and me involved my telling him a synchronistic dog story by letter. He replied:

> I am in some state of altered consciousness as I finish reading your account. There is a sense of astonishing integration, of inner and outer, of human, canine and created order, of this world and the other, of the mundane and the ethereal, of light and dark, of wholeness and apparent impairment, of eros and agape, of saints and sinners, of pain and bliss, of eternal flow and precise moment in time... [Mungo] opens up the blessed communion of All Saints, All Souls and All Sorts.

Using myself as a sample human once again, I note that I was excited to hear this, not only for the quality of the state Julian claimed, but also because his altered state of consciousness added to enough experiences by others in connection with Mungo to firm up another 'elephant'.

Although this whole area of contact with spirits (or God) is controversial, it does have a long history as part of mainstream religious tradition, and within folk religion and many ordinary people's lives it remains significant (Hay 1982). Any open consideration of spirituality and its part in therapy needs to be cognizant of these phenomena, as indeed some writers have discussed (Thorne 2002; Jenkins 2006).

I have found the above to be true in my practice (*without* Mungo's explicit presence) among spiritually 'ordinary people' in a prison, but intriguingly, prisoner-clients have mentioned the supernatural and/or the religious more to me since I came to have more credence and ease in such matters myself through my Mungo relationship and study. Sometimes they have related to me their initial hesitation to tell me about, say, visionary experiences or ghostly events that either had an impact on their lives at some other time or even as they were happening to them at that very moment. They have wondered things like 'Will she think I'm off my trolley?' or 'Will she trample this special thing?'. But then, they report, they sensed it was OK, one even saying, 'A voice told me you can tell her.'

I value this improved, therapeutically helpful 'airability' of such things for those clients with me, and at this point I also own that I would be well pleased if, by being clear, transparent and concrete enough in this chapter, I were to have increased such 'airability' elsewhere too. If we have readier words and notions to aid our conversations, together with steadier personal feelings born of more familiarity with the arena, then we can better meet those of our clients who do – and sometimes most tentatively or timidly – bring issues about spirit encounters and related phenomena to counselling.

## Conclusion

I am myself indebted to the transparency of Rennie (1994b), who wrote:

> I found that dealing with both [aspects of a certain research project] was overwhelming... yet also in the same article... human scientists address phenomena in their full complexity instead of reducing the complexity through fragmentation...

My study suggests Mungo to be allied to a 'herd of elephants', each 'elephant' increasing the remarkability of the 'herd' for me. Avoiding both herd fragmentation and being personally overwhelmed realistically means that I must situate my research against others' work, with much of the detail sacrificed to breadth. So be it – for now.

This does touch on a question which several people have posed: *If* Mungo and/or 'all this' partakes of spiritual intelligence, *then* why has it chosen me? Why not choose someone with a bigger mind or an easier life situation, then there could be both detail and breadth? Turning that around, I note (most conjecturally) that maybe what I do bring includes:

- A situation so tight, especially with caring duties, as to have needed and thus highlighted the seemingly synchronistic help.
- Starting unforeseeably *after* my PhD by a mere few days, that tight situation blocked my 'adequate' early reading-round-the-field, perforce turning my research into a qualitatively very different tale of meeting such events with significant naïveté.
- Similarly, I am by nature and nurture in the very 'bandwidth' of the sceptical–persuadable spectrum as to have instructively *felt* (as well as thought) this heuristic journey, not only sitting on the fence but also often wobbling (which is another story).

- With a yen for logic and a first degree in physics and maths, I probably explore how an unknown acts (call it 'black box' or 'x' or 'Mungo') differently to a purer humanities researcher.

Whether or not I was chosen, the above reflexive points do bear on how the reader may assess my research (Etherington 2004). As to my own assessment of the quality of Mungo work, I find myself currently persuaded in favour of 'him' due to such hallmarks as the following (which might serve as yardsticks for other spiritual helpers or sources):

- The phenomenon acted with respectful, skilled pitching.
- It helped a significant proportion of participants, and was reported to harm none, even when I double-checked by asking them to *please, please tell me any misgivings, that I may avoid harm to others in the future.*
- It was growthful, bringing seemingly intelligent surprises and outside-the-box ways forward.
- It promoted interconnectedness, between me and my participants' lives and research, and with its own 'herd of elephants'.
- It acted so as to promote scrutiny of itself.

Now I can put forward my tentatively general suggestion as promised, and I feel that the vernacular will express this best. Basically, if one seems to have come into collaboration with an intelligent spiritual source, and if one remains adequately supervised and vigilantly willing to close the proceedings if harmfulness ensues, then give it enough research rope to hang itself. Only thus can one ever know if it would have hanged itself, or fallen flat or tied itself up in knots – or, say, roped in a variety of helping modes and/or lessons and/or 'elephants' worth the having and the sharing.

## Discussion points

1. How do you think the world of therapy should engage with such spiritual gifts?
2. How can we face the overlaps between delusion or mental illness and spiritual gifts?
3. Where do we draw the line with innovative therapeutic practice such as that described in this chapter?

# 11
## Psychic Energy in Counselling

*Marie Wardle*

## Introduction

In this chapter I consider the spiritual and healing experiences that can occur within counselling using the framework of psychic energy. I explore what is meant by psychic energy and draw on my research findings into psychic experiences in counselling practice. Such work raises a number of key issues that are addressed, including those related to ethics and supervision. The implications for practitioners are explored and some tentative guidelines for practice offered.

## Psychic experiences

One way of understanding the extraordinary work of a spiritual and healing nature that can occur in counselling is to frame it in terms of psychic energy. It is not uncommon for clients to present their counsellors with issues that they categorize as specifically of a spiritual nature. The therapist might prepare themselves for working with their clients' spiritual issues by having an understanding of what falls under the umbrella of spirituality in counselling. These might include communication with spirit guides, channelling, clairvoyance, pre-cognition, telepathy, out-of-body experiences, spiritual awakening and spiritual crises, to name just a few. I offer an opening vignette:

A new client arrives for a counselling appointment. The counsellor knows nothing about this client's past or reason for wanting to see her. Following the client through the door, the counsellor can see the presence of a boy, quite tall with blond streaky hair. He is wearing blue shorts and t-shirt and looks to be in his mid-teens. He stands very close to this woman and the room feels profoundly full of love. The counsellor begins to feel emotional and speaks to the boy tele-pathically as the client sits in silence trying to compose herself. She too is overcome with emotion. The boy tells the counsellor that he is here to help his mother come to terms with his sudden death. This was the beginning of a profoundly moving encounter. The counsel-lor became a channel between a mother and son, who had so much left unsaid and was touched by the power of love that physical death does not sever. Both were transformed by this experience.

This vignette may seem strange and not mainstream to counselling, but there is a growing literature and debate around such experiences in counselling (Criswell and Herzog 1977; Hastings 1983; Carpenter 1988; West 1997, 2004a). McLeod (1997) suggests that either modern counselling is seen as a new set of techniques from the time of Freud or it is a continuation of forms of helping that date back some time. West (2004a) would argue that this also includes shamans, witches, priests, healers and psychics. Strupp (1972) adds that the modern psychothera-pist relies to a large extent on the same psychological mechanisms.

Often people disregard terms with which they are unfamiliar, just because they do not understand them. I believe that our clients deserve us to be as truly present as we can using all of our abilities, but that this may need careful contracting and clear ethical guidelines. Counselling is a relatively young profession. Shamans and psychics have worked for thousands of years without organizations, through word-of-mouth referral. In another 40 years' time we may have other labels.

Schiller (1967) points out that many people insist on explaining, understanding and taking a yardstick to everything and will tolerate nothing vague, obscure or inaccessible. However, the need for more definite knowledge of our place in nature is no mere academic one. My work is then a step, a modest advance in the exploration of the unrecog-nized boundaries of counselling that are being creatively and ethically tested in my research.

Psychic experiences certainly seem mysterious (Carpenter 1988), but do we really understand how counselling works? Both therapist and client discover many things that have previously remained hidden and this may come about by strange images, feelings and thoughts that  appear to come from nowhere. By the process of both therapist and client coming together, something mysterious and yet often not really understood occurs in the counselling room. At such times, one cannot say where or how this occurs, or give adequate explanations.

## Background

As long as people have reported psychic experiences, there must have been many more who have suffered from these experiences (Kramer 1993). Kramer says that parapsychology and paranormal phenomena have been neglected by the established sciences and by medicine. He further states that the emotional problems related to such experiences were not recognized and were often classified either as exaggerated behaviour or as part of traditional psychiatric patterns and hence treated accordingly. In testing psychics, the emotional feelings and needs of the person are often neglected by the parapsychologists. Hastings (1983) and Kramer (1993) describe how counsellors, psychologists and other professionals may encounter such people who have had apparent psychic experiences and wish to explore the emotional and psychological aspects of such occurrences.

This area of research is very much about exploring new developments in practice. I have been interviewing a group of people who have not been explored much and I am aware that for many this is very much about breaking a taboo (West 1995). While the topic up for discussion is problematic traditionally, I am not the first researcher to acknowledge this fact. In Chapter 9 Roy Moodley and Olga Oulanova term such practice traditional healing working alongside western therapy.

I am nevertheless challenging some outdated views and treading the line between mainstream psychology and unorthodox psychology. My research over many years has allowed me to collect some highly controversial and revealing data, which challenge our established ways of understanding counselling. My research seeks to encourage voices that have previously been marginalized and oppressed to come forward. Research that I carried out (Wardle 2004a, 2006, 2008) revealed that the psychic phenomenon is very much present in some counsellors' working practice. This fact has important implications for counselling research. Wilber (2000: 85) states that 'each new generation of counsellors has a chance to move the integral vision forward in some way simply because new information, data and discoveries are constantly being made'. This research is concerned with what actually occurs between the therapist and the client.

This chapter will offer some guidelines for practitioners and focus on five discussion points:

- What is meant by the term 'psychic energy'?
- What experiences are occurring in counselling sessions with clients?
- How is psychic energy viewed in supervision?
- What are the implications for the counsellor, client and the counselling profession?
- What are the ethical issues?

## What is psychic energy?

The term psychic energy has long been in use. We find it as early as Lipps (1897), Freud (1905) and Jung (1916). We have Lipps to thank for the distinction between psychic energy and psychic force, when he said that psychic force is the possibility of processes arising in the psyche. He defines psychic energy, on the other hand, as the inherent capacity of these processes to actualize this force in themselves. Jung (1917, 1948) wrote extensively on psychic energy and tells us that we must expect to find it in the unconscious. For the purpose of this study, I suggest that psychic energy is the counsellor's undervalued resource.

Jung (1948), Ruskan (1993) and Hunt (1996) all make reference to psychic energy as repressed information, surfacing and sometimes manifesting in non-verbal forms of psychic communication, which does not come through the normal five senses (Rhine 1937). A psychic atmosphere develops as a result of, and compensation for, loss of contact and unexpressed experiences. Although both verbal and non-verbal channels provide useful information, they offer only partial components of communication (Pulvino 1975). The inconclusiveness of our present understanding of communication indicates that a substantial portion of communication occurs at a different level, more than can be measured through verbal interchange.

## Experiences in practice

Many counsellors tell me they believe that the essence of communication is more than just words and that when they work with psychic energy, they are moving beyond words. Ruskan (1993) explains that the level where suppressed energy is stored can be quite tangible on the psychic level and may be felt and seen by a psychic. Such a place or level may be what Harding (1963) refers to as the threshold, which between the conscious and unconscious part of the psyche. ~~...~~llors that took part in my research (Wardle 2008) tell me that ~~...~~nergy is not tangible; it goes above and beyond the five senses a~~...~~ ~~...~~urs outside the sensory mode.

Mastering the native language of energy is not easy, but, as pointed out by Eden (1998), for a psychic who is working outside the five senses it is possible to be able to read it, see it, hear it and converse with it. Her view is that you cannot know in advance how you will register subtle energies; it may be through seeing, hearing, smelling and even tasting the energy. Ruskan (1993) suggests that a person with ordinary though sensitive perceptions can sometimes sense that something is being repressed or blocked, but that a psychic has more defined and detailed information about the content that is unexpressed. He believes that where the energy of a feeling is not released, it does not go away, but stays with us, in latent form, attached to the psychic energy body. A psychic is described as someone who is able to decode communication that has been passed to them so that they can pass it on to someone else, as discussed in Eisenbud (1970) and Mintz (1983). If we now look at the term 'psychic counsellor', Heron (2003) describes such a person as someone who has causal vision and is able to see outside the usual visionary parameters.

The practitioners who took part in my research tell me that somebody who is psychic can pick up things or give things out about another person, but that psychic energy is something that is exchanged. A transaction takes place and energy is exchanged from one level to another, from dark to light, and the two levels have to operate synchronistically and be tuned in. We saw in Chapter 8 a discussion of energy exchange that occurs in the process of healing. I interviewed 30 therapists as part of my doctoral studies (Wardle 2008) and found that not only is there an exchange of energy, but that both the therapist and the client are affected when this occurs. Oschman (2000) describes this process as coupling, when the combining of two people's energies changes the frequency. It is in the changing of the frequency of the energy pattern which determines the success or failure. The counsellors tell me that they are able to engage with their client at a different level. The psychic bit is about being able to be in tune with this other level. Within clinical practice, the practitioners tell me that the following themes are present with their clients:

- Working on a different level/frequency
- Different time and space
- Working at the threshold/crossing a line
- Beyond words, pre-language, language barrier

- Metaphors, symbols
- Transforming something where energy is exchanged/retrieved
- Soul-to-soul connection
- Signals: bodily and visual
- Working with ancestor or spirit guides

I will now summarize the above themes. Sometimes it is possible for counsellors to engage in an energy or level of existence other than the one you can see right now within clinical practice. When both therapist and client meet in a psychic space, both may occupy the same space at the same time. This now becomes a two-way communication link. Extra-sensory perception (ESP) is present and this can be experienced in different ways, namely clairvoyance, clairaudience, clairsentience, telepathy, pre-cognition.

When the counsellor makes a connection with their client on this 'other' level, something is synchronized and time and space appear to be significantly different. They tell me that energy is exchanged and energy is retrieved and brought back over a threshold. Some clients describe a transaction taking place and sometimes a reconciling symbol is seen at the time of the transference. The language changes and barriers dissolve. Occasionally the counsellor has an awareness of either a spirit guide or a deceased ancestor present in the counselling room. Sometimes the work feels too risky or there is an awareness that it is not the right time to work at this 'other' level. The thought processes are different, the process appears to change the energetic frequency and the room feels different. Clients have described being in an altered state of consciousness on these occasions and can feel a little disoriented until they adjust back to the normal level.

A choice has to be made by the counsellor about whether they are going to work with this energy. I suggest that to some degree the client is also making an informed choice about whether to work at this level. I would say that this 'other' level is where the soul of the counsellor meets the soul of the client and I have called this the soul-to-soul connection.

Scientific evidence suggests that when we die we cease to exist in the space–time continuum – that is, the dimension that composes the material world – and are therefore no longer able to communicate within the parameters of the five senses. Based on my findings, what is repressed and lost from consciousness also falls outside the space–time continuum. Consequently, physical death and loss of experiences and memories (loss of energy) are both subject to a psychic atmosphere. Psychic energy is energy lost from consciousness or lack of quality of consciousness (Jung 1948) and this energy needs to be transferred back into consciousness, but may need some extra help in bringing it back; this is where the counsellor steps in.

Having discussed some aspects of working with psychic energy, this leads me to discuss some of the key issues that arise around supervision.

## Supervision issues

My research suggests that there is very little literature available relating to psychic energy in counselling supervision. This is not surprising when we consider that many of the counsellors who took part in my study were reluctant to disclose their psychic work to their supervisors. Those who do disclose prefer to leave the word 'psychic' out of it and talk about such occurrences in terms of energy, as this feels less risky.

Those who do speak to their supervisors about their experiences are reluctant to change their supervisors and may be staying with them for too long and for the wrong reasons. The reason for this is that they feel that it has taken them many years to build the trust and it feels too daunting to try to find someone else.

West (1995) also found that therapists were reluctant to talk about such experiences with their supervisors. One of the difficulties he found was that the difference in the language and articulation of what actually occurred in the session made it more difficult. Finding a supervisor who speaks the same language is essential. My findings indicate that when two people communicate psychic energy, the language barrier disappears and the language is no longer clumsy. When this does not occur the counsellors report that they end up losing the experience and it then gets changed into something different. Tudor and Worrall (2004) say that a supervisor may become remote or disempowered if they have fears of their own about certain matters that their supervisee is bringing to the relationship. Some counsellors report that some supervisors have either refused to work with the counsellor or admitted that the matter is outside their expertise and suggested finding a different supervisor.

Research by West (2000b) found that those counsellors who are working with spiritual interventions (of which he includes clairvoyance, channelling and spirit guides) require high-quality supervision from a supervisor who is familiar with such experiences. Rowan (2002a) sees it also as absolutely crucial that the counsellor who is psychospiritually aware can find a supervisor who is connecting in this level. Some counsellors tell me that they are receiving supervision from another dimension. This appears to be happening particularly with those who are not able to talk to their supervisors about their experiences or to find a suitably qualified supervisor to help them with their clinical work. At first glance, this might seem extraordinary and pushing the boundaries too far in contemplating that some counsellors do get supervision from their spirit guides.

Klimo (1987), Rowan (2002b) and Fontana (2005) refer to channelling and the arrival of spirit guides to help a distressed person. Information is passed through to the therapist and it is then at the discretion of the therapist how they make use of this information, which determines the success or failure of such guidance. Fontana (2005) describes a spirit guide as a particular spiritual entity that takes an interest in an individual and offers them useful information. Shine (1998) also refers to a spirit guide as a doorkeeper, which leads me to consider that supervision in counselling is also a form of doorkeeping. In psychic and spiritual circles it is not unusual that the term doorkeeper is used to describe someone who helps the psychic or medium to filter the communication that comes through them. In exploring this unrecognized boundary, the participants of my study were quick to remind me:

- If one is going to work on another level this requires supervision on two levels.
- Spiritual supervisors act as a doorkeeper if the counsellor oversteps a boundary; supervision is supposed to stop you leaking. Leakage can occur while switching from different levels.
- It would be unethical not to have a spiritual supervisor/doorkeeper.
- The counsellors say that they are only aware of their spiritual guides or helpers coming in when they are stuck or require additional energy.

Let us now look at the implications of the above information.

## Implications for practice

My findings bring the counselling profession into ethically muddy waters and produce questions around whether there is a power imbalance. Working in a different space requires a different approach and different training, and raises the question of whether sufficient training, professional and personal development allows counsellors to work ethically. The research described in this chapter is intended to:

- Increase awareness of the difficulties of integrating paranormal occurrences and monitoring the appropriateness of such an intervention while checking for inappropriate use.

- Inform through professional research undertaken in higher education and by researching professionals in their own settings.
- Strive to reduce barriers to participation and learning for marginalized groups of people.
- Provide other leaders in this field with knowledge that will underpin their work. This will increase ethical practice and reduce unethical practice.

Some counsellors who are working with psychic energy do not really understand the implications and the risks involved. Little (1986) refers to the psychoanalyst, who has undergone quite substantial training and is at a far advanced level of insight into psychological states. She says that they can still be naïve about what actually occurs and takes risks, because they have no understanding of the consequences of merging their energy with a client:

> Not all analysts have to be willing to make adaptations, but an analyst who is not willing to do so may have to limit either his choice of patients or the expectations of his results; it is a matter of investment. (Little 1986: 151)

There are other factors in relation to fears and risks that have emerged in this research, namely:

- Being pathologized, as discussed in Russell et al. (1987).
- Being misunderstood, as discussed in Irwin (1994) and Tart (2000).
- Fear of the level of intimacy with their client, as discussed in Thorne (2006).
- Risk of disclosure and ownership of working psychically to their professional status, as discussed in Wardle (2004a, 2004b, 2006). The fears are directed at other peers, supervisors and the professional governing body of which they are members finding out about what they do.

Thorne (2006) talks about the difficulties in presenting controversial material and the apparent unwillingness of professional psychology and psychotherapy to engage with what Rogers (1980: 134) referred to as 'the cutting edge of our ability to transcend ourselves', both proclaiming that this comes at a heavy price for the therapist.

Ankrah (2002) discovered that when she wanted to speak about unusual experiences related to spiritual emergency, she learned very quickly

that people were afraid of what she was saying and her experiences a.
consequently became afraid of her. She learned that it was not OK to
talk about this kind of phenomenon because she soon realized that she
had a fear of being pathologized. Eventually, she learned to keep quiet.
As Tart (2000: 21) comments, 'Disclosure of working from a paranormal
perspective has brought criticism and this has brought about a defensive stance from such disclosure.'

Like Ankrah (2002), many of the counsellors I interviewed worry
about whether they should disclose or not disclose to their client that
they are psychic. One participant in my study said that she gets around
this by telling her clients that she is very perceptive and will often pick
up things that may be helpful in their work. She feels that this is less
threatening to the client and there is absolutely no need to mention the
word psychic; the decision about whether to disclose, or how much to
disclose, to the client is always going to be a tricky one. West (2000a)
believes that it is the therapist's attitude to such experiences that can
have a crucial bearing on how easily the client can integrate those
experiences. It is important that the client does not come to see the
counsellor as having all the power (Wardle 2004a), because the essence
of counselling is about empowering the client.

Thorne (2006) has an ongoing interest in the cutting-edge work
that arises when spirituality and healing can take their rightful place
within the therapeutic encounter. He says that to work in this way
can be very challenging to the therapist. Indeed, in some of his work,
Thorne believes that the boundaries of counselling are being creatively
and ethically tested to benefit the client, but does not say anything
here about the safety, or should I say lack of safety, and regard for the
counsellor.

Some of the participants in my study fear the loss of boundaries
in work with their clients. Wilber (1979) infers that a dissolving of
boundaries will occur as we move through different levels of development. Cameron (2004) reminds us that as practitioners we all need to
be acutely aware of our own energetic boundaries. It is really important to keep the layers/levels separate until the time is right, which
leads me to consider that it is at the point of merging/crossing over
the threshold where leakage can occur. It is crucial that the counsellor
knows how to keep good boundaries, on this other level, and knows
how and when to break off this connection with their client. This
leads me to think about that crucial ingredient required at the point
of merging and crossing over, integrity or the lack of it, and this will
now be discussed.

## Ethical issues

Jung (1960: 152) explains:

> the energy charge of the repressed contents adds itself, in some measure to that of the repressing factor, whose effectiveness is increased accordingly. The higher its charge, the nearer it comes to conversion into its opposite and the more the ego forfeits its practical importance. The ego keeps its integrity only if it does not identify with one of its opposites, and if it understands how to hold the balance between them.

In other words, if the counsellor has unresolved suppressed psychic energy of their own, they will not be able to achieve this integrity with their client. At the point of crossing over, at the threshold, here is where we see whether the counsellor has the integrity and intentions that are honourable and trustworthiness to be at this privileged place with their client.

Some counsellors feel that when working on different levels, ethics are still there though in a different way; that one tries to make them the same, but they are not. Jung's (1916) theory on the adaptation of releasing energy back into consciousness tells us that this will have an impact on the ethical standpoint. Based on both viewpoints, I suggest that as an individual moves towards greater individualization, they reduce the tendency to conform to mass ethical guidelines and it is then that one's ethical and moral position has to be one's own. It is at this stage that some counsellors are arguing something really profound: that it is their own morals that they are questioning and that this is a big place to be because no other body has decided on all this.

A few counsellors felt that it was perfectly ethical to make use of any psychic communication as long as it does not disrupt the client's own process. Making an informed choice and backing it up ethically is a sort of art, not a science, of counselling and we make that informed choice at a gut level. Working as a humanistic counsellor, rather than, say, a cognitive behavioural therapist or psychodynamic counsellor, there is greater flexibility in the way we work, but it is always going to be costly and risky to that counsellor; perhaps that is another ethical consideration. Making an informed choice about whether we work with a psychic link or not is no different to any other counselling intervention we use; what matters is how we use it and whether we are being responsible. When I asked some counsellors whether they thought that it was ethical to work with their psychic side, they responded similarly and said that you cannot not do this, and that it is unethical to deny who you are. As Bell (2002) said, when one is living an ethical life it will inevitably also be a courageous one as one has to challenge the status quo.

It is necessary to mention that there are people who are irresponsible and uneducated in the nature and process of psychic work (Benor and Mohr 1986; Wardle 2004b). Their motives may be anything from greed to ego needs. Benor and Mohr infer that most serious, balanced psychic counsellors conduct their practice with dignity and professional attitudes. They take their work seriously, because they see it as counselling and not merely as sensational exploitation of psychic abilities. This research is only concerned with professionally qualified counsellors who have undertaken rigorous training and have a solid psychological base with which to underpin their work. Having said that, a counsellor who is working with psychic energy will need to have reached a certain level of development.

West (2000a) explores ethical issues related to both spiritual and cultural differences. He discusses whether the therapist is competent to work with their client around spirituality and whether they have had sufficient training and personal development to hold the space needed to work on such a level. The BACP Ethical Framework (2002) stipulates that practitioners should give careful consideration to the limitations of their training and experience and work within these limits.

Research cannot move forward unless people come forward. People will not come forward unless they feel safe to do so. Innovative research cannot be done unless people are prepared to go against the majority and doing so can still be an indicator of ethical practice. Bond (2004) says that some of the major challenges come from inequality, difference, risk and uncertainty.

Rapp (2001) looks at working with difference and diversity. She says that to offer effective and ethical counselling, it is important to be able to distinguish between differences that are cultural, biological and sociopolitical and differences due to inequality. Both kinds of difference can result in psychological distress and damage to all parties concerned, by which I mean supervisor, supervisee and client. Rapp says that despite the complexities of working with people who have experiences and beliefs that are totally different to our own, we must have a map, a matrix by which we can still work ethically and safely. This matrix may come down to each individual 'work[ing] out for themselves how they interpret the spirit of the law both in light of the specific ethical codes of their own professional body, and their own ethical values and moral precepts' (Rapp 2001: 137).

## Guidelines for practitioners

Successful integration of counselling and para-psychological interventions raises questions about whether counselling professionals have the expertise and training to integrate these in an ethical way. Counsellors who are working with psychic energy, channelling and using psychic interventions must have a supervisor who has the expertise and training to help the counsellor work safely, ethically and appropriately with their clients. This is discussed extensively in Chapter 8.

It is important for counsellors to learn to distinguish among three categories of client with regard to their claims of psychic experiences or abilities. There are people who are having genuine psychic experiences free of pathology, and then there are some who are mentally ill and who may have unasked-for psychic experiences. Lastly, there are those who are delusional and believe they are having genuine psychic experiences but are not.

## Conclusions

Rhine (1937, 1962, 1972), a well-known scholar in the field of parapsychology, said that the psychic phenomenon is likely to become more comprehensible and successfully understood through studies in psychology. It is through the porthole of counselling that I believe there is greater promise of the experiences of our clients and counsellors becoming more demonstrable, which can shed more light on this issue. Counsellors, as opposed to psychologists, rely more on the therapeutic use of self and that is why the counselling profession is more likely to experience psychic abilities than are traditional psychologists. I believe that the real threat of the psychic phenomenon in the counselling and psychology professions is predominantly confined to the West, because it constitutes a threat to their frames of reference. In the East it is not so, although the East–West divide is changing rapidly. Slowly and with care more acceptance may be obtained; integration of new ideas takes time.

I suggest that it is not psychics who are confused but psychologists, because the parapsychologist recognizes distinctiveness in their field. Parapsychology has a more clearly definable boundary line than many of the more established sciences, because it deals only with psychic phenomena and these are neatly identifiable as extrasensory motor exchanges between persons and environment. Many recognize this as ESP (Rhine 1962, 1972). Because of the non-physical nature of these extrasensory and extra-motor interactions, they afford what is at present one of the most definite natural lines of division in the known natural order. This difference has been so impressive that it has led people to categorize such occurrences as 'miraculous', 'extraordinary' and 'supernatural', although not of course in parapsychology. Psychoanalysts and transpersonal psychologists have found a way of making it safe to talk about this kind of phenomenon without scaring people, because the language they use tames the fear around psychic occurrences and breaks down some of the tension.

I think that paranormal occurrences within counselling and psychotherapy are underestimated and underdeveloped, but may well hold the key that unlocks some psychological and psychiatric states. If we can let go of our fears as practitioners, we hold such a key which would allow us to reduce the gap and the tension between the two modalities.

## Discussion points

1. What does the term 'psychic energy' mean to you?
2. What psychic experiences are you aware of occurring in counselling sessions with clients?
3. What are the implications for the therapist, the client and the therapy profession?
4. What are the ethical and supervisory issues?

# Part Three
# Research and Practice

# 12
# Research in Spirituality and Healing

*William West*

## Introduction

In this chapter I explore some of the challenges we face in researching therapy, spirituality and healing. Some of these issues are common to any research involving people. Some have a specific relevance when spirituality and healing are considered. I will look at what factors contribute to successful therapeutic outcomes, before discussing some exemplars of spirituality research and practice. Reference to some key research texts should prevent us from reinventing the wheel or feeling that only we think, feel or experience spirituality and healing in the way we do. I then briefly address the question of research methodology: research into spirituality and healing could be regarded as constituting a problem area, but it also invites the use of innovative methodologies. Finally, I will put forward some guidelines for researching counselling, spirituality and healing.

## Background

It is important that we think carefully about the ethics involved in researching our fellow human beings. 'Above all do no harm' is a good starting point. The BACP and other professional bodies provide some very useful ethical guidelines for research (Bond 2004). Because of the taboo around disclosing human spiritual and healing experiences and because of the importance of spirituality and religion to many people, anyone researching in any depth in this area needs to approach research with great sensitivity and care. Issues like confidentiality, care of research participants and self, data protection and informed consent all need appropriate consideration (West 2002b; West and Burne 2009).

189

Approaching the broader issue of researching therapy, it needs to be acknowledged that it is a challenging process in itself. Researching therapy, spirituality and healing is even more challenging. We can now be fairly confident in claiming that therapy does help people: the widespread use of therapeutic services bears this out. However, more detailed research questions such as 'Which therapy helps best with which client problem and why?' remain frustratingly difficult to answer. Indeed, there seems to be more variation between individual practitioners from the same school than between the different schools of therapy. So it is apparent that the question we need to ask is not *What works for whom?* but rather *Who works with what?*

## Successful outcomes

Research has consistently shown over more than 60 years that a good therapeutic alliance – that is, the relationship established between therapist and client – is a key factor in a successful outcome. It has also become clear that there was little difference in outcomes when varying therapeutic approaches with clients with the same problems were compared, for example Wampold (2001: 77), 'Meta-analytic evidence throughout the 1980s and 1990s supported the contention that all psychotherapies intended to be therapeutic produce equivalent outcomes'.

Terry Hanley's rigorous literature review into the therapeutic alliance (2008) offers the following figures as factors that affect therapeutic progress (drawn from Asay and Lambert 2000; Lambert and Barley 2002):

* 40% extra-therapeutic, specific client characteristics, outside events etc.
* 30% relationship, variables found across therapies
* 15% placebo, belief in treatment etc.
* 15% techniques, specific characteristics of the model of therapy

From these figures, it is apparent that the biggest factor (40 per cent) in a good outcome for a client is what actually happens in their life outside of therapy. Perhaps this is where innovative research and practice should actually focus? Can we discover what these extra-therapeutic factors are and encourage clients to make best use of them? In terms of the contribution of therapy itself to client change, the biggest factor is clearly the therapeutic alliance (30 per cent) and in an ideal world this is where most of the research money and interest should and would reside.

It is noticeable that placebo and client belief in the treatment are of equal importance to techniques, yet there is so little research into the creative use of placebos and beliefs. Most of the research is devoted to specific techniques which, as already stated, when therapeutic approaches are compared show little variation.

When we add the question of researching the effectiveness of spiritual or healing interventions into this situation, some interesting if difficult issues arise:

- We are dealing with only a small part (15 per cent) of the factors that contribute to client change. However, since this part attracts most of the current research funding and accompanying research interest, it is appropriate to research it.
- Even where spiritual and healing interventions have been, or could be proven to be, helpful, they are unlikely to improve significantly the outcomes for mainstream therapists working with mainstream clients, given that such research would be aiming to improve on only 15 per cent of what contributes to client change, as mentioned above.
- There could be scope to exploring the impact of the spiritually informed therapist on the therapeutic alliance. It is possible that spiritually informed therapists have better alliances with spiritually minded clients. For example, a spiritually minded therapist who used therapeutic *presence*, as described by Rogers (1980), would be likely have a qualitatively different therapeutic alliance with the clients involved.
- The whole question of client adherence to therapy is a key one that is often ignored. When we are presented with research findings, our attention is rarely drawn to the number of clients who drop out. It is possible that the lack of a spiritual approach on the part of the therapist might be a key factor in unsuccessful outcomes for religiously minded clients.
- Where research into spiritual and healing interventions would prove useful is if it focused on the moment-by-moment encounter in the therapy session. Such an encounter, captured on video, could then be played back for client and therapist comment. I have explored such research in relation to helpful events in therapy supervision (West and Clark 2004). However, such research work is very labour intensive.
- There is also some important survey research to be done around therapists working with spirituality and healing in therapy, including

which interventions are used and with which clients. Further research would also be useful to discover therapists' own relationship with spirituality, their attitude to mystical and spiritual experiences and their use of spiritual assessments.

## What has already been done?

There is a view put forward by Glaser and Strauss (1967) – who invented grounded theory, which is a qualitative research methodology that has been especially used in therapy research thanks to the pioneering work of David Rennie (1994a, b) – that researchers should not read too much literature before approaching data gathering so that they are not biased in their understandings by previous knowledge. While this is an attractive notion, few of us will approach research without some prior suppositions; indeed, many researchers research topics they are passionately interested in. The challenge instead is to find a way to research that can draw on previous understanding but to be open to being surprised by what is new in the data. In any case, as the philosopher Rorty makes clear:

> no description of how things are from a God's-eye point of view, no skyhook provided by some contemporary or yet-to-be-developed science, is going to free us from the contingency of having been acculturated as we were. Our acculturation is what makes certain options live, or momentous, or forced, while leaving others dead, or trivial, or optional. (Rorty 1991: 13)

There is another reason for reading the literature: it can inspire and uplift us and show us that what felt like our own personal understandings were in fact common understandings. As Rogers put it, 'the very feeling which has seemed to me most private, most personal, has turned out to be an expression for which there is a resonance in many other people' (Kirschenbaum and Henderson 1990: 27).

There are some classic texts that will sensitize people to the whole topic of therapy, spirituality and healing. For example, Buber (1970), Rogers (1980), Wilber (1980, 2001), Thorne (1991, 2002) and Rowan (2005) all give excellent points of departure. Taking these authors in turn:

- *Martin Buber* was a Jewish philosopher who made an important contribution to our understanding of spirituality in human encounters when he suggested that there were two ways in which people could relate to one another: I/It in which people treat other people as objects or I/Thou in which we treat each other like kin. Buber reckoned that it was not possible to stay in the I/Thou way of relating endlessly. So I/Thou are experienced as special, and usually spiritual, moments of encounter between people. Buber insisted that I/Thou moments were not possible in unequal relationships such as between teachers and pupils and therapists and clients. Nonetheless, there is a lot of interest in the humanistic therapy world in I/Thou moments and many people claim that they have experienced such moments.

- *Carl Rogers* drew on painstaking research and clinical practice to present his view of the successful therapeutic relationship based on careful use of the core conditions of empathy, unconditional positive regard and congruence (Rogers 1951). He then considered adding the more spiritually informed quality of presence (Rogers 1980, discussed previously). However, while he described presence in clear and striking terms, it was left to future researchers like Shari Geller (Geller and Greenberg 2002) to address the meanings and implications of the use of presence more fully.

- *Ken Wilber* is not a therapist but shows a good understanding of the possibilities and limitations of therapy. He constructed a 10-stage model of human spiritual development that wove together secular western ideas of human development and spiritual eastern ideas of human development. His model articulates the developmental tasks at each stage and lists the best fit in terms of therapy or spiritual approach for that stage. This opens up some useful thinking about offering people the help that fits the challenges they are facing rather using a 'one-size-fits-all' approach. Wilber is not without his critics, including John Heron (1992, 1998), who regard Wilber's model as too rigid.

- *Brian Thorne* has doggedly insisted on talking about spirituality in therapy even within a Christian framework, which is not always well received. Thorne (1991) has articulated a notion of 'tenderness', which he acknowledges overlaps in many ways with Rogers' 'presence' but which spells out the experience from the point of view of the therapist in even more detail. Thorne is an exemplar of someone writing about spirituality and counselling drawing on deep reflection arising from vast clinical experience. Inevitably, quite a few people do accept that spirituality is relevant to therapy practice and even more challenge the notion that it can or should be Christian.

- *John Rowan* is a key British humanistic and transpersonal author, theoretician and practitioner. His writings are infused with a deeply transpersonal spiritual perspective, underpinned by a strong and wide-ranging scholarship. He takes the stance (Rowan 2005) that all therapists should be pursuing their own spiritual development. He has taken Wilber's model of human spiritual development and explored people's experiences of Wilber's levels of consciousness in workshops. In so doing, he has brought Wilber's theory into actual practice in a way that has profound implications for psychotherapy.

Focusing more specifically on research, Richards and Bergin's (2005) book on spiritual strategies in counselling and psychotherapy is a classic summary of the literature (and more), albeit US and deistically biased. This groundbreaking book, first published in 1997, shows how much more research into spiritual interventions had been undertaken than many of us thought at the time. Their advice to practitioners is also especially useful and they have published other relevant books (Richards and Bergin 2000, 2003).

With regard to the practice of spiritual assessment, which they advocate as a routine part of the assessment process, they maintain:

> For psychotherapists who believe that God can inspire and enlighten human beings, a religious and spiritual assessment will always be more than just gathering and conceptualizing information that has been gathered... for such therapists, a spiritual assessment includes an effort to seek and remain open to spiritual impressions and insights about clients and their problems that may come from the divine source. (Richards and Bergin 1997: 198)

Readers who are able to look beyond the deistic language they use will find their work of great benefit.

John Swinton's (2001) book *Spirituality and Mental Health Care* is a classic, not merely for the quality of the research he undertook but also the depth of his excellent literature review and how he brought the two together. The results of his research (see Swinton 2001: 112–31) are particularly worthy of study. His themes on depression derived from his qualitative interviews are evocative even just from their titles: the meaningless abyss of depression, questioning everything, abandonment, clinging on, the desire to relate and the failure of relationships, grinding me down, trapped into living and the crucible of depression.

Reading through these themes and the extracts from Swinton's interviews with his participants, one can begin to feel really weighed down. However, under the heading 'restoring meaning' he offers two further themes that are hopeful: the healing power of understanding, and liturgy and worship. This second theme may not at first glance be that clear, but it is about the value of belonging to a welcoming church community.

## Approaching methodology

> Spirituality relates to such things as love, hope, meaning, purpose – things which cannot be fully captured by the traditional methodologies of science. (Swinton 2001: 93)

In choosing an appropriate methodology to research spirituality and healing in therapy, it is all too easy to become dazzled by methodological theories, especially those of a qualitative nature, although quantitative methods have their own glittering appeal. I myself have enjoyed the delights of methodological writing and debate (West 2001b, 2007). However, research is above all about doing, and therapy research should make some contribution to better therapeutic practice, indeed to a better life for at least some of humankind.

Most research projects begin with a passionate desire to know something about some topic or other and possibly even answer a burning question or two about the topic. It is then a matter of what methodology and what methods will best answer this passion. At such a point things can get difficult. How do you make a choice out of the many methodologies and methods available?

This is rather akin to choosing what kind of therapist out of the 400+ schools available. You can try to simplify matters by dividing methodologies into qualitative, quantitative and mixed methods. That, however, will only get you so far. If you choose to do qualitative or mixed methods, John McLeod (2001) suggests that philosophy will be more useful than psychology. You will need to decide whether you are drawn to hermeneutics or phenomenology, since he insists that all qualitative research methods are based on hermeneutics or phenomenology or a mixture. Even after that one is spoilt for choice: grounded theory in its various forms is the most popular; other options include heuristics, interpretive phenomenological analysis, narrative analysis, a/r/t/ography and autoethnography. Many of these approaches have been used and described by the authors in this book.

A good question to pose is: In what way will a particular methodology cast light on my intended research topic? In other words, what kind of questions can it usefully answer? Another question to as is: What is the role of the researcher within this methodology? Also, more pragmatically: How easy is it to use? What is its pedigree?

My discussion so far has mostly kept within schools of methodology, akin to schools of therapy. However, there are researchers equivalent to integrative or eclectic therapists who use techniques from one or more approaches. One way of thinking about this to use the notion of researcher as bricoloeur, producing a bricolage (Denzin and Lincoln 2005). Some have seen their research as more akin to a quilt.

It is apparent that all researchers have a stance in relationship to their research. (I am indebted to my colleague Dr Clare Lennie for the notion of stance as applied to quantitative researchers.) This stance may be made explicit or remain implicit. For example, anyone conducting quantitative research will present their work as empirical, as objective, as rigorous, as hard science and this will be an expression of their stance.

Qualitative researchers, while aiming to be equally rigorous in their approach to research, are encouraged to share their worldview and to explicate their relationship with their research. Such openness on the part of the qualitative researcher enables the reader to understand the research in context and to be clear about the researcher's role in the research process.

In the context of qualitative research into spirituality and healing, the stance of the researcher becomes even more crucial. Spirituality and healing are both topics that can produce strong and passionate reactions in people. It is also exceedingly difficult to define a neutral position on these topics and indeed, many people will not participate in such research without feeling that the researcher is accepting of the subject matter. Spirituality and spiritual healing remain in tension with our modern, westernized, secular society and hence they have a troubled, and at times taboo, relationship with the world of therapy and therapeutic practice.

The challenge for the researcher is to be frank about their stance without that inhibiting or unduly influencing the researchee's participation in the research process. This challenge could be seen as quite daunting to the novice therapist-researcher. However, it is just this careful approach to relating that is part of the therapist's training. The nuanced understandings and use of transference and countertransference, empathy and congruence as applied in the therapeutic encounter are, in effect, transferable skills of great value for the researcher. (I am not saying that the research interview is the same as the therapy encounter, merely that many of the therapy skills and insights can be put to use by the researcher.) This careful reflection on practice during the therapy session and afterwards in supervision are skills that would be useful as part of what is referred to as researcher reflexivity.

Kim Etherington has written extensively about reflexivity in research:

> I understand researcher reflexivity as the capacity of the researcher to acknowledge how their own experiences and contexts (which might be fluid and changing) inform the process and outcomes of inquiry. If we can be aware of how our own thoughts, feelings, culture, environment and social and personal history inform us as we dialogue with participants, transcribe their conversations with us and write our representations of the work, then perhaps we can come closer to the rigour that is required of good qualitative research. By using reflexivity in research we close the illusory gap between researcher and researched and between the knower and what is known. (2004: 31–2)

Inevitably, this issue of the stance of the researcher includes the whole process of data analysis. In previously discussing this (West 2004a) I suggested that how the researcher wrestles with the data could be viewed as *inner data analysis*. Such an approach honours the depth of the researcher's engagement with spirituality and healing, but also uses them as a site of, or place for, making sense of the data. This implies that data analysis can be both a systematic process and also a profoundly intuitive one.

If this seems too farfetched, it is worth remembering that David Rennie, who is largely and single-mindedly responsible for the frequent use of grounded theory in therapy research, uses the phrase 'It rises from my guts' in his approach to categorization. This means that when the category to be used is finally chosen, it feels right in a holistic sense. In this way, Rennie feels he is balancing realism and relativism. Fortunately, I do not have to address all of the philosophical issues involved. However, Rennie is claiming here – as Rogers (1980) and Moustakas (1990) both would – that there is a universal level to human experiencing that can be tapped into.

My own jury is out on this. I do believe I can mystically connect with the whole of creation, but when I try to talk about it I am culturally bound. So I prefer to say, 'These are my findings based on my use of this method. This is what I think is important about these findings, you might think different, indeed such discussions become yet another form of data and development of the original research.'

I feel a certain reluctance to open up the question of postmodernity. This is partially because I have two contradictory views on postmodernism.

First, it would be useful to define it, although that in itself opens up a whole new can of worms. If the pre-modern world was identifiable by a belief in God(s), then modernism was about a belief in objective truth and reality – the beliefs of a secular world. The postmodern view, which arose out of the apparent failure of modernism (Polkinghorne 1992), is 'characterised by a loss of belief in an objective world and an incredibility towards meta-narratives of legitimation' (Kvale 1992: 32).

What I find true about postmodernism is this insistence that the grand narratives are losing their appeal and dying out. This is how I feel about Christianity. Postmodernism is also one way of understanding the huge flux in modern urban western living and the role of the internet and cyberspace in modern life. Postmodernism shares with qualitative research the focus on, and the relevance given to, local knowledge and the doubt attached to explanations which claim a universality. Nonetheless, I also feel that I agree with Pittu Laungani (2003) who, while acknowledging how much cultures are mixing (which we could consider to be a postmodern phenomenon), says, 'behind closed doors, when each individual enters his/her own house, the apparent similarity ends, and life takes on a specific culture-centred dimension'.

It is worth reflecting on how a postmodern approach to research would be congruent with postmodern spirituality as practised and understood within the modern world. If we conflate spirituality with organized traditional religion, we are simply missing out on what is actually happening. Modernism might well have undermined Christianity and other traditional religions, but it has not apparently reduced people's spiritual beliefs and their desire to engage in spiritual practices.

## Approaching the topic

Researching therapy, spirituality and healing presents its own unique dilemmas. These include the question of researcher stance, discussed above. If we hold a positive view of spirituality and also have a spiritual faith, it is a real challenge to attempt to stand outside that position. Also many spiritual experiences are simply ineffable, they are beyond words, occurring in altered states of consciousness. To try to *talk* about any human experience is obviously not the same as *having* the experience. With regard to spiritual experiences, this presents a whole other level of difficulty. As one of my research respondents put it:

> In the I/Thou in which we are one, yet there's also a sense in which we are still separate. I think it may be a problem where we're trying

to use language to define things that aren't easily defined. (West 1995: 303)

In my work with a client I called Matthew (West 2004a) I found myself in a very deep meditative space, but was able to communicate with Matthew from within that space. Usually talking would bring me out of the space. I was also aware that if Matthew had not been present or if I had given up my role as a therapist, I would have dropped into an even deeper space.

The question arises: Are these experiences real and healthy? In the light of postmodernism discussed above and in the spirit of Rogers' (1980) respect for the client's reality (and by extension the therapist's reality also), if an experience is true to the client then it is true. Are these experiences invariably healthy? No. Are there sometimes mental health issues to be addressed? Yes. This is a huge topic, discussed in West (2000a) and Swinton (2001). It is important to distinguish between the immediate impact of such an experience – it can be frightening, exciting, life changing and so on – and the context for that person and how the experience sits with them over time.

I find Lukoff's (1985) mapping of mystical experiences and psychosis very helpful and this applies whether or not one considers psychosis to be a real and useful diagnosis. We can best understand his model by imagining a spectrum with pure mystical experience at one end and pure psychosis at the other. In between we can have varying mixtures of mystical experiences with psychotic features or psychotic experiences with mystical features. Lukoff also makes a useful distinction between temporary psychotic episodes and long-term psychosis.

This might seem like merely an intellectual exercise, but Lukoff invites us to think about the kind of support a person undergoing such challenging experiences might need. Sometimes the mere naming and describing of a mystical experience can have a calming effect on the person involved. It is common for people to think: 'Am I mad?' So to hear that this is fairly common, that it is part of many people's lives, is reassuring. This is not to deny that when psychotic features are involved people will need varying degrees of support. Lukoff (1985) provides us with a useful map for exploring and making appropriate decisions about the support needed.

There are also profound cultural and subcultural issues around spiritual and healing experiences. For example, some Christian churches will only accept healing in the name of Jesus and may still view some healing phenomena in terms of the devil. Spiritual healing was illegal in Britain until the 1950s and prosecution was possible under the Witchcraft Act. Some of the folk religious and healing practices seem clearly pagan and are practised by pagans today. (For a useful discussion of paganism and therapy, see Seymour 2005.) I think there is a deep mistrust and a curiosity within white British culture about these phenomena. I do not think that any of us come to this territory unaffected by our cultural background; often this is unconscious.

## Guidelines for researching therapy, spirituality and healing

It is always very useful to examine one's own assumptions about important matters, none more so than the approach to therapy, spirituality and healing. Designing a research project in this whole area needs to begin with a careful indwelling (Moustakas 1990) on the topic chosen, irrespective of what methodological approach one initially and finally chooses.

In terms of guidelines:

1. Think carefully about your own attitude to human spirituality and healing.
2. Carefully explore your own experiences, both good and bad.
3. Choose a topic in relation to human spirituality and/or healing about which you are passionate.
4. Chose a methodology to which you are drawn and which looks like it will deliver findings in a form that appears useful to you; which will (hopefully) cast fresh light on your topic; and which will hopefully answer the questions you have in relation to your research topic.
5. With support as necessary, design a suitable project that does not dispel the passion with which you initially approached your topic and which also deeply addresses the various ethical issues that will be present in any research involving people.
6. You may well need to repeat steps 3–5 several times before achieving a good enough research design.
7. Check what has been done before in your chosen research area (and nearby) so that you are not reinventing the wheel. Learn what you can from such research, including making contact with the researchers involved.
8. Have a down-to-earth conversation with a colleague about how to resource your research.
9. Get research supervision from someone you trust.

10. Attend one or more relevant conferences while doing your research.
11. Write your research up with as much support as you can get from others.
12. Disseminate your findings as creatively and as far as you can via conferences, websites, blogs, articles in professional journals, academic papers and conversations.

Most of these above guidelines apply, of course, to all research into therapy. Focusing specifically on research into therapy, spirituality and healing, some areas especially worthy of research are apparent:

- Exploration of clients' and therapists' experience of spirituality and healing within and outside of therapy.
- Careful examination of audio and video recordings of spiritual and healing moments in therapy sessions. This could also involve playing back such tapes to the participants separately using interpersonal process recall.
- Studies focusing on particular spiritual or healing interventions. These might include prayer; discussing theological concepts and making references to scriptures; using spiritual relaxation and imagery; encouraging forgiveness; helping clients live congruently with their spiritual values; self-disclosure of spiritual beliefs or experiences; consulting with religious leaders, using religious bibliotherapy and use of spiritual intuition.
- Outcome and case studies of therapists who habitually use such interventions.
- Surveys into which kind of spiritual and healing interventions are used by which therapists with which client groups.

## Conclusion

In this chapter I have considered the challenges that arise when researching therapy, spirituality and healing. Many of these challenges are not unique, but by engaging with such an important, tender and often taboo area the challenges involved take on a new level of difficulty. The bottom line, I feel, is to find an ethically appropriate way of exploring these aspects of human experience so as to illuminate practice with current and future therapy clients, to their benefit. Research done in this spirit almost invariably also benefits research participants and the researchers themselves.

## Discussion points

1. What in your view is the most important research into therapy, spirituality and healing that needs to be done and why?
2. What is your own view of spiritual and healing phenomena and where does that view come from? How would this view inform your selection and design of a suitable research project?
3. In your view are mystical experiences ever healthy? How might they be worked with in therapy? How might they be researched?

# 13
## Emergent Spirituality

*David Paul Smith*

## Introduction

This chapter suggests that we approach spirituality in an experiential, person-centred way and uses a phenomenological method in order to take a non-pathological viewpoint of this emerging aspect of human experience. It begins with examples from history, from fieldwork and from the contributors of this book. The chapter conclusion is that a focus on a respectful attitude to spiritual experience within psychotherapy would benefit both client and therapist.

## Background

Spirituality has become a very popular topic within psychological research. It has expanded almost exponentially in the past decade and a half. This interest may be considered curious in the modern world among an arguably secular profession. Since Freud's *The Future of an Illusion* (1961), the religious and cultural contexts that frame spiritual experience have been criticized as illusory and irrational. Recent books such as *God Is Not Great: How Religion Poisons Everything* by Christopher Hitchens (2007) and *The End of Faith* by Sam Harris (2005) argue that it is time to give up religion, as it provides a poor, even dangerous basis for personal guidelines and public policy. It is irrational. Nevertheless, even Harris suggests in his final chapter that 'mysticism', or at least spiritual practice such as meditation, can be rational (Harris 2005: 235).

The debate rages on as researchers adopt different methods, often at odds with each other, and approach the topic from diverse assumptive worlds. For example, a researcher can be religiously committed or not. If the researcher adheres strongly to a particular religious tradition, they may assume that their belief system is correct. Thus, they see other perspectives as, at best, approximations to the truth. These 'apologists' often engage in research to find support for the validity of their particular view. Their psychological interpretations are set in an assumptive world that is both theological and ideological; it is not questioned.

Others, as Freud did, may start with an atheist bias in a psychiatric Weltanschauung. They apply a western medical bias when they interpret spiritual phenomena. In the worst cases, they pathologize people's experience, even when it is unwarranted; that is, the person is not 'crazy'. Similar to the religious ideologue, scientists often use clinical heuristics that become basic claims about reality. Then, the ideological form of consciousness blocks, prevents or renders unnoticeable contrary evidence or arguments. This promotes a false consciousness in a sense (see Pippin 2005: ch. 11).

This chapter suggests a way out of these traps. First, we must take an experiential and 'person-centred' approach in the research of spiritual phenomena. That is, we should consider spiritual experience as an emergent property of personal development. We must start by respectfully addressing the indigenous perspective as it is related by our subjects. Then, it behoves us to turn to the methodology of experiential phenomenology in the social sciences. The influence of an experiential and phenomenological method in ethnomethodology can be traced back to Eugene T. Gendlin (Liberman 1997). Today, fields such as psychological anthropology utilize a phenomenological approach, as summarized by Gendlin to 'seek to articulate experience as actually had, rather than laying some invented theoretical scheme on experience' (Gendlin 1973).

An experiential and phenomenological method can avoid the pitfalls of falling back into strictly archaic and traditional explications of phenomena, as well as avoid the dismissive and pathologizing tendencies of an ideological science. To begin, I will present examples from history, from my own fieldwork and from the contributors of this book. In these examples, I suggest that there is an experiential basis that we refer to as spiritual that is then contextualized in some sort of cultural frame. Looking at spirituality as an emergent phenomenon starts with experience first. This experience is perhaps rare, but not as rare as one may think.

The question is not to dismiss the problems of our hermeneutic circle (Rabinow and Sullivan 1987). That is, I am not arguing that spiritual experience is free from religious interpretation or not framed by cultural context. It is. However, the question remains what is the most appropriate interpretation. As I have argued earlier, both modern medicine and psychiatry as well as traditional religious views can present a problematic bias. The question remains: What is the best and most useful interpretation of these experiences?

## Two contemporary examples of spiritual leaders

Religious figures often have similar experiences at an early age that are then interpreted in terms of the religious context in which they grew up. The experiences are spontaneously rooted in the person's development. This development is immediately influenced by cultural forces. So, what issues relate to nature and what issues relate to nurture are difficult to tease out. However, utilizing a phenomenological and experiential approach can lead us to identify common denominators and begin to ask the right questions.

I start with two examples of contemporary spiritual leaders. One is Shri Sai Baba, head of the ashram Prashanti Nilayam in Puttaparthi, India. Sai Baba has millions of devotees around the world. The other is Mata Amritanandamayi, often referred to as Amma, the hugging saint, whose ashram is in the state of Kerala, India. She became better known after a French documentary *Darshan-L'etreinte*, directed by Jan Kounen, was released in 2005. She has won numerous awards and recognition for her humanitarian efforts.

There are numerous stories of unique events in Sai Baba's early childhood. Here, I discuss events that started in March of 1940. At that time Baba, in his early teens, fell prey to a drastic change in mental status that lasted for several days. After a period of unconsciousness, he regained consciousness but refused to eat or drink. He presented as oblivious to goings-on around him. He appeared to be hearing voices, described by biographers as conversations with 'spiritual beings'. His family took him to various healers. but a variety of doctors and traditional healers failed to bring him back to normality.

The family retuned to their home. At that time, his grandfather read in a sacred text that the avatar Rama went through a similar listlessness at the same age. Sai Baba's moods appeared to fluctuate from excessive energy to weak and listless. During this time he read poetry and praised the Lord. Finally, his odd behaviour ended in May, more than two months after he first fell unconscious. At this time, he is reported to have produced candy and flowers, materializing them from nothing. After these miraculous events he announced his mission and his true identity as an avatar (Kheirabadi 2005).

Mata Amritanandamayi is reported to have started speaking when she was nearly six months old. It is reported that she exhibited a passion to sing divine names as soon as she began to speak fairly well. Her biography suggests that without instruction from anyone, she began saying prayers and sang songs in praise of Shri Krishna. These devotional behaviours continued through her childhood. She is described as continually keeping a picture of Lord Krishna on her person. She began to sit for long periods in what appeared to be meditative silence, spontaneously and without instruction. Her biographer states that it was not uncommon to find her sitting in solitude with closed eyes and when she was aroused from her meditation, she seemed distracted and distant.

As she grew older, her devotional moods grew more intense and she became more absorbed in ecstatic reverie, dancing and long periods of silence. Aside from her daily chores in school, she spent her free time in prayer and meditation. Religious obsessions caused conflict with her family and there were times where she was physically punished for not behaving like other children. (This is an experience that she shared with Sai Baba, who was also beaten at various points in his childhood for not behaving in a normal manner.) Her biographer records her as performing her first miracle in September of 1975, where she turned water to milk (Aswarupananda 1994).

These two examples of living spiritual masters can easily be construed as modern myths developed by devotees to lend divine characteristics to their objects of devotion. However, we can pinpoint some clear common denominators. Both experienced altered states of consciousness at an early age, such as spontaneous absorption in trance states. Also, they gravitated towards religious devotion. Neither ended up exhibiting the type of dysfunction that we associate with psychopathology in the West. Both have built large followings and have become social reformers and both contribute to social improvement, giving millions of dollars to education, medicine and social infrastructure.

## Further historical examples in the West

HP Blavatsky in the nineteenth century was described as continually hearing voices and communicating with spiritual entities throughout her childhood. She went on to establish the Theosophical Society and arose as an internationally renowned figure who reportedly communicated telepathically with 'spiritual masters' hidden somewhere in the Himalayas. While this was controversial, it was nonetheless part of her personal story (Aveni 2002; Albanese 2007).

Another figure, Rudolf Steiner, who broke from theosophy and established the discipline of anthroposophy, may provide a better example. Steiner is also responsible for the development of the Waldorf schools. His work has influenced fields as diverse as education, medicine, agriculture, architecture, art, religion, social organizations and more. His biographers describe him as a young boy who was sensitive to spiritual phenomena, aspects of reality 'not perceived with the physical senses'. For example, he was reported to have perceived a relative who requested assistance from him although she had already been dead due to suicide committed in a remote location. His biographers describe this experience as a 'clairvoyant ability' that deepened more and more throughout his life (Barnes 1997; Lachman 2007).

A further example is Krishnamurthi, who as a child in India was adopted by the theosophist Charles Walter Leadbeater, a British mystic and leader of the Theosophical Society. Leadbeater 'recognized' Krishnamurthi as a special child and the society took responsibility for his education. Krishnamurthi eventually went his own way. In 1922, as a young man, he moved to California. In August, he suffered a succession of ailments involving pains in his neck and spine. He would tremble, faint and enter a semiconscious state. He experienced a 'fire' that started at the base of his spine and rose to the nap of his neck. This fire or heat moved to the left of his head and then to the right side, and finally met in the forehead, between his eyes. Later these vegetative functions of his nervous system were interpreted as a manifestation of *kundalini* or spiritual force, referred to in Hindu sacred texts (Lutyens 1975; Jayakar 1985).

Many examples can be found in the annals of spiritual biographies. The history of religious personalities often includes profound experiences of otherworldly phenomena. However, it is interesting to note that many of our friends and family also have experiences of this nature. As early as the 1970s, Fr. Andrew Greeley, a sociologist and Catholic priest affiliated with the University of Chicago, published a study suggesting that mystical experiences among the general public are not uncommon (Greeley 1975). Furthermore, in an article titled 'The paranormal is normal: A sociologist looks at parapsychology', Dr Greeley suggested that paranormal phenomena are experienced by over 50 per cent of people in the general population, based on research done in the United States. This theme is reflected in books such as *Ordinary People as Monks and Mystics: Lifestyles for Spiritual Wholeness* by Marsha Sinetar (2007). In the next section, I share some of my own stories and those related to me by friends and colleagues.

## Emergent spirituality

During a period of my life when spiritual experiences started to become more prominent and prevalent, I happened to attend a conference on psychotherapy research in the UK. I spent some time with a friend, colleague and author who conducts similar research. I had a great opportunity to share my experiences with him. Around the summer equinox, walking among the stones at the ancient stone monolith site of Arbor Low, he related the following story.

In the 1970s, he was actively involved with the work of Wilhelm Reich. Reich's theory of orgone energy involves the manipulation or intensification of what he construed as bio-energy, the life force that regulates physical health. At some point during his work, my colleague began to see light around people, or auras. The experience was clearly egodistonic and he began to become concerned. He thought that he might be losing his mind. However, a friend of his suggested that he went to see a therapist in London who explained to him that, considering the work he was doing, this type of experience was not uncommon. She suggested that he stop worrying about it and simply get on with his work. He found this information a great relief and did just that. I believe that he still sees auras.

Interviewing another colleague, I asked her why she had become a disciple of Sai Baba, mentioned earlier in this chapter. She stated that she had been involved in work with a spiritual group where she lived. At one point after involvement with this group, she had a vivid dream of a visually distinct individual. The person was distinctive but no one she had seen before, only in her dream. However, within the next few days she saw a photograph of the person she had seen in her dream. It was a photo of Sai Baba. This story is quite common for many people who come to follow this leader. Similar stories are related in a variety of books and documentaries on him (Murphet 1971; Berenstein 1998).

Another colleague shares a common experience with Rudolf Steiner. While growing up, she often saw images and gained impressions of people who were no longer living. The stories were corroborated by the people who were, of course, alive. However, on some occasions she would gain insight into people's lives that had not been shared openly or verbally. For example, what does one do when a dead parent or child appears to you providing some information and the individual is still struggling with their death? What if they are there, in the room with that person?

Finally, a further colleague related a story of how she came to believe that she was in communication with a dead saint. Over a period of time, she began to encounter the same symbol over and over again. Images and messages were encountered in a synchronistic manner, coming into her life unexpectedly but having some significance. On a trip to Glasgow she began to see this crest or emblem in many places and eventually she entered a church. Exploring the church, she walked into the crypt and noticed a tour group. Not able to withhold her curiosity and pressured by these nagging events, she approached the tour guide and asked if she knew the meaning of this symbol. The guide explained that it was the crest associated with St Mungo, founder of the city of Glasgow. At that moment, the colleague turned and realized that she was standing in front of his very burial spot. This event, to some extent, changed her view of reality and changed the direction of her life.

All these stories share examples of altered mental state, synchronicities and spontaneous changes in life that were not planned or expected. While in the case of the dream our auras, spiritual or therapeutic practices preceded the experience, the experience itself emerged in an unexpected and surprising manner. The stories unfold with meaningful relationships, but are not planned, predicted or determined by individuals' efforts (Main 2007; Richo 2007).

These phenomena emerge out of lived experience, rooted in raw perception and sensation in the body. They often open the individual to a new way of understanding the world and their place in it. I would argue that the subjective nature of each phenomenon combined with the type of meaning provided in people's lives constitute these stories as spiritual.

## Two examples from my research

The next example comes from my work in the study of traditional healing practices. I had gone to interview traditional Anishinabe healers who worked in Ontario, Canada on the Serpent River Reservation in 2006. These were friends and family of a close friend and colleague on whom I had published previously, Donald Beaucage, a Native American counsellor who introduced me to the 'sweatlodge' (Smith 2005).

The following is a short excerpt from a healing ritual called the Cedar Bath, a process that has historically been used along with medicinal and psychospiritual interventions (Grim 1983). The practice of the Cedar Bath appears to be undergoing some revitalization in Canada.

The Cedar Bath ceremony involves the use of a water solution that is prepared in part with boiling cedar branches. Cedar is considered to be a plant that is associated with the release of strong emotions and is used

in a variety of rituals and among various indigenous cultures throughout North America (Savinelli 2002). The following excerpt is part of a
longer narrative describing a Cedar Bath (Moodley et al. 2010).

> During the course of the ritual, as the assistants rubbed down my
> arms and legs, my muscles began to twitch spontaneously. The sub-
> jective sensation was analogous to a sneeze or cough. The muscles
> in my arms and legs would shudder and my arms and legs began to
> move in an arrhythmic manner. All this took place as I continued
> to cry with deep sobs. The gut wrenching sobs accompanied by a
> thrashing about continued while the healers continued to wash my
> arms, chest and legs.

> As my crying and spasms increased, Isabelle encouraged me to not
> hold back and let forth even stronger emotions. She asked if I remem-
> bered Primal Scream Therapy. She suggested screaming as the crying
> intensified. She encouraged me to scream and I complied. I screamed
> as loud as I could, over and over again several times. She also encour-
> aged me to vomit if I felt the need and stated there were basins to my
> side. Let it all out, she encouraged, in a nurturing fashion as a mother
> might support her child in the throws of a reaching flu.

The traditional healers who utilize this method of medicine explain
that they invoke the help of spirits and then pull trauma and emotional
blockage from the body. This is done in collaboration with the spirits
and involves working with 'energy' in the body.

From a phenomenological level, I can say the following. The method
is body based and group based. The technique involves hypnotic
induction, the facilitation of abreactive and cathartic responses, guided
imagery and group therapy. These are all approaches used in standard
psychotherapy. However, although there are sometimes strong abreactive processes induced in psychotherapy, I still cannot account for the
spontaneous and powerful muscle spasms and undulating movements I
experienced throughout my body. This introduction to the Cedar Bath
has led me to explore the work being done in energy medicine, bio-
energy work and energy psychology. It has also renewed my interest
in Wilhelm Reich and those he influenced, such as Alexander Lowen
(Reich 1961; Lowen 1990).

At times, research in spirituality can change the very core of one's
worldview and sense of reality. I recall looking at a book on 'healing
hands' not so many years ago, while I was in graduate school at the

University of Chicago. I thought to myself: What is that kind of garbage doing in a bookstore around here? Now, I'm not as critical.

The spontaneous emergence of spiritual experiences in one's life often leads to radical changes in one's sense of onself and the world one lives in. It can often shake the foundation of one's personal sense of self and what is real, as I mentioned with my friend who sees auras. If I emphasize anything in this chapter, it is this: we must be able to approach this subject in a respectful manner. While we may question a person's interpretation of their own experience, we must at least assume that a fair number of people are merely being honest with statements such as seeing or hearing what others may not. To dismiss this flippantly as hallucination or fantasy does not fit the social facts; and certainly to relegate these experiences to psychopathology does not fit the standards of our diagnostic criteria.

Reality is fairly malleable. It may be that we not only interpret reality in various ways but, due to our training and cultural context, we may notice things that other people do not. This clearly leads one to the work of ontology and epistemology, beyond the scope of this particular chapter. Anthropologists have contributed extensively to this issue. Psychological anthropologists look at how people can live in different realities, shifting from one epistemic frame to another (Duerr 1985; Luhrmann 1989).

Let me give one more story from my own research. I have worked with a group of Sufi students and mediators who live in Canada in the city of Toronto. Sufism is the term generally applied to mystical currents in Islam. The word is derived from *suf* (Arab for 'wool'), pointing to the woollen frocks of Middle Eastern ascetics (Smith 1995). These students work with a Shaykh whom I will refer to as Dr J. Dr J's major orientation is the Chisti lineage. According to him, there are four major lineages in Sufism: Qadri, Chisti, Naqshbandi and Shorverd. Dr J. reported that his teacher gave him permission to teach from all four lineages.

Dr J. is also a psychiatrist in his mid-50s. I work closely with him in Chicago and he is a close friend. He worked as an internal medicine physician for 21 years. Then he respecialized in psychiatry at the age of 49. We talk about our cases and when we have time, we talk about spirituality. I often have difficulty in reconciling the two worlds of Sufism and psychiatry, two worlds he seems to live in comfortably.

In Sufism, the Shaykh is an important conduit between the student and Allah. Meditation often focuses on the teacher as an assistant to know God directly. Thus, an intimate emotional relationship is established by virtue of the training system. Dr J has mentioned many events that leave me food for thought.

For example, one evening when he was upset with one of his children, he was sitting in front of his computer experiencing a fair amount of anger (not a typical state of emotion for him, based on my personal experience). At that moment his head student called from Canada and Dr J's wife answered the phone. The student said, 'Tell him to stop doing what he is doing or my head is going to explode!' On another occasion, Dr J intentionally tried an experiment, and began thinking about his student in an intense fashion. Again, his student called from Canada asking what was going on and why he was bothering him. These types of experience beg for formal research. However, we can at least categorize them as synchronistic events; that is, meaningful moments that are not causally related in any type of concrete or clearly understandable fashion.

## Conclusion

I would like to start my conclusion with a quote from Carl Rogers. In 'Do We Need "A" Reality?', he describes a case of a 'hardheaded businessman' who, 'after some puzzling experiences, found himself one night floating up to the ceiling of his room, looking down on his own body and that of his wife'. Rogers goes on to describe this case and asks, 'One cannot help but ponder the question: What "reality" can encompass such experiences, as well as the "real" experiences I know?' (Rogers 1978).

Spiritual experiences involve the most important and essential characteristics of our personal development: the edge of meaning and the verge of our emerging selves. Research suggests that spirituality involves how we understand the world, how we make meaning out of life and, as Paul Tillich suggested, 'issues of ultimate concern' (Elkins at al. 1988; Smith and Orlinsky 2000).

Merely defining spiritual beliefs as cultural and historical artifacts does them a disservice. Furthermore, our beliefs are often not only what we are taught in Sunday school, but often a desperate attempt to make sense of our own experience. These experiences frequently break the bounds of what we understand to be real and challenge our concept of who we are.

Defining these experiences merely as wish fulfilment or, worse yet, pathological processes does not help. In fact, many of these processes are related to experiences of personal wellness and wholeness. These experiences help enrich and enlighten our lives. Clearly, after decades of research on spiritual personalities, shamans and mystics are *not typically* crazy (Torrey 1972).

At the same time, turning to traditional views or popular explanations of our experience may not be adequate. Assuming that our own personal religion has the 'right' answer is rife with cultural bias and often arrogant. Furthermore, many religious explanations fall flat in the face of modern science and medicine. We cannot ignore the hard-learned knowledge of over 100 years of medicine, psychiatry and psychology.

The study of spirituality in a scientific context has not only become popular, I argue that it is quite important. In my own research, the clear benefits of traditional healing, such as the Cedar Bath, warrant significant scientific attention and community resources. Why? Because they are so effective. Many more people could benefit if more support was provided to the traditional therapists who have mastered these techniques. However, this has yet to happen on a wide scale (Smith 2005).

The question we are left with is how to best explain and approach the study of these phenomena. Modern psychiatry and psychotherapy research often do a disservice to spiritual efforts and phenomena. Therapists who use spiritual techniques and religious concepts leave modern scientists shaking their heads or confused. We need a new way to understand these phenomena. Clearly, we need to start on a phenomenological level and lend a respectful eye to the cultural frames that inform these practices. The collaboration between traditional views and modern science can help lead to a new way of understanding these processes. Finally, starting by looking at psychotherapists who have personal spiritual experiences, as this book has done, is a good contribution towards that end.

## Discussion points

1. What kind of psychology must we develop to encompass the kind of spiritual experiences discussed in this chapter?
2. What is 'spiritual energy' and what might help us address this question?
3. What is the difference between scientific rhetoric and religious rhetoric? How does a chemist or physicist frame reality compared to a poet or a mystic?
4. How do 'spiritual events' and synchronistic occurrences relate to experience and the making of meaning?
5. What is the difference between experience and belief? How do they relate?

# 14
# Practice around Therapy, Spirituality and Healing

*William West*

## Introduction

In this chapter I will address what I regard as key issues around therapeutic practice including spirituality and healing. These consist of the challenges faced by the therapist working in the realms of therapy, spirituality and healing; models for working with spirituality and healing in therapy; a discussion of whether and how therapists should explore their spirituality in training; and finally I will offer some suggestions for the training and practice of therapists.

It is worth bearing in mind that therapeutic practice around spirituality and healing remains controversial, which points us towards the great care needed if as a practitioner we are going to engage or find ourselves engaged with our clients in these ways. There remains the ethical challenge: if we do know something that will benefit a client struggling with a problem, we should offer our best endeavours to help them.

## Challenges for the therapist in working with spirituality and healing

One way to think about this whole question of therapeutic practice around spirituality and healing would be to imagine possible supervision issues that might arise. Regular meetings with a supervisor – usually a more experienced and senior colleague – is a professional demand made of psychotherapists and counsellors working in Britain. Within these supervisory meetings therapists are expected to review their work with clients in order to improve their practice. Typically, any innovative or unusual interventions or experiences arising from their work would be carefully explored.

From such a perspective, namely that of a clinical supervisor, it is possible to highlight and explore some of the more challenging aspects of therapeutic practice presented in this book. These would include:

- prayer occurring within the therapy session
- accessing spiritual guides in the session
- use of psychic energy
- deliberate use of spiritual healing methods in a therapy session

With myself as putative supervisor of a therapist offering each of the above approaches, I will reflect on issues that are likely to arise.

## Use of prayer

This is largely outside of my usual practice as a counsellor and as a supervisor. I have often wished the best for my clients after difficult sessions. In some of these instances I have said to the client involved, 'I will be thinking of you.' I have never prayed with a client, it simply does not appeal to me as a possible intervention. I might or might not if asked. It would depend on the context in which the request arose, my gut reaction to the request and my thoughts and feelings about the implications for the client and our work together. From a supervisory point of view, I would want my supervisee to be very clear about any use of prayer and its impact on the client and the therapeutic alliance, and its potential contribution to a successful outcome.

## Accessing spirit guides

Christa Gorsedene makes her apparent use of a spirit guide very transparent in her chapter. Spirit guides are not a direct experience of mine. I do feel helped from time to time in my work from what I take to be a spiritual source, but I do not tend to think of this as being the actions of a spirit guide. I think of it more in Jungian terms of the collective unconscious. With regard to supervision, I would want the therapist using spirit guides to be very clear on their impact on the therapy as indicated above around the use of prayer.

I would tend to see the use of spirit guides as actually stepping outside of the usual therapy boundaries into a different kind of relationship. This is not necessarily any less helpful to the client, but is a different kind of relationship. This is not a reason per se for not using spirit guides to help a client, more indicative of a need to think through the boundaries of what seems to me to be a different kind of professional relationship.

## Use of psychic energy in therapy

I would find this easier to supervise, as aura work and intuition were used by a number of my participants in my doctoral research into therapy and spiritual healing (West 1995). Marie Wardle's chapter, indeed, does offer some clear ways of thinking about this whole area. I am, however, left with some questions regarding sense making around such altered states as Marie describes, and I think that such work can also be usefully understood within a transpersonal therapeutic framework.

## Use of spiritual healing methods

This raises the same set of questions for me as those around the use of prayer. I present my thoughts about helping models for spirituality and healing in therapy in the next section of this chapter.

One of the telling points that Peter Gubi makes in discussing the use of prayer therapy (Gubi 2003) is his analogy between how we, as a practitioner, might approach the use of, say, a Gestalt two-chair exercise and how we might approach the use of prayer. (A Gestalt therapist might use a two-chair exercise when a client is in two minds about a particular important decision in their life. Each chair represents one 'mind' and enables a dialogue to occur out loud and to be witnessed by the therapist.) In both cases we might consider the ethics and the practice issues of introducing something that we feel could be of benefit to our client.

You might however feel, with some justification, that the use of prayer is different in a number of ways to the use of the Gestalt two-chair exercise. Potentially the Gestalt exercise is not any different to inviting the client to take part in a relaxation exercise, explore a recent disturbing dream or pick up crayons and draw. I feel that prayer changes the relationship between therapist and client by introducing a specifically spiritual element. If the client wants the therapist to pray for them, the therapist might then be seen by the client as a religious figure, akin to a religious teacher or minister. This implies a change of boundaries, a change of rules to this relationship.

On one level it is not, it is merely a question of integrating such an intervention into our modelling of how we work with clients. The world of therapists is divided between those who maintain they stick to a pure model of working and those who draw on a range of approaches integratively or eclectically. However, as Hollanders (2000a, b) has shown, 'pure' therapists are not as pure as they might think. It seems apparent that the largest group of therapists consists of those who view themselves as 'eclectic' or 'integrative'.

This process of integrative or eclectic practice is based on the thera-pists' exposure to, and willingness to draw on, interventions from other schools than the one(s) they were initially trained in. We find, for example, that many therapists use relaxation techniques, work with visualization, get clients to rate their problems and so on (Hollanders and McLeod 1997). The question arises as to where the individual thera-pist draws the line. It is much easier to be told 'do this, don't do that' and this is probably a helpful place to start from, especially for those in training. However, over time questions can begin to arise, such as: 'Why not offer this intervention I have just come across on a workshop?' It gets harder when we have moments of intuition and feel drawn to act in ways which we cannot logically justify (Rogers 1980). Or even: 'My client has asked me to do this, should I?'

## Models for working with spirituality and healing in therapy

I would dearly like to have one model to offer for all occasions of work-ing therapeutically with clients around spirituality and healing. There are models that are helpful in a variety of contexts. This word 'con-text' is actually a helpful one. When I had clients who came to me for therapy or spiritual healing, I had pretty clear models from my time as a trainee in each discipline to draw on. However, I found these models restrictive at times and they were not especially helpful when a therapy client asked for spiritual healing from me.

When would-be clients come to me and in effect say 'draw on whatever you know to help me', I find this notion very freeing, but I still struggle with what a model for my work would look like. I remember, during my doctoral studies, thinking of a spectrum with spiritual healing at one end and psychotherapy at the other, and viewing myself as working with any one client at any one point in their process as being at some point on such a spectrum. Useful questions arise about where on the spectrum I might find myself working with any one client and why.

When I came to examine the experiences of the 30 respondents in my doctoral research I noticed that they could be fitted into a developmen-tal model of four stages:

1. The practitioner is initially either a therapist or a healer.
2. The practitioner becomes both therapist and healer and uses both separately with different sets of clients.
3. The practitioner begins to integrate the one with the other.

4. True integration occurs and transcends both roles. For example, I was told 'I can move around in what I've learned quite easily from one thing to another' or 'I no longer make distinctions now [between therapy and healing]' (West 1995: 377). Or 'I don't call myself an anything. It's a very interesting place somehow. It's like more and more about not having an agenda... What I am actually interested in is how we get beyond technique to something much more basic, which is like spirit and presence' (West 1995: 353).

However, developing a model that integrated both therapy and healing and that could answer some of the questions, issues and dilemmas raised was another matter. For example, one respondent was moved to say to me when he recognized that no label existed for the part of his work that was spiritual: 'We haven't got practitioners of what you're talking about' (West 1995: 305).

The best fit for me was, and is, Wilber's model; discussed briefly in Chapter 8. Wilber offers us a 10-stage model of human spiritual development in which each successive stage includes the previous ones, rather like the Russian babushka dolls. The higher up the model you get, the more explicitly spiritual it becomes. The lower stages of the model more or less coincide with Freudian ideas of human personal development. The upper stages correlate more with eastern ideas of human spiritual development. Wilber, provocatively, recommends western therapy followed by eastern spiritual development.

What I especially like about Wilber's model is that it is big and inclusive of therapy, spirituality and healing. He suggests that there are particular developmental challenges associated with each stage and consequently the best fit for the kind of help needed. This could link into my idea (presented above) of a spectrum with secular therapy at one end and spiritual healing at the other. If I also view it as a dynamic model, then any one client could need me to be in differing roles over time depending on the therapeutic work they need to do.

For example, one of my respondents described a 'quantum leap' in his work with one client:

I don't think I've ever experienced anything quite like it; it was just a totally different level of functioning of consciousness for us. Often the work we're doing is quite sort of nuts and bolts, sort of spade work... the room was filled with an incredible sort of soothing energy, totally undemanding sort of energy... At the same time it wasn't just about being, because he also made sort of momentous decisions about what he was going to do. (West 1995: 288–9)

It is also possible within such a model as Wilber's to name the work that needs to be done by the client but not to feel one has to be their facilitator, or that one is even necessarily capable of facilitating the named work. For example, the upper and more overtly spiritual levels of Wilber's model require the helper to be in the role of spirit guide. Many therapists would reject such a role, but perhaps they are actually realizing this when they feel a need to refer on.

There is a bigger problem here with Wilber's model and that is around any common agreement about what the spiritual tasks are that are connected with the higher levels of his model. Or rather, he might seem clear on these matters but are the people who offer spiritual guidance actually in agreement with him? For example, is spiritual direction within a Christian context actually very similar to that within Islam, Sikhism, Hinduism and Native American spirituality, as Wilber (1980) suggests? Wilber does seem to believe that all roads properly engineered lead to Rome. I am not sure. How we talk about and envisage these matters – and remember, we are talking about territory that is beyond words, beyond ordinary states of consciousness – must interrelate with where we arrive.

This leads back to notions of what the good life is and where therapy and spirituality or religion can take us to. The bottom line, I feel, is *knowing* what is true by the process of sitting with what you believe it to be in a process of meditation, contemplation and prayer. You might call this discernment, contact with your soul or Higher Self or with the God/dess within. This process is not always simple and true, and we need help and support with it, but some of our best decisions seem to have come by this route.

## Therapists exploring their spirituality

John Rowan (1993, 2005) argues that therapists should develop themselves spiritually via spiritual practices. He maintains that this would help equip them for working with spiritual issues in their clients' lives. I am tempted to agree, since I find that the benefits of regular yoga, retreat going, spiritual friendships and attending religious services profoundly affect me on many levels of my being. However, I do not think that it can, or should, be insisted on.

There is a counter argument that can be put forward akin to the arguments around personal therapy and personal development groups in therapy training courses. On many training programmes these are course requirements for personal development groups and individual therapy for trainees, despite the lack of convincing research evidence as to their efficacy. However, if therapy, or indeed any individual therapist, is serious about competence with regard to spirituality, then a case can be made for therapists' personal exposure to a variety of spiritual teaching and practices. This is not the same as the therapist needing to be on their own spiritual journey, which is the implication of John Rowan's view.

In the current absence of clarity and somewhat limited professional guidance on this matter (see Harborne 2008 for recent BACP guidelines), we could usefully follow Jonathan Wyatt's conclusion to his research into responding to clients' expression of religious faith:

> When I am clear about my faith and comfortable with it – whatever it looks like – then that is good. I know what I think. I know what I believe and I know what I do not believe. I know what, my values are, or I know that I don't know. Then, when I am like that, I can listen to clients. (2002: 182)

What I especially like about this suggestion is that it allows the practitioner to change their stance over time.

So I would insist that we need, at the very least, to have explored what religious faith means to us. In the training context this might not prove to be easy as Chris Jenkins found out in his research (see his earlier chapter):

> The message there [on the Personal Development Group] was that a lot of counsellors had anti-religious feelings... So I suppose there too there is a message being given that it is not okay to talk about your spirituality... certainly never in my [counsellor] training have we talked about religion. (Jenkins 2006)

In my own experience of facilitating personal development groups for counsellors in training, I have been shocked at times by the strength of the anti -religious views that have been expressed.

What I find curious, when invited to talk to trainee counsellors and psychotherapists, is how personally interested they often are in their own spirituality, and that a number also show some interest and engagement in religion. I suspect that younger trainees might differ from their trainers on this matter. I reckon that many trainers of my generation – post Second World War 1950s – had difficult childhood experiences around Christianity in particular. The other point to reflect on is how much is expected to be covered in therapists' training, leading to a challenge around how to fit everything in.

There is a final and crucial point to be made with regard to training: being white, heterosexual, middle class, educated and female is the default position on therapists' training courses in Britain. So issues of culture and diversity when addressed are usually about exploring sexual and ethnic minorities and sometimes non-Christian religions. These topics for many are 'Other' and hence it is possible for many people to train without reflecting publicly and deeply on their own experience of spirituality and religion; or, if so, only in contrast to the Other.

With regard to practitioners rather than trainees, the situation might well be different. One of the surprises from Peter Gubi's research into prayer and counselling (see Chapter 4) was how many counsellors were praying for their clients. Peter surveyed just over half of BACP-accredited practitioners and 43 per cent (247) replied. Of his respondents, 59 per cent had used prayer covertly with clients and 12 per cent had used it overtly with Christian clients. Only 24 per cent of those who used prayer had ever discussed it in supervision. Given that many counsellors are spiritually or religiously minded, maybe this use of prayer should not be surprising. Of course, since it is does not fit with the largely secular models of therapy, perhaps it is also not a surprise to find that such use of prayer is often not taken to supervision.

Going back to Peter's figures, it works out that about one in eight of BACP-accredited practitioners at the time of his survey were using prayer covertly. Clearly this use of prayer makes sense to the counsellor, but its low rate of discussion in supervision leaves me feeling somewhat uneasy and also that our models of training of therapists do not sufficiently address the way trainees are likely actually to practise around this key topic.

There is a phrase from Alexander Pope (1734) that I probably overuse: 'Fools rush in where angels fear to tread.' Maybe in wanting to cast light on the use of spiritual interventions by therapists I am upsetting a comfortable *modus vivendi* or tolerance of practice. However, since I have found in my research into spirituality and healing (West 1995, 1998b) many examples of problems in supervision, I remain concerned that practice is this area is not always benefiting from appropriate training, supervision and informed discussion. It seems to be that clients are being short-changed and that the taboo that remains in some circles around discussing these matters needs to be broken.

## Guidelines for training and practice of therapists around spirituality and healing

I offer here some of the basic principles that can, and should, underpin guidelines to both training and practice. Many of these principles apply to innovative interventions of any kind, but some comments are especially addressed to those involving spirituality and healing.

In order best to protect both client and therapist, all practice needs to be done from a clear ethical perspective laid down by the relevant professional body, and this includes any innovations in practice. Any such innovative intervention used needs to be carefully explored in supervision, preferably before its use. If current supervision arrangements cannot meet this need, then extra supervision should immediately be sought elsewhere.

Innovative interventions should be carefully consented to by the client involved and the client should not be made to feel pressurized to accept such an intervention. The therapist needs to develop a rationale for their use of any innovative interventions and these should be based on potential client benefit and also open to, and defendable in, debate and challenge.

It is important that therapists in training get to hear of innovative interventions, not to encourage them to use them immediately, but to offer a perspective of mature practice that is inclusive of healing and spirituality. It is also important that trainees, practitioners, supervisors and trainers are aware of the rationale for these practices, enabling appropriate decision making to occur within therapeutic practice.

We need more research into all forms of innovative practice, especially that involving spirituality and healing. Further surveys into the use of such interventions would enable research to be targeted at the most promising and/or the most commonly used interventions.

## Finally

I hear a small voice saying, 'Why bother? Who knows if innovative practice of a spiritual or healing kind advocated in this book will benefit clients more than existing practice? Indeed, why take the risk?' Innovations in therapeutic practice and other aspects of our lives come about because people feel moved to make them. Without innovation, practice could get dull and lifeless and the vital connection between therapist and client that is the key outcome variable could wither away. Who knows whether a particular innovation might not become the next big breakthrough in therapeutic practice? Even if it does not, innovation at the very least keeps therapists on their toes, engaged with their clients. This is surely the place from which they need to practise.

There is a further and final point to be made. My best work with clients, indeed with my students, comes from when I am most present and most engaged with them. It is my experience that the same is true for them. If a vital part of human experience is denied its rightful place in these human encounters, we are all diminished. This is not just an argument for being spiritually present to one another, it covers all that we are or could be. And if we are ever going to respond sufficiently to the challenges of climate change, of making the Earth a fit and fruitful place for all of its people and creatures, then we have to be more fully present to one another. As Gandhi said: 'If you don't find God in the next person you meet you won't find him anywhere.'

## Discussion points

1. Make your own list of the most challenging interventions discussed in this book.
2. Consider which of these you would feel comfortable to use/may already being using and which not.
3. In what circumstances, if any, would you consider using interventions from your 'not' list above?
4. What is your personal experience and understanding of spirituality? Notice the words you are drawn to use to describe it and the range of feelings involved.

# Bibliography

Albanese, C. L. (2007) *A Republic of Mind and Spirit: A Cultural History of American Metaphysical Religion*, New Haven, CT: Yale University Press.

Alexander, F. (1961) *The Scope of Psychoanalysis*, New York: Basic Books.

Alexander, F. and French, T. M. (1946) *Psychoanalytic Therapy: Principles and Application*, New York: Ronald Press.

Alison, J. (2003) *On Being Liked*, London: Darton Longman and Todd.

Al-Krenawi, A. (1999) 'An overview of rituals in Western therapies and intervention: Argument for their use in cross-cultural therapy', *International Journal for the Advancement of Counselling* 21: 3–17.

Al-Krenawi, A. and Graham, J. R. (1999) Gender and biomedical/traditional mental health utilization among the Bedouin-Arabs of the Negev, *Culture, Medicine, and Psychiatry* 23: 219–43.

Allman, L. S., De Las Rocha, O., Elkins, D. N. and Weathers, R. S. (1992) 'Psychotherapists' attitudes towards clients reporting mystical experiences', *Psychotherapy* 29(4): 654–9.

Amritaswarupananda, Swami (1994) *Ammachi: The Life of the Holy Mother Amritanandamayi*, San Ramon, CA: Mata Amritanandamayi Center.

Ankrah, L. (2002) 'Spiritual emergency and counselling: An exploratory study', *Counselling and Psychotherapy Research* 2(1): 55–60.

APA (1993) 'Guidelines for providers of psychological services to ethnic, linguistic and culturally diverse populations', *American Psychologist* 48: 45–8.

APA (2003) *Ethical Principles of Psychologists and Code of Conduct*, Washington DC: American Psychological Association.

Arnold, W. V. (1982) *Introduction to Pastoral Care*, Philadelphia, PA: Westminster Press.

Asay, T. and Lambert, M. (2000) 'The empirical case for the common factors in therapy: Quantitative findings', in M. Hubble, B. Duncan and S. Miller (eds) *The Heart and Soul of Change: What Works in Therapy*, Washington, DC: American Psychological Association, 33–56.

Asuni, T. (1986) 'African and Western psychiatry: A comparison', in J. L. Cox (ed.) *Transcultural Psychiatry*, London: Croom Helm.

Ataudo, E. S. (1985) 'Traditional medicine and biopsychosocial fulfillment in African health', *Social Science and Medicine* 21: 1345–7.

Aveni, A. (2002) *Behind the Crystal Ball: Magid, Science, and the Occult from Antiquity Through the New Age*, revd edn, Boulder, CO: University Press of Colorado.

BACP (2002) *Ethical Framework for Good Practice in Counselling and Psychotherapy*, Rugby: British Association for Counselling and Psychotherapy.

Barnes, H. (1997) *A Life for the Spirit: Rudolf Steiner in the Crosscurrents of Our Time* (Vista Series, V.1), Hudson, NY: Anthroposophic Press.

Bart, M. (1998) 'Spirituality in counselling finding believers', *Counseling Today* 6: 1, Dec.

Beals, J., Novins, D. K., Spicer, P., Whitesell, N. R., Mitchell, C. M. et al. (2006) 'Help seeking for substance use problems in two American Indian reservation populations', *Psychiatric Services* 57(4): 512–20.

Bell, D. (2002) *Ethical Ambition: Living a Life of Meaning and Worth*, London: Bloomsbury.

Benor, D. J. and Mohr, M. (1986) 'The overlap of psychic readings with psychotherapy', *Psi Research* March/June: 56–78.

Berenstein, M. (1988) *Sai Baba for Beginners*, New York: Writers and Readers Publishing.

Berg, A. (2003) 'Ancestor reverence and mental health in South Africa', *Transcultural Psychiatry* 40(2): 194–207.

Berne, E. (1968) *Games People Play*, Harmondsworth: Penguin.

Bhugra, D. and Bhui, K. (1998) 'Psychotherapy for ethnic minorities: Issues, context and practice', *British Journal of Psychotherapy*, 14(3): 310–26.

Boadella, D. (1987) *Lifestreams: An Introduction to Biosynthesis*, London: Routledge & Kegan Paul.

Bochner, A. P. and Ellis, C. (2003) 'An introduction to the arts and narrative research: Art as inquiry', *Qualitative Inquiry* 9: 506.

Bojuwoye, O. (2005) 'Traditional healing practices in South Africa: Ancestral spirits, ritual ceremonies, and holistic healing', in R. Moodley & W. West (eds) *Integrating Traditional Healing Practices into Counseling and Psychotherapy*, Thousand Oaks, CA: Sage, 196–209.

Bond, T. (2004) 'Ethical guidelines for researching counselling and psychotherapy', *Counselling and Psychotherapy Research* 4(2): 10–19.

Braud, W. and Anderson, R. (1998) *Transpersonal Research Methods for the Social Sciences: Honoring Human Experience*, Thousand Oaks, CA: Sage.

Brennan, B. A. (1988) *Hands of Light: A Guide to Healing through the Energy Field*, New York: Bantam Books.

Buber, M. (1970) *I and Thou*, Edinburgh: T and T Clark.

Buhrmann, M. V. (1986) *Living in Two Worlds: Communication between a White Healer and her Black Counterpart*, Chicago, IL: Chiron.

Bullis, R. K. (2001) *Sacred Calling, Secular Accountability: Law and Ethics in Complementary and Spiritual Counselling*, Philadelphia, PA: Brunner-Routledge.

Bunyan, J. (1988[1678]) *The Pilgrim's Progress*, London: Marshall Cavendish Partworks.

Burns, D. D. and Nolen-Hoeksema, S. (1992) 'Therapeutic empathy and recovery from depression in cognitive-behavioral therapy: A structural equation model', *Journal of Consulting and Clinical Psychology* 60: 441–9.

Cameron, R. (2004) 'Shaking the spirit: Subtle energy awareness in supervision, in K. Tudor and M. Worrall (eds) *In Freedom to Practise*, Ross-on-Wye: PCCS.

Campbell, A. (1985) *Paid to Care?* London: SPCK.

Canadian Psychological Association (2001) *Canadian Code of Ethics for Psychologists*, Ontario: Canadian Psychological Association.

Canales, M. K. (2004) 'Taking care of self: Health care decision making of American Indian women', *Health Care for Women International* 25: 411–35.

Canda, E. R. (1990) 'An holistic approach to prayer for social work practice', *Social Thought* 16: 3–13.

Cannon, W. B. (1915) *Pain, Hunger, Fear and Rage,* New York: D. Appleton and Company.

Cannon, W. B. (1939) *The Wisdom of the Body,* 2nd edn, New York: W.W. Norton.

Carpenter, J. C. (1988) 'Parapsychology and the psychotherapy session: Their phenomenological confluence', *Journal of Parapsychology* 52: 214–24.

Carroll, R. (2003–2004) *Training Seminar: Embodiment and Emotion: A New Relationship between Neuroscience and Psychotherapy,* London: Confer.

Carter, R. (1995) *The Influence of Race and Racial Identity in Psychotherapy: Towards a Racially Inclusive Model,* New York: John Wiley & Sons.

Chang, D. F., Tong, H., Shi, Q. and Zeng, Q. (2005) 'Letting a hundred flowers bloom: Counseling and psychotherapy in the People's Republic of China', *Journal of Mental Health Counseling* 27(2): 104–16.

Chen, N. N. (2003) *Breathing Spaces: Qigong, Psychiatry, and Healing in China,* New York: Columbia University Press.

Chireau, P. Y. (2003) *Black Magic: Religion and the African American Conjuring Tradition,* Berkeley, CA: University of California Press.

Chisti, Sheikh H. M. (1991) *The Book of Sufi Healing,* Rochester, VT: Inner Traditions International.

Chopra, D. (1995) *Journey to the Boundless: Exploring the Intimate Connection between our Mind, Body and Spirit.* Tape 1. Chicago, IL: Nightingale Conant.

Christodoulidi, F. (2006) 'Spirituality and Culture in Counselling and Psychotherapy: Practitioners' Perspectives', MSc thesis, University of Manchester.

Clarkson, P. (1995) *The Therapeutic Relationship,* London: Whurr.

Clarkson, P. (1998) 'Beyond schoolism', *Changes* 16(1): 1–11.

Clarkson, P. (2002) *The Transpersonal Relationship in Counselling and Psychotherapy,* London: Whurr.

Clebsch, W. A. and Jaekle, C. R. (1975) *Pastoral Care in Historical Perspective,* New York: Harper.

Clements, J., Ettling, D., Jenett, D. and Shields, L. (1998) 'Organic research: Feminine spirituality meets transpersonal research' in W. Braud and R. Anderson (eds) *Transpersonal Research Methods for the Social Sciences: Honoring Human Experience,* London: Sage.

Comas-Diaz, L. (2006) 'Latino healing: The integration of ethnic psychology into psychotherapy', *Psychotherapy: Theory, Research, Practice, Training,* Special Issue: Culture, Race, and Ethnicity in Psychotherapy, 43(4): 436–53.

Corey, G. (1996) *Theory and Practice of Counselling and Psychotherapy,* 5th edn, Pacific Grove, CA: Brooks/Cole.

Cortright, B. (1997) *Psychotherapy and Spirit: Theory and Practice in Transpersonal Psychotherapy,* Albany, NY: State University of New York Press.

Craig, E. (1978) 'The heart of the teacher: A heuristic study of the inner world of teaching', doctoral dissertation, Boston University, *Dissertation Abstracts International,* 38.

Criswell, E. and Herzog, L. (1977) 'Psychic counselling', *Psychic* 7(6): 42–6.

Crofoot Graham, T. L. (2002) 'Using reasons for living to connect to American Indian healing traditions', *Journal of Sociology and Social Welfare* 29(1): 55–75.

D'Andrea, M., Daniels, J. and Beck, R. (1991) 'Evaluating the impact of multicultural counsellor training', *Journal of Counselling and Development* 70: 143–50.

D'Ardenne, P. and Mahtani, A. (1989) *Transcultural Counselling in Action*, London: Sage.

Darou, W. G. (1987) 'Counselling and the northern native', *Canadian Journal of Counselling* 21: 33–41.

Davie, G. (1994) *Religion in Britain since 1945*, Oxford: Blackwell.

Davies, B., Browne, J., Gannon, S., Honan, E., Laws, C., Muller-Rockstroh, B. and Bendix, E. (2004) 'The ambivalent practice of reflexivity', *Qualitative Inquiry* 10: 360–68.

Dawkins, R. (2007) *The God Delusion*, London: Black Swan.

Deeks, D. (1987) *Pastoral Theology: An Inquiry*, London: Epworth Press.

Dein, S. and Sembhi, S. (2001) 'The use of traditional healing in South Asian psychiatric patients in the UK: Interactions between professional and folk psychiatries', *Transcultural Psychiatry* 38(2): 243–57.

Denzin, N. K. and Lincoln, Y. S. (eds) (2005) *Handbook of Qualitative Research*, 3rd edn, London: Sage.

de Vaus, D. (2002) *Surveys in Social Research*, 5th edn, London: Routledge.

Dobbins, R. D. (2000) 'Psychotherapy with Pentecostal protestants', in P. S. Richards and A. E. Bergin (eds) *Handbook of Psychotherapy and Religious Diversity*, Washington DC: American Psychological Association.

Donald, D. R. and Hlongwane, M. M. (1989) 'Issues in the integration of traditional Africa healing and Western counseling in school psychological practice', *School Psychology International* 10: 243–9.

Duan, C. and Hill, C. E. (1996) 'Theoretical confusions in the construct of empathy: A review of the literature', *Journal of Counseling Psychology* 43: 261–74.

Duerr, H. P. (1985) *Dreamtime: Concerning the Boundary Between Wilderness and Civilization*, trans. F. Goodman, New York: Basil Blackwell.

Duran, E. (1990) *Transforming the Soul Wound*, Delhi: Arya Offset Press.

Eden, D. (1998) *Energy Medicine*, New York: Penguin Putnam.

Edge, D. (2006) 'Perinatal depression: Its absence among Black Caribbean women', *British Journal of Midwifery* 14(11): 646–52.

Edge, D. and Rogers, A. (2005) 'Dealing with it: Black Caribbean women's response to adversity and psychological distress associated with pregnancy, childbirth, and early motherhood', *Social Science and Medicine* 61: 15–25.

Edwards, S. D. (1986) 'Traditional and modern medicine in South Africa: A research study', *Social Science and Medicine* 22(11): 1273–6.

Eisenbud, J. (1969) 'Chronologically extraordinary psi correspondences in the psychoanalytic setting', *Psychoanalytic Review* 56: 9.

Eisenbud, J. (1970) *Psi and Psychoanalysis*, New York: Rune & Stratton.

Eleftheriadou, Z. (2003) 'Cross-cultural psychology', in R. Woolfe, W. Dryden and S. Strawbridge (eds) *Handbook of Counselling Psychology*, London: Sage.

Eliade, M. (1964) *Shamanism*, New York: Princeton University Press.

Elkins, D. N., Hedstorm, J. L., Hughes, L. L., Leaf, J. A. and Saunders, C. (1988) 'Toward a humanistic-phenomenological spirituality', *Journal of Humanistic Psychology* 28(4): 5–18.

Etherington, K. (2004) *Becoming a Reflexive Researcher*, London: Jessica Kingsley.

Farsimadan, F., Draghi-Lorenz, R. and Ellis, J. (2007) 'Process and outcome of therapy in ethnically similar and dissimilar therapeutic dyads', *Psychotherapy Research* 17(5): 567–75.

Feltham, C. (1995) *What Is Counselling?* London: Sage.

Ferrer, J. N. (2002) *Revisioning Transpersonal Theory*, Albany, NY: State University of New York Press.

Field, N. (1990) 'Healing, exorcism and object relations theory', *British Journal of Psychotherapy* 6: 274–84.

Fontana, D. (2005) *Is There an Afterlife?* Oakland, CA: O Books.

Foskett, J. and Lynch, G. (2001) 'Pastoral counselling in Britain: An introduction', *British Journal of Guidance and Counselling* 29(4): 373–9.

Frank, J. D. (1974) 'Psychotherapy: The restoration of morale', *American Journal of Psychiatry* 131: 272–4.

Frank, J. and Frank, J. (1993*) Persuasion and Healing: A Comparative Study of Psychotherapy*, Baltimore, MD: Johns Hopkins University Press.

Freud, S. (1905) *On Psychotherapy*, Standard edition, London: Hogarth Press.

Freud, S. (1932) *The Dissection of the Psychical Personality*, Standard edition, London: Hogarth Press.

Freud, S. (1961) *The Future of an Illusion*, New York: Norton.

Fukuyama, M. A. (1990) 'Taking a universal approach to multicultural counselling', *Counsellor Education and Supervision* 30: 6–17.

Fukuyama, M. A. and Sevig, T. D. (1997) 'Multicultural and spiritual issues in counselling: A new course', *Counselor Education and Supervision* 36: 233–44.

Fukuyama, M. A. and Sevig, T. D. (1999) *Integrating Spirituality in Multicultural Counseling*, London: Sage.

Ganje-Fling, M. A. and McCarthy, P. (1996) 'Impact of childhood sexual abuse on client spiritual development: Counseling implications', *Journal of Counseling and Development* 74: 253–8.

Garrett, M. T. and Carroll, J. J. (2000) 'Mending the broken circle: Treatment of substance dependence among Native Americans', *Journal of Counseling and Development* 78(4): 379–88.

Garzon, F. L. (2005) 'Inner healing prayer in "spirit-filled" Christianity', in R. Moodley and W. West (eds) *Integrating Traditional Healing Practices into Counseling and Psychotherapy*, Thousand Oaks, CA: Sage, 148–58.

Geller, S. and Greenberg, L. (2002) 'Therapeutic presence: Therapists' experience of presence in the psychotherapy encounter', *Person-Centred and Experiential Therapies* 1: 71–86.

Gendlin, E. T. (1973) 'Experiential phenomenology,' In M. Natanson (ed.) *Phenomenology and the Social Sciences*, Evanston, IL: Northwestern University Press.

Gilbert, P. (ed.) (2005) *Compassion: Conceptualisations, Research and Use in Psychotherapy*, New York: Routledge.

Gilbert, P. and Irons, C. (2005) 'Focused therapies and compassionate mind training for shame and self-attacking', in P. Gilbert (ed.) *Compassion: Conceptualisations, Research and Use in Psychotherapy*, New York: Routledge, 263–325.

Glaser, B. and Strauss, A. (1967) *The Discovery of Grounded Theory*, Chicago: Aldine.

Gomez, B. (2007) 'Psychotherapy in Argentina: A clinical case from an integrative perspective', *Journal of Clinical Psychology: In session* 63(8): 713–23.

Gonzalez Chevez, L. (2005) 'Latin American healers and healing: Healing as a redefinition process', in R. Moodley and W. West (eds) *Integrating Traditional Healing Practices into Counseling and Psychotherapy*, Thousand Oaks, CA: Sage, 196–209.

Good, B. J. and Good, M.-J. D. (1982) 'Towards a meaning-centred analysis of popular illness categories: 'Fright-illness' and 'heat distress' in Iran', in A. J. Marsella and G. M. White (eds) *Cultural Conceptions of Mental Health and Therapy*, Dordrecht: Reidel.

Grabosky, T. K. (2005) 'The encounter with self through the process of cross-cultural transition: The perspective of Japanese women who study in higher education institutions in the United States', *Dissertation Abstracts International Section A: Humanities and Social Sciences*, Vol 65(9-A): 3288.

Graham, E. (1996) *Transforming Practice*, London: Mowbray.

Graham, E. (2002) *Transforming Practice*, Oregon: Wipf and Stock.

Greeley, A. (1975) 'Are We a Nation of Mystics?' *New York Times Magazine*, January 26.

Grim, J. A. (1983) *The Shaman: Patterns of Religious Healing among the Ojibwa Indians*, Norman, OK: University of Oklahoma Press.

Grof, C. and Grof, S. (1989) *Spiritual Emergency: When Personal Transformation Becomes a Crisis*, Los Angeles, CA: Tarcher.

Grof, S. (1972) 'Varieties of transpersonal experiences and observations from LSD psychotherapy', *Journal of Transpersonal Psychology* 4(1): 45–80.

Grumet, M. R. (1991) 'The politics of personal knowledge', in C. Witherell and N. Noddings (eds) *Stories Lives Tell: Narrative and Dialogue in Education*, New York: Teachers College Press, 66–77.

Gubi, P. M. (1999) 'Prayer and psychotherapy: An exploration of the therapeutic nature of Christian prayer and its possible use with Christian clients in secular psychotherapy', Unpublished MTheol dissertation, University College Chester (University of Liverpool).

Gubi, P. M. (2001) 'An exploration of the use of prayer in mainstream counselling', *British Journal of Guidance and Counselling* 29(4): 425–34.

Gubi, P. M. (2002) 'Practice behind closed doors: Challenging the taboo of prayer in mainstream counselling culture', *Journal of Critical Psychology, Counselling and Psychotherapy* 2(2): 97–104.

Gubi, P. M. (2003) 'Integrating prayer and counselling: An enquiry into mainstream counsellors whose work includes prayer', Unpublished PhD thesis, University of Manchester.

Gubi, P. M. (2004) 'Surveying the extent of, and attitudes towards, the use of prayer as a spiritual intervention among British mainstream counsellors', *British Journal of Guidance and Counselling* 32(4): 461–76.

Gubi, P. M. (2007) 'Exploring the supervision experience of some mainstream counsellors who integrate prayer in counselling', *Counselling and Psychotherapy Research*, 7(2): 114–21.

Gubi, P. M. (2008) *Prayer in Counselling and Psychotherapy: Exploring a Hidden Meaningful Dimension*, London: Jessica Kingsley.

Gurley, D., Novins, D. K., Jones, M. C., Beals, J., Shore, J. H. and Manson, S. M. (2001) 'Comparative use of biomedical services and traditional healing options by American Indian veterans', *Psychiatric Services* 52(1): 68–74.

Halmos, P. (1965) *The Faith of the Counsellors*, London: Constable.

Hankey, A. (2005) 'The scientific value of Ayurveda', *Journal of Alternative and Complementary Medicine* 11(2): 221–5.

Hanley, T. (2008) The therapeutic alliance in online counselling, PhD thesis, School of Education, University of Manchester.

Harborne, L. (2008) *Working with Issues of Spirituality, Faith or Religion*, BACP Information Sheet G13, Lutterworth: BACP.

Harding, M. E. (1963) *Psychic Energy: Its Source and Its Transformation*, New York: Pantheon Books.

Harris, S. (2005) *The End of Faith: Religion, Terror, and the Future of Reason*, New York: W.W. Norton.

Hastings, A. (1983) 'A counselling approach to parapsychological experience', *Journal of Transpersonal Psychology* 15: 143–67.

Hay, D. (1982) *Exploring Inner Space: Scientists and Religious Experience*, Harmondsworth: Penguin.

Hay, D. and Hunt, K. (2000) *Understanding the Spirituality of People Who Don't Go to Church*, Nottingham: Centre for the Study of Human Relations, Nottingham University.

Hay, D. and Morisy, A. (1978) 'Reports of ecstatic, paranormal, or religious experiences in Great Britain and the United States – a comparison of trends', *Journal for the Scientific Study of Religion*, 17(3): 255–68.

Heber, A. S., Fleisher, W. P., Ross, C. A. and Stanwick, R. S. (1989) 'Dissociation in alternative healers and traditional therapists: A comparative study', *American Journal of Psychotherapy* 43: 562–74.

Hegel, G. (1974) *Hegel: The Essential Writings*, ed. F. Weiss, New York: Harper Torchbooks.

Helminiak, D. A. (1982) 'How is meditation prayer?' *Reviews for Religion* 41(5): 774–82.

Hentschel, U. (2005) 'Therapeutic alliance: The best synthesizer of social influences on the therapeutic situation? On links to other constructs, determinants of its effectiveness, and its role for research in psychotherapy in general', *Psychotherapy Research* 15(1/2): 9–24.

Heron, J. (1987) *Confessions of a Janus Brain*, London: Endymion Press.

Heron, J. (1992) *Feeling and Personhood*, London: Sage.

Heron, J. (1998) *Sacred Science, Person-Centred Inquiry into the Spiritual and Subtle*, Ross-on-Wye: PCCS Books.

Heron, J. (2003) *Confessions of a Janus-brain*, revd edn, e-book at South Pacific Centre for Human Inquiry, http://homepages.ihug.co.nz/-jnheron/expsrcon.htm, retrieved January 29, 2003.

Hikmet, K. (1979) 'The most beautiful sea', in M. Kaunein (ed.) *Punainen Omena* [The Red Apple], Helsinki: Tammi.

Hill, C. E., Knox, S., Thompson, B. J., Williams, E. N., Hess, S. and Ladany, N. (2005) 'Consensual qualitative research: An update', *Journal of Counseling Psychology* 52: 196–205.

Hill, C. E., Thompson, B. J. and Williams, E. N. (1997) 'A guide to conducting consensual qualitative research', *The Counseling Psychologist* 25: 517–72.

Hilton, B. A., Grewal, S., Popatia, N., Bottorff, J. L., Johnson, J. L. et al. (2001) 'The Desi ways: Traditional health practices of South Asian women in Canada', *Health Care for Women International* 22: 553–67.

Hinksman, B. (1999) 'Tranference and countertransference in pastoral counselling', in G. Lynch (ed.) *Clinical Counselling in Pastoral Settings*, London: Routledge.

Hitchens, C. (2007) *God is Not Great: How Religion Poisons Everything*, New York: Twelve.

Hohmann, A. A., Richeport, M., Marriott, B. M., Canino, G. J., Rubio-Stipec, M. & Bird, H. (1990) 'Spiritism in Puerto Rico: Results of an Island-wide community study', *British Journal of Psychiatry* 156: 328–35.

Hollanders, H. (2000a) 'Eclecticism/integration: Historical developments', in S. Palmer and R. Wolfe (eds) *Integrative and Eclectic Counselling and Psychotherapy*, London: Sage.

Hollanders, H. (2000b) 'Eclecticism/integration: Some key issues and research', in S. Palmer and R. Wolfe (eds) *Integrative and Eclectic Counselling and Psychotherapy*, London: Sage.

Hollanders, H. and McLeod, J. (1997) 'Theoretical orientation and reported practice: A survey of eclecticism among counsellors in Britain', *British Journal of Guidance and Counselling* 27(3): 405–14.

Holmes, J. (1985) 'The language of psychotherapy: Metaphor, ambiguity, wholeness', *British Journal of Psychotherapy* 1(4): 240–54.

Horvath, A. (2005) 'The therapeutic relationship, research and theory', *Psychotherapy Research* 15(1/2): 3–8.

Hunt, V. (1996) *Infinite Mind: Science of the Human Vibrations of Consciousness*, Malibu, CA: Malibu Publishing.

Hunter, L. M., Logan, J., Goulet, J.-G. and Barton, S. (2006) 'Aboriginal healing: Regaining balance and culture', *Journal of Transcultural Nursing* 17(1): 13–22.

Hurdle, D. E. (2002) 'Native Hawaiian traditional healing: Culturally based interventions for social work practice', *Social Work* 47(2): 183–92.

Ineichen, B. (1990) 'The mental health of Asians in Britain: Little disease or underreporting?' *British Medical Journal* 300: 1669–70.

Irwin, R. L. and De Cosson, A. (2004) *A/R/T/ography: Rendering Self through Arts-Based Living Inquiry*, Vancouver: Pacific Educational Press.

Janesick, V.J. (2001) 'Intuition and creativity: A pas de deux for qualitative researchers', *Qualitative Inquiry* 7: 531.

Jarmey, C. and Mojay, G. (1991) *Shiatsu: The Complete Guide*, London: Thorsons.

Jayakar, P. (1985) *Krishnamurti: A Biography*, New York: Harper & Row.

Jenkins, C. A. (2006) 'A Voice Denied, Clients' Experience of the Exclusion of Spirituality in Counselling and Psychotherapy', PhD Thesis, University of Manchester.

Jenkins, C. A. and West W. (2006) 'Honouring spirituality in therapy: A Dialogue'. in J. Moore and C. Purton (eds) *Spirituality and Counselling, Experiential and Theoretical Perspectives*, Ross-on-Wye: PCCS Books.

Johnson, D. H. and Grand, I. (eds) (1998) *The Body in Psychotherapy, Inquiries in Somatic Psychology*, Berkeley, CA: North Atlantic Books.

Jorge, A. (1995) 'Mesa blanca: A Puerto Rican healing tradition', in L. L. Adler and B. R. Mukherji (eds) *Spirit versus Scalpel: Traditional Healing and Modern Psychotherapy*, Westport, CT: Bergin & Garvey, 109–20.

Jung, C. G. (1916) *Psychology of the Unconscious: A Study of the Transformations and Symbolisms of the Libido*, New York: Moffat, Yard & Co.

Jung, C. G. (1917) 'On the Psychology of the Unconscious', *Collected Works of C. G. Jung, Vol. 7*. New York: Princeton University Press.

Jung, C. G. (1948) 'On Psychic Energy', *Collected Works of C.G. Jung, Vol. 8*, New York: Princeton University Press.

Jung, C. G. (1953) *Psychology and Alchemy*, London: Routledge & Kegan Paul.

Jung, C. G. (1960) *Jung on the Nature of the Psyche*, London: Routledge.

Jung, C. G. (ed.) (1964) *Man and His Symbols,* London: Picador.

Jung, C. G. (1967) *Memories, Dreams, Reflections,* London: Fontana.

Jung, C. G. (1973) 'Synchronicity: An Acausal Connecting Principle', *Collected Works of C. G. Jung, Vol. 8.* New York: Princeton University Press.

Jung, C. G. (1991) 'Psychology of the Unconscious: A Study of the Transformations and Symbolisms of the Libido,' *Collected Works of C. G. Jung, Supp. Vol. B,* New York: Princeton University Press.

Juntunen, C. L. and Morin, P. M. (2004) 'Treatment issues for Native Americans: An overview of individual, family, and group strategies', In D. R. Atkinson (ed.), *Counseling American Minorities,* New York: McGraw-Hill.

Kabat-Zinn, J. (1994) *Wherever You Go, There You Are: Mindfulness Meditation in Everyday Life,* NewYork: Hyperion.

Kahn, M. S. and Kelly, K. J. (2001) 'Cultural tensions in psychiatric nursing: Managing the interface between Western mental health care and Xhosa traditional healing in South Africa', *Transcultural Psychiatry* 38(1): 35–50.

Kakar, S. (1982) *Shamans, Mystics and Doctors,* Oxford: Oxford University Press.

Karasu, T. B. (1986) 'The specificity against nonspecificity dilemma: Towards identifying therapeutic change agents', *American Journal of Psychiatry* 143: 687–95.

Kareem, J. and Littlewood, R. (eds) (1992) *Intercultural Therapy: Themes, Interpretations and Practice,* Oxford: Blackwell.

Keleman, S. (1975) *Your Body Speaks Its Mind,* New York: Simon and Schuster.

Kellner, D. (1995) *Media Culture: Cultural Studies, Identity and Politics between the Modern and the Postmodern,* New York: Routledge.

Kenyon, G. (1994) 'Oman tarinan kertomisen merkityksesta. The Meaning of Telling One's Own Story', *Gerontologia* 8: 196–204.

Kessler, R. C., Davis, R. B., Foster, D. F., Van Rompay, M. I., Walters, E. E. et al. (2001) 'Long-term trends in the use of complementary and alternative medical therapies in the United States', *Annals of Internal Medicine* 135: 262–8.

Kheirabadi, M. (2005) *Sri Satya Sai Baba,* Series Spiritual Leaders and Thinkers, Philadelphia, PA: Chelsea House Publishers.

Kirmayer, L. J. (2003) 'Asklepian dreams: The ethos of the wounded – healer in the clinical encounter', *Transcultural Psychiatry* 40: 248–77.

Kirschenbaum, H. and Henderson, V. (eds) (1990) *The Carl Rogers Reader,* London: Constable.

Kleinman, A. (1980) *Patients and Healers in the Context of Culture,* Berkeley, CA: University of California Press.

Klimo, J. (1987) *Channelling,* Los Angeles, CA: Jeremy Tarcher.

Knox, S., Catlin, L., Casper, M. and Schlosser, L. Z. (2005) 'Addressing religion and spirituality in psychotherapy, client's perspectives', *Psychotherapy Research* 15(3): 287–303.

Kohut, H. (1977) *The Restoration of the Self,* New York: International Universities Press.

Kramer, W. M. (1993) 'Recent experiences with psi counselling in Holland', in L. Coly and J. McMahon (eds) *Psi and Clinical Practice,* New York: Parapsychology Foundation.

Kreimer, J. C. (1997) *Krishnamurti for Beginners,* New York: Writers and Readers Publishing.

Krueger, R. A. (1994) *Focus Groups: A Practical Guide for Applied Research*, 2nd edn, Thousand Oaks, CA: Sage.

Kumar, M., Bhugra, D. and Singh, J. (2005) 'South Asian (Indian) traditional healing: Ayurvedic, shamanic, and Sahaja therapy', in R. Moodley and W. West (eds) *Integrating Traditional Healing Practices into Counseling and Psychotherapy*, Thousand Oaks, CA: Sage, 196–209.

Kumaraswamy, N. (2007) 'Psychotherapy in Brunei Darussalam', *Journal of Clinical Psychology: In session* 62(8): 735–45.

Kurihara, T., Kato, M., Reverger, R. and Rai Tirta, I. G. (2006) 'Pathway to psychiatric care in Bali', *Psychiatry and Clinical Neurosciences* 60: 204–10.

Kurtz, R. (1990) *Body-Centred Psychotherapy: The Hakomi Method*, Mendocino, CA: Life Rhythm.

Kutz, I., Borysenko, J. Z. and Benson, H. (1985) 'Meditation and psychotherapy: A rationale for the integration of dynamic psychotherapy, the relaxation response and mindfulness meditation', *American Journal of Psychiatry* 142: 1–8.

Kvale, S. (1992) 'Postmodern psychology: A contradiction in terms?' in S. Kvale (ed.), *Psychology and Postmodernism*, London: Sage.

Lachman, G. (2007) *Rudolf Steiner: An Introduction to His Life and Work*, Edinburgh: Floris Books.

Ladany, N. (2004) 'Psychotherapy supervision: What lies beneath', *Psychotherapy Research* 14(1): 1–19.

Lago, C. and Thompson, J. (1996) *Race, Culture and Counselling*, Buckingham: Open University Press.

Lake, J. (2002) 'Qigong', in S. Shannon (ed.) *Handbook of Complementary and Alternative Therapies in Mental Health*, San Diego, CA: Academic Press, 183–207.

Lake, J. H. and Spiegel, D. (2007) *Complementary and Alternative Treatments in Mental Health Care*, Washington, DC: American Psychiatric Publishing.

Lama, Dalai (1999) *Ethics for a New Millennium*, New York: Riverhead Books.

Lama, Dalai (2001) *The Dalai Lama's Book of Love and Compassion*, Glasgow: Thorson.

Lambert, M. J. and Barley, D. E. (2002) 'Research summary on the therapeutic relationship and psychotherapy outcome', in J. C. Norcross (ed.) *Psychotherapy Relationships that Work: Therapist Contributions and Responsiveness to Patients*, New York: Oxford University Press, 17–32.

Lambert, M. J. and Bergin, A. E. (1994) 'The effectiveness of psychotherapy', in A. E. Bergin and S. L. Garfield (eds) *Handbook of Psychotherapy and Behaviour Change*, 5th edn, London: John Wiley & Sons.

Lange, M. A. (1983a) 'Prayer and psychotherapy: Beliefs and practice', Unpublished D.Psych thesis, La Mirada, CA: Rosemead School of Psychology.

Lange, M. A. (1983b) 'Prayer and psychotherapy: Beliefs and practice', *Journal of Pastoral Counseling* 2(3): 36–49.

Lannert, J. (1991) 'Resistance and countertransference issues with spiritual and religious clients', *Journal of Humanistic Psychology* 31(4): 68–76.

Laungani, P. (1999) 'Culture and identity: Implications for counselling', in S. Palmer and P. Laungani (eds) *Counselling in a Multicultural Society*, London: Sage, 35–70.

Laungani, P. (2005) 'Cross-cultural psychology: A handmaiden to mainstream Western psychology: a personal view', Keynote address to 1st International South Asia Regional Conference, Mumbai, India, December.

Laungani, P. (2007) *Understanding Cross-Cultural Psychology*, London: Sage.

Lee, C. C. and Armstrong, K. (1995) 'Indigenous models of mental health interventions: Lessons from traditional healers', in J. Ponterotto, J. M. Casas, L. A. Suzuki and C. M. Alexander (eds) *Handbook of Multicultural Counseling*, London: Sage, 441–56.

Lee, C. C., Oh, M. Y. and Mountcastle, A. R. (1992) 'Indigenous models of helping in non-western countries: Implications for multicultural counseling', *Journal of Multicultural Counseling and Development* 20: 3–10.

Liberman, K. (1997) 'Meaning reflexivity: Gendlin's contribution to ethnomethodology', in D. M. Levin (ed.) *Language Beyond Postmodernism: Saying and Thinking in Gendlin's Philosophy*, Evanston, IL: Northwestern University Press.

Linehan, M. (1992) *Cognitive Behavioral Treatment of Borderline Personality Disorder*, New York: Guilford.

Lipps, T. (1897) 'Der Begriff des Unbewussten', Third International Congress for Psychology, Munich, 4–7 August.

Little, M. (1986) *Transference, Neurosis and Transference Psychosis*, London: Free Association Press.

Littlewood, R. (1990) 'From categories to contexts: A decade of the "new cross-cultural psychiatry"', *British Journal of Psychiatry* 156: 308–27.

Locke, D. C. (1990) 'A not so provincial view of multicultural counselling', *Counsellor Education and Supervision* 30: 18–25.

Lorimer, D. and Drew, J. (eds) (1995) *Ways Through the Wall: Approach to Citizenship in an Interconnected World*, Lydney: First Stone Publishing.

Lowen, A. (1958) *Physical Dynamics of Character Structure*, New York: Grune & Stratton.

Lowen, A. (1990) *The Spirituality of the Body: Bioenergetics for Grace and Harmony*, New York: Macmillan.

Luhrmann, T. M. (1989) *Persuasions of the Witch's Craft: Ritual Magic in Contemporary England*, Cambridge, MA: Harvard University Press.

Luhrmann, T. M. (2000) *Of Two Minds: The Growing Disorder in American Psychiatry*, New York: Knopf.

Lukoff, D. (1985) 'The diagnosis of mystical experiences with psychotic features', *Journal of Transpersonal Psychology*, 12(2): 155–181.

Lutyens, M. (1975) *Krishnamurti: The Years of Awakening*, London: John Murray.

Macmin, L. and Foskett, J. (2004) 'Don't be afraid to tell', *Mental Health, Religion and Culture* 7(1): 23–40.

Magaletta, P. R. and Brawer, P. A. (1998) 'Prayer in psychotherapy: A model for its use, ethical considerations and guidelines for practice', *Journal of Psychology and Theology* 26(4): 322–30.

Maiello, S. (1999) 'Encounter with an African healer: Thinking about the possibilities and limits of cross-cultural psychotherapy', *Journal of Child Psychotherapy* 25(2): 217–38.

Main, R. (2007) *Revelations of Chance: Synchronicity as Spiritual Experience*, Albany, NY: State University of New York Press.

Markham A. N. (2005) '"Go ugly early"': Fragmented narrative and bricolage as interpretive method', *Qualitative Inquiry* 11: 813.

Marshall, R. (2005) 'Caribbean healers and healing: Awakening spiritual and cultural healing powers', in R. Moodley and W. West (eds) *Integrating Traditional*

*Healing Practices into Counseling and Psychotherapy*, Thousand Oaks, CA: Sage, 196–209.

McCabe, G. H. (2007) 'The healing path: A culture and community-derived indigenous therapy model', *Psychotherapy: Theory, Research, Practice, Training*, 44(2): 148–60.

McCormick, R. (1996) 'Culturally appropriate means and ends of counselling as described by the First Nations people of British Columbia', *International Journal for the Advancement of Counselling* 18: 163–72.

McCormick, R. (2000) 'Aboriginal traditions in the treatment of substance abuse', *Canadian Journal of Counselling*, Special Issue: Counselling First Nations people in Canada, 34(1): 25–32.

McDonald, D. (1999) 'Body language and spirituality', *Search – A Church of Ireland Journal*, Spring.

McLeod, J. (1997) *Narrative and Psychotherapy*, London: Sage.

McLeod, J. (1999) *Practitioner Research in Counselling*, London: Sage.

McLeod, J. (2001) 'Counselling as a social process', in P. Milner and S. Palmer (eds) *The BAC Reader, Vol 2*, London: Sage.

McMinn, M. R. (1996) *Psychology, Theology and Spirituality in Christian Counseling*, Wheaton, IL: Tyndale House Publishers.

Mearns, D. and Cooper, M. (2005) *Working at Relational Depth in Counselling and Psychotherapy*, London: Sage.

Medawar, P. (1984) *The Limits of Science*, Oxford: Oxford University Press.

Melbourne Academic Mindfulness Interest Group (2006) 'Mindfulness-based psychotherapies: A review of conceptual foundations, empirical evidence and practical considerations', *Australian and New Zealand Journal of Psychiatry* 40: 285–94.

Merry, T. (1995) *Invitation to Person Centred Psychology*, London, Whurr.

Mindell, A. (1984) *Dreambody: The Body's Role in Revealing the Self,* London: Routledge & Kegan Paul.

Mindell, A. (1990) *Working on Yourself Alone: Inner Dreambody Work*, Harmondsworth: Arkana.

Mindell, A. (1995) *Metaskills: The Spiritual Art of Therapy*, Las Vegas, NV: New Falcon Publications.

Mindell, A. (2000) *The Quantum Mind, Journey to the Edge of Psychology and Physics*, Portland, OR: Lao Tse Press.

Mindell, A. (2004) *Quantum Mind and Healing: How to Listen and Respond to Your Body's Symptoms*, Charlottesville, VA: Hampton Roads Publishing.

Mintz, E. E. (1983) *The Psychic Thread*, New York: Human Sciences.

Monteiro, N. M. (2004) 'The conceptualization of mental illness in Ethiopia: A survey of attitudes, beliefs and practices', *Dissertation Abstracts International: Section B: The Sciences and Engineering,* 65(2-B): 1034.

Moodley, R. (1998a) '"I say what I like": Frank talk(ing) in counselling and psychotherapy', *British Journal of Guidance and Counselling* 26(4): 495–508.

Moodley, R. (1998b) 'Cultural returns to the subject: Traditional healing in counselling and therapy', *Changes: International Journal of Psychology and Psychotherapy* 16(1): 45–56.

Moodley, R. (1999a) 'Challenges and transformation: Counselling in a multicultural context', *International Journal for the Advancement of Counselling* 21: 139–52.

Moodley. R. (1999b) 'Psychotherapy with ethnic minorities: A critical review', *Changes: International Journal of Psychology and Psychotherapy* 17: 109–25.

Moodley, R. (2000) 'Representation of subjective distress in black and ethnic minority patients: Constructing a research agenda', *Counselling Psychology Quarterly* 13(2): 159–74.

Moodley, R. (2005) 'Shamanic performances: Healing through magic and the supernatural', in R. Moodley and W. West (eds) *Integrating Traditional Healing Practices into Counseling and Psychotherapy*, Thousand Oaks, CA: Sage, 2–14.

Moodley, R. (2006) 'Cultural representations and interpretations of "subjective distress" in ethnic minority patients', in R. Moodley and S. Palmer (eds) *Race, Culture and Psychotherapy*, London: Routledge.

Moodley, R. (2007a) '(Re)placing multiculturalism in counselling and psycho-therapy', *British Journal of Guidance and Counselling* 35(1): 1–22.

Moodley, R. (2007b) 'The role of traditional healers in counselling, health pro-motion and education, at Ontario Institute for the Studies in Education at the University of Toronto'. Centre for Diversity in Counselling and Psychotherapy, http://cdcp.oise.utoronto.ca.

Moodley, R. and Palmer, S. (2006) *Race, Culture and Psychotherapy*, London: Routledge.

Moodley, R. and West, W. (2005) *Integrating Traditional Healing Practices into Counseling and Psychotherapy*, Thousand Oaks, CA: Sage.

Moodley, R., Rai, A. and Alladin, W. (Eds.) (2010) *Bridges East–West Psychology and Counselling: Exploring the Work of Pittu Languani*, New Delhi: Sage.

Morse, J. M., Young, D. E. and Swartz, L. (1991) 'Cree Indian healing practices and Western health care: A comparative analysis', *Social Science and Medicine* 32(12): 1361–6.

Moulton, J. (2007) 'Examining the impact of wide-scale structural change of a Church movement on its leadership', Master's dissertation, School of Education, University of Manchester.

Moustakas, C. (1990) *Heuristic Research, Design, Methodology, and Applications*, London: Sage.

Moustakas, C. (1994) *Phenomenological Research Methods*, London: Sage.

Mullen, C. A. (2003) 'A self-fashioned gallery of aesthetic practice', *Qualitative Inquiry* 9(2): 165–81.

Murphet, H. (1971) *Sai Baba: Man of Miracles*, Boston, MA: Weiser Books.

Nathan, T. (2005) 'The Djinns: A sophisticated conceptualization of pathologies and therapies', in R. Moodley and W. West (eds), *Integrating Traditional Healing Practices into Counseling and Psychotherapy*, Thousand Oaks, CA: Sage, 196–209.

Neki, J. S. (1975) 'Sahaja: An Indian ideal of mental health', *Psychiatry* 36: 1–11.

Nelson-Jones, R. (2002) *Essential Counselling and Therapy Skills: The Skilled-Client Model*, London, Sage.

NFSH (2008) 'What is spiritual healing?' from www.nfsh.org.uk, accessed 31 March 2008.

Nicholls, V. (2002) *Taken Seriously: The Somerset Spirituality Project*, London: Mental Health Foundation.

Nielsen, S. L. (2004) 'A Mormon rational emotive behaviour therapist attempts Qur'anic rational emotive behaviour therapy', in P. S. Richards and A. E. Bergin (2004) *Casebook for a Spiritual Strategy in Counselling and Psychotherapy*, Washington DC: APA.

Nolan, G. (2008) 'Mirrors and echoes: Meaning-moments in counselling supervision', Doctorate in Counselling Studies thesis, School of Education, University of Manchester.

Norcross, J. C. (ed.) (2002) *Psychotherapy Relationships that Work: Therapist Contributions and Responsiveness to Patients*, New York: Oxford University Press.

Novins, D. K., Beals, J., Sack, W. H. and Manson, S. M. (2000) 'Unmet needs for substance abuse and mental health services among northern plains American Indian adolescents', *Psychiatric Services* 51(8): 1045–7.

Novins, D. K., Beals, J., Moore, L. A., Spicer, P., Manson, S. M. and AI-SUPERPFP Team (2004) 'Use of biomedical services and traditional healing options among American Indians: Sociodemographic correlates, spirituality, and ethnic identity', *Medical Care* 42(7): 670–79.

Önder, M. (1993) *Mevlana and the Mevlana Museum*, Istanbul: Aksit Kultur Turizm Sanat Ajans.

Oschman, J. L. (2000) *Energy Medicine: The Scientific Basis*, London: Churchill Livingstone.

Palmer, S. (ed.) (2002) *Multicultural Counselling: A Reader*, London: Sage.

Palmer, S. and Woolfe, R. (2000) (eds) *Integrative and Eclectic Counselling and Psychotherapy*, London: Sage.

Pargament, K. I. (1997) *The Psychology of Religion and Coping*, New York: Guilford Publications.

Pargament K. I., Murray-Swank, N. A. and Tarakeshwar, N. (2005) 'An empirically-based rationale for a spiritually-integrated psychotherapy', *Mental Health, Religion and Culture* 8(3): 155–65.

Pattison, S. (1988) *A Critique of Pastoral Care*, London: SCM.

Pattison, S. (2000) *Shame: Theory, Therapy, Theology*, Cambridge: Cambridge University Press.

Pedersen, P. B. (1997) *Culture-Centered Counseling Interventions: Striving for Accuracy*, London: Sage.

Pert, C. (1999) *Molecules of Emotion: Why You Feel the Way You Feel*, New York: Simon and Schuster.

Pettifor, J. L. (2001) 'Are professional codes of ethics relevant for multicultural counselling?' *Canadian Journal of Counselling* 35(1): 26–35.

Pierrakos, J. (1990) *Core Energetics*, New York: Synthesis Press.

Pippin, R. B. (2005) *The Persistence of Subjectivity: On the Kantian Aftermath*, New York: Cambridge University Press.

Pirsig, R. M. (1974) *Zen and the Art of Motorcycle Maintenance*, London: Bodley Head.

Poincaré, J. H. (1982[1913]) *The Foundations of Science: Science and Hypothesis, the Value of Science, Science and Method*, trans. G. B. Halstead, New York: University of America Press.

Polkinghorne, D. E. (1992) 'Postmodern epistemology of practice', in S. Kvale (ed.), *Psychology and Postmodernism*, London: Sage.

Poonwassie, A. and Charter, A. (2001) 'An Aboriginal worldview of helping: Empowering approaches', *Canadian Journal of Counselling* 35(1): 63–73.

Poonwassie, A. and Charter, A. (2005) 'Aboriginal worldview of healing: Inclusion, blending, and bridging', in R. Moodley and W. West (eds) *Integrating Traditional Healing Practices into Counseling and Psychotherapy*, Thousand Oaks, CA: Sage, 15–25.

Poulin, P. A. and West, W. (2005) 'Holistic healing, paradigm shift, and the New Age', in R. Moodley and W. West (eds.) *Integrating Traditional Healing Practices into Counselling and Psychotherapy*, Thousand Oaks, CA: Sage, 257–68.

Powers, R. (2005) 'Counseling and spirituality: A historical review', *Counseling and Values* 49: 217–25.

Praglin, L. J. (2005) 'Jewish healing, spirituality, and modern psychology', in R. Moodley and W. West (eds) *Integrating Traditional Healing Practices into Counseling and Psychotherapy*, Thousand Oaks, CA: Sage, 170–81.

Prigogine, I. (1977) *Self-Organization in Nonequilibrium Systems*, New York: John Wiley & Sons.

Prigogine, I. (1980) *From Being to Becoming: Time and Complexity in the Physical World*, New York: John Wiley & Sons.

Prigogine, I. (1984) *Order Out of Chaos*, New York: Bantam Books.

Propst, L. R., Ostrum, R., Watkins, P., Dean, T. and Masburn, D. (2002) 'Comparative efficacy of religious and non-religious cognitive behavioural therapy for the treatment of clinical depression in religious individuals', *Journal of Consulting and Clinical Psychology* 60: 94–103.

Pulvino, C. J. (1975) 'Psychic energy: The counsellor's undervalued resource, *Personal and Guidance Journal* 54(1): 28–32.

Rabinow, P. and Sullivan, W. M. (1987) *Interpretive Social Science: A Second Look*, Berkeley, CA: University of California Press.

Rack, P. (1982) *Race, Culture and Mental Disorder*, London: Tavistock Publications.

Rao, D. (2006) 'Choice of medicine and hierarchy of resort to different health alternatives among Asian Indian migrants in a metropolitan city in the USA', *Ethnicity and Health* 11(2): 153–67.

Rapp, H. (2001) 'Working with difference and diversity: The responsibilities of the supervisor', in S. Wheeler and D. King (ed.) *Supervising Counsellors*, London: Sage.

Reich, W. (1961) *Wilhelm Reich Selected Writings: An Introduction to Orgonomy*, New York: Noonday Press.

Rennie, D. L. (1994a) 'Clients' deference in psychotherapy', *Journal of Counseling Psychology* 41(4): 427–37.

Rennie, D. L. (1994b) 'Human science and counselling psychology: Closing the gap between research and practice', *Counselling Psychology Quarterly* 7(3): 235–50.

Restoule, B. (1997) 'Providing services to Aboriginal clients', *Guidance and Counseling* 12: 13–17.

Rhine, J. B. (1937) *New Frontiers of the Mind*, New York: Farrar & Rinehart.

Rhine, J. B. (1962) *Extra-Sensory Perception*, Boston, MA: Bruce Humphries.

Rhine, J. B. (1972) 'Parapsychology and man', *Journal of Parapsychology* 36(2): 102–21.

Richards, P. S. and Bergin, A. E. (1997) *A Spiritual Strategy for Counselling and Psychotherapy*, Washington DC: American Psychological Association.

Richards, S. and Bergin, A. E. (eds) (2000) *Handbook of Psychotherapy and Religious Diversity*, Washington, DC: American Psychological Association.

Richards, S. and Bergin, A. E. (eds) (2003) *Spiritual Strategies Case Studies*, Washington, DC: American Psychological Association.

Richards, P. S. and Bergin, A. E. (2005) *A Spiritual Strategy for Counselling and Psychotherapy*, 2nd edn, Washington DC: APA.

Richardson, L. (2000) 'Introduction – Assessing alternative modes of qualitative and ethnographic research: How do we judge? Who do we judge? Who judges? (Also, evaluating ethnography)', *Qualitative Inquiry* 6(2): 251–5.

Richo, D. (2007) *The Power of Coincidence: How Life Shows Us What We Need to Know*, Boston, MA: Shambhala Press.

Robinson, W. (1997) 'Can we hear one another?' Talk to Quaker Retreat Group, Savio House, Macclesfield, March.

Rogers, C. (1951) *Client Centered Therapy*, London: Constable.

Rogers, C. R. (1957) 'The necessary and sufficient conditions of therapeutic personality change', *Journal of Consulting Psychology* 21: 95–103.

Rogers, C. (1978) 'Do We Need "A" Reality?' in H. Kirschenbaum and V. L. Henderson (eds) *The Carl Rogers Reader*, New York: Houghton Mifflin.

Rogers, C. (1961) *On Becoming a Person*, Boston, MA: Houghton Mifflin.

Rogers, C. R. (1980) *A Way of Being*, Boston, MA: Houghton Mifflin.

Rogers, C. (1985) *Encounter Groups*, Harmondsworth: Penguin.

Rorty, R. (1991) *Objectivity, Relativism, and Truth: Philosophical Papers, Volume 1*, Cambridge: Cambridge University Press.

Rose, J. (1993) The integration of prayer and practice in the counselling relationship, Unpublished MSc dissertation, Roehampton Institute of Higher Education (University of Surrey).

Rose, J. (1996) *A Needle-Quivering Poise – Between Prayer and Practice in the Counselling Relationship*, Monograph No. 6, Edinburgh: Contact Pastoral.

Rose, J. (1999) 'Pastoral counselling and prayer', in G. Lynch (ed.) *Clinical Counselling in Pastoral Settings*, London: Routledge.

Rose, J. (2002) *Sharing Spaces? Prayer and the Counselling Relationship*, London: Darton, Longman & Todd.

Ross, R. (1992) *Dancing with a Ghost: Exploring Indian Reality*, Markham, Ontario: Octopus Publishing Group.

Rowan, J. (1989) 'A late developer', in W. Dryden and L. Spryling (eds) *On Becoming a Psychotherapist*, London: Tavistock/Routledge.

Rowan, J. (1993) *The Transpersonal, Psychotherapy and Counselling*, London: Routledge.

Rowan, J. (2001) 'Supervision and the psychospiritual levels of development', *Transpersonal Psychology Review* 5(2): 12–21.

Rowan, J. (2002a) *Supervision and the Psychospiritual Levels of Development*, JohnRowan@compuserve.com, 12–21.

Rowan, J. (2002b) 'Self and Society. Volume 30. No. 3, review', in E. Watkins (ed.) *Handbook of Psychotherapy Supervision*, Chichester: John Wiley & Sons.

Rowan, J. (2004) 'Three levels of therapy', *Counselling and Psychotherapy Journal* 15(9): 20–22.

Rowan, J. (2005) *The Transpersonal: Spirituality in Psychotherapy and Counselling*, 2nd edn, London: Routledge.

Rumi, J. (1995) Excerpt from *The Essential Rumi*, trans. C. Barks and J. Moyne, San Francisco: HarperCollins.

Rumi, J. (2002) *Rumi: The Mathnawi*, trans. E.H. Whinfield, London: Watkins Publishing.

Ruskan, J. (1993) *Emotional Clearing: Releasing Negative Feelings and Awakening Unconditional Happiness*, London: Rider.

Ryde, J. (2009) *Being White in the Helping Professions: Developing Effective Intercultural Awareness*, London: Jessica Kingsley.

Sachs, J. (2007) *Reith Lectures*, Lecture 3, audio, London: BBC.

Safran, J. D. (2003) *Psychoanalysis and Buddhism*, Boston, MA: Wisdom Publications.

Salzberg, S. (1995) *Loving-kindness: The Revolutionary Art of Happiness*, Boston, MA: Shambhala.

Sayed, M. A. (2002) 'Arabic psychiatry and psychology: The physician who is a philosopher and the physician who is not a philosopher: Some cultural considerations', *Social Behaviour and Personality* 30(3): 235–42.

Schiller, F. (1967) *On the Aesthetic Education of Man*, Oxford: Clarendon Press.

Schore, A. N. (1997) 'Early organization of nonlinear right brain and development of a predisposition to psychiatric disorders', *Development and Psychology*, 9: 595–631.

Schore, A. (2003a) *Affect Dysregulation and Disorders of the Self*, Hove: Lawrence Erlbaum.

Schore, A. (2003b) *Affect Regulation and Repair of the Self*, New York: Norton.

Schwartz, G. (2002) *The Afterlife Experiments: Breakthrough Scientific Evidence of Life After Death*, New York: Atria Books.

Scott, A. (2008) 'The effect of doing qualitative research on novice researchers', *European Journal for Qualitative Research in Psychotherapy* 3: 10–18.

Segal, Z., Williams, J. M. G. and Teasdale, J. (2002) *Mindfulness-Based Cognitive Therapy for Depression: A New Approach to Preventing Relapse*, New York: Guilford.

Seymour, P. (2005) 'Pagan approaches to healing', in R. Moodley and W. West (eds.) *Integrating Traditional Healing Practices into Counseling and Psychotherapy*, Thousand Oaks, CA: Sage.

Shafranske, E. P. and Malony, H. N. (1990) 'Clinical psychologists' religious and spiritual orientations and their practice of psychotherapy', *Psychotherapy* 17(1): 72–8.

Shapiro, D. H. (1980) *Meditation: Self-Regulation and Altered States of Consciousness*, Hawthorne, NY: Aldine.

Sheldrake, R. (1995) *A New Science of Life: The Hypothesis of Morphic Resonance*, Vermont: Park Street Press.

Shine, B. (1998) *A Mind of Your Own*, London: Harper Collins.

Sima, R. G. and West, W. (2005) 'Sharing healing secrets: Counselors and traditional healers in conversation', in R. Moodley and W. West (eds.) *Integrating Traditional Healing Practices into Counseling and Psychotherapy*, Thousand Oaks, CA: Sage, 196–209.

Smith, D. P. (2008) 'Engaging spiritual practice and the rectification of scientific distance: A phenomenological comparison of Native American, Sufi and Hindu spiritual therapeutics', Bridges to Wellness: Conference on Multicultural Counselling, Bangalore, India.

Smith, D. P. (2005) 'The sweat lodge as psychotherapy: Congruence between traditional and modern healing', in R. Moodley and W. West (eds) *Integrating Traditional Healing Practices into Counseling and Psychotherapy*, Thousand Oaks, CA: Sage.

Smith D. P. (2006) 'The value of a traditional religious framework in order to provide effective mental health: A Native American solution', Presented paper, Conference for the North American Society for Psychotherapy Research, Burr Oak, OH.

Smith, D. P and Orlinsky, D. (2000) 'The spiritual and religious orientation of psychotherapists: Research and philosophical speculations, Presented paper, International Conference for the Society for Psychotherapy Research, Chicago, IL.

Smith, J. A. (1996) 'Beyond the divide between cognition and discourse: Using interpretative phenomenological analysis in health psychology, *Psychology and Health* 11: 261–71.

Smith, J. A., Jarman, M. and Osborn, M. (1999) 'Doing interpretative phenomenological analysis', in M. Murray and K. Chamberlain (eds) *Qualitative Health Psychology: Theories and Methods*, London: Sage.

Smith, J. Z. (ed.) (1995) *Harper Collins Dictionary of Religion*, Associate ed. W. S. Green, American Academy of Religion, San Francisco, CA: Harper San Francisco.

Sinetar, M. (2007) *Lifestyles for Spiritual Wholeness*, Nahwah, NJ: Paulist Press.

Solomon, A. and Wane, N. (2005) 'Indigenous healers and healing in a modern world', in R. Moodley and W. West (eds) *Integrating Traditional Healing Practices into Counseling and Psychotherapy*, Thousand Oaks, CA: Sage, 196–209.

Sperry, L. (2001) *Spirituality in Clinical Practice*, Philadelphia, PA: Brunner-Routledge.

Sperry, L. and Shafranske, E. P. (eds) (2005) *Spiritually Oriented Psychotherapy*, Washington DC: American Psychological Association.

Stokes, F. (2006) *The Great Debates*, BBC Radio 4, 11 January.

Storti, C. (2001) *The Art of Crossing Cultures*, Yarmouth, ME: Intercultural Press.

Strupp, H. H. (1972) 'On the technology of psychotherapy', *Archives of General Psychiatry* 26: 270–78.

Sue, D. W. and Sue, D. (1999) *Counselling the Culturally Different: Theory and Practice*, New York: John Wiley & Sons.

Sue, D. W., Arrendondo, P. and McDavis, R. J. (1992) 'Multicultural counseling competencies: A call to the profession', *Journal of Counseling and Development* 70: 477–86.

Sussman, N. M. (2000) 'The dynamic nature of cultural identity throughout cultural transitions: Why home is not so sweet', *Personality and Social Psychology Review* 4(4): 355–73.

Swinton, J. (2001) *Spirituality and Mental Health Care*, London: Jessica Kingsley.

Swinton, J. (2005) *Why Psychiatry Needs Spirituality*, Royal College of Psychiatrists Spirituality Special Interest Group, www.rcpsych.ac.uk/college/sig/spirit/publications/index.htm, accessed 11 December 2005.

Swinton, V. (2007) 'Researching spirituality in counsellor training', *Thresholds, Counselling with Spirit*, Autumn: 16–19.

Tan, S. Y. (1996) 'Religion in clinical practice: Implicit and explicit integration', in E. P. Shafranske (ed.) *Religion and the Clinical Practice of Psychology*, Washington DC: American Psychological Association.

Targ, R. and Hastings, A. (1987) 'Psychological impact of psychic abilities', *Psychological Perspectives* 18(1): 38–51.

Tart, C. (2000) 'Fear of psychic phenomena', *Transpersonal Hypnosis: Gateway to Body, Mind and Spirit*, Boca Raton, FL: CRC Press.

Taton, R. (1963) *Ancient and Medieval Science*, trans. A. J. Pomerans, London: Thames and Hudson.

Ten Eyck, C. C. R. (1993) 'Inner healing prayer: The therapist's perspective', Unpublished EdD thesis, University of South Dakota.

Thorne, B. (1991) *Person-Centred Counselling: Therapeutic and Spiritual Dimensions*, London: Whurr.

Thorne, B. (1994) 'Developing a spiritual discipline', in D. Mearns (ed.) *Developing Person-Centred Counselling*, London: Sage.

Thorne, B. (1997) *Counselling and the Spiritual Journey*, Birkenhead: Time & Space.

Thorne, B. (1998) *Person-Centred Counselling and Christian Spirituality: The Secular and the Holy*, London: Whurr.

Thorne, B. (2002) *The Mystical Path of Person-Centred Therapy: Hope beyond despair*, London: Whurr.

Thorne, B. (2006) 'The gift and cost of being fully present', in J. Moore and C. Purton (eds) *Spirituality in Counselling: Experiential and Theoretical*, Ross-on-Wye: PCCS.

Torrey, E. F. (1972) *The Mind Game: Witch Doctors and Psychiatrists*, New York: Bantam Books.

Tseng, W. S. and Hsu, J. (1979) 'Culture and psychotherapy', in A. J. Marsella, R. G. Tharp and T. J. Ciborowski (eds) *Perspectives on Cross-Cultural Psychology*, New York: Academic Press, 333–45.

Tseng, W. S. and McDermott, J. F. (1975) 'Psychotherapy: Historical roots, universal elements, and cultural variations', *American Journal of Psychiatry* 132: 378–84.

Tudor, K. and Worrall, M. (2004) *Freedom to Practise: Person-Centred Approaches to Supervision*, Ross-on-Wye: PCCS.

Ulanov, A. and Ulanov, B. (1982) *Primary Speech: A Psychology of Prayer*, Louisville, KY: John Knox Press.

Underwood, L. G. (2002) 'The experience of compassionate love', in S. G. Post, L. G. Underwood, J. Schloss and W. B. Hurlbut (eds) *Altruism and Altruistic Love*, Oxford: Oxford University Press, 72–88.

Young-Eisendrath, P. and Muramoto, S. (2002) *Awakening and Insight: Zen Buddhism and Psychotherapy*, Hove: Brunner-Routledge.

Van der Wal, J. (2006) 'The embryo in motion: The speech of the embryo', Presented paper, Biosynthesis Conference, Lisbon University.

Vaughan, F. (1991) 'Spiritual issues in psychotherapy', *Journal of Transpersonal Psychology* 23(2): 105–19.

Vicary, D. A. and Bishop, B. J. (2005) 'Western psychotherapeutic practice: Engaging Aboriginal people in culturally appropriate and respectful ways', *Australian Psychologist*, 40(1): 8–19.

Vieira, W. (1996) *Penta: Manual Personal Energetic Task*, trans. K. de La Tour and S. de La Tour, Rio de Janeiro: International Institute of Projectiology and Conscientiology.

Vivino, B. L., Thompson, B. T., Hill, C. E. and Ladany, N. (2009) 'Compassion in psychotherapy: The perspective of therapists nominated as compassionate', *Psychotherapy Research* 19(2): 157–71.

Von Franz, M.-L. (1980) *On Divination and Synchronicity*, Toronto: Inner City Books.

Vontress, C. E. (1991) 'Traditional healing in Africa: Implications for cross-cultural counselling', *Journal of Counseling and Development* 70(1): 242–9.

Vontress, C. E. (1999) 'Interview with a traditional African healer', *Journal of Mental Health Counseling* 21: 326–36.

Waldram, J. B., Herring, D. A. and Young, T. K. (2006) 2nd edn, *Aboriginal Health in Canada*, Toronto: University of Toronto Press.

Wampold, B. (2001) *The Great Psychotherapy Debate: Models, Methods and Findings*, Mahwah, NJ: Lawrence Erlbaum Associates.

Wansbrough, H. (ed.) (1985) *The New Jerusalem Bible*, London: Darton, Longmann & Todd.

Wardle, M. (2004a) 'Counsellors' experiences of extrasensory perception whilst working with their clients', MA thesis, University College Chester.

Wardle, M. (2004b) 'Presenting psychic energy in counselling', *Transpersonal Psychology Review* 8(2): 20–27.

Wardle, M. (2006) 'Working with suppression via the bridge of psychic energy: An integrative counsellor's perspective', *Journal of Critical Psychology, Counselling and Psychotherapy* 6(4): 210–14.

Wardle, M. (2008) 'Psychic energy in counselling', PhD thesis, University of Manchester.

Watson, G., Batchelor, S. and Claxton, G. (eds) (1999) *The Psychology of Awakening: Buddhism, Science and our Day-to-Day Lives*, London: Rider.

Webster, J. P. (1992) 'Verbal prayer in psychotherapy: A model for pastoral counsellors', Unpublished STD thesis, San Francisco Theological Seminary.

Welwood, J. (1999) 'Realization and embodiment: Psychological work in the service of spiritual development', in G. W. Watson, S. Batchelor and G. Claxton (eds) *The Psychology of Awakening: Buddhism, Science, and Our Day-to-Day Lives*, London: Rider. 137–66.

West, W. (1994a) 'Clients' experience of bodywork psychotherapy', *Counselling Psychology Quarterly* 7(3): 287–303.

West, W. (1994b) 'Post Reichian therapy', in D. Jones (ed.) *Innovative Therapy: A Handbook*, Buckingham: Open University Press.

West, W. (1995) 'Integrating psychotherapy and healing', Doctoral thesis, Department of Applied Social Studies, Keele University.

West, W. (1997) 'Integrating counselling, psychotherapy and healing: An inquiry into counsellors and psychotherapists whose works includes healing', *British Journal of Guidance and Counselling* 25(3): 291–312.

West, W. (1998a) 'Therapy as a spiritual process', in C. Feltham (ed.) *Witness and Vision of the Therapists*, London: Sage.

West, W. (1998b) 'Developing practice in a context for religious faith: A study of psychotherapists who are Quakers', *British Journal of Guidance and Counselling* 26(3): 365–75.

West, W. (2000a) *Psychotherapy and Spirituality: Crossing the Line between Therapy and Religion*, London: Sage.

West, W. (2000b) 'Supervision difficulties and dilemmas for counsellors and psychotherapists around healing and spirituality', in B. Lawton and C. Feltham (eds) *Taking Supervision Forwards: Dilemmas, Insights and Trends*, London: Sage.

West, W. (2000c) 'Eclecticism and integration in humanistic therapy', in S. Palmer and R. Woolfe (eds) *Integrative and Eclectic Counselling and Psychotherapy*, London: Sage, 218–32.

West, W. (2001a) 'Issues relating to the use of forgiveness in counselling and psychotherapy', *British Journal of Guidance and Counselling* 29(4): 415–23.

West, W. (2001b) 'Beyond grounded theory: The use of a heuristic approach to qualitative research', *Counselling and Psychotherapy Research* 1(2): 126–31.

West, W. (2002a) 'Being present to our clients' spirituality', *Journal of Critical Psychology, Counselling and Psychotherapy* 2(2): 86–93.

West, W. (2002b) 'Some ethical dilemmas in counselling and counselling research', *British Journal of Guidance and Counselling* 30(3): 261–8.

West, W. (2003) 'An introduction to the Symposium on Counselling and Armed Conflicts', *British Journal of Guidance and Counselling* 31(4): 355–8.

West, W. (2004a) *Spiritual Issues in Therapy: Relating Experience to Practice*, Basingstoke: Palgrave.

West, W. (2004b) 'Pittu Laungani in conversation with William West', *British Journal of Guidance and Counselling* 32(3): 419–35.

West, W. (2007) 'The role of the researcher and methodological choices: Pragmatics, Russell, Einstein and Newton', *Journal of Critical Psychology, Counselling and Psychotherapy* 7(3): 168–74.

West, W. (2009) 'Situating the researcher in qualitative psychotherapy research around spirituality', *Counselling Psychology Quarterly* 22(2): 187–95.

West, W. and Burne, J. (2009) 'Some ethical concerns about counselling research', *Counselling Psychology Quarterly* 22(3): 309–18.

West, W. and Clark, V. (2004) 'Learnings from a qualitative study into counselling supervision: Listening to supervisor and supervisee', *Counselling Psychotherapy Research*, 4(2): 20–26.

White, R. A. (1998) 'Becoming more human as we work: The reflexive role of exceptional human experiences', in W. Braud and R. Anderson (eds) *Transpersonal Research Methods for the Social Sciences: Honoring Human Experience*, London: Sage.

Whitmore, D. (2000) *Psychosynthesis Counselling in Action*, London: Sage.

Wilber, K. (1979) *No Boundary*, Boston, MA: Shambhala.

Wilber, K. (1980) *The Atman Project*, Wheaton, IL: Quest.

Wilber, K. (2000) *Integral Psychology: Consciousness, Spirit, Psychology, Therapy*, London: Shambhala.

Wilber, K. (2001) *A Theory of Everything: An Integral Vision for Business, Politics, Science and Spirituality*, Dublin: Gateway.

Williams, V. (2003) 'Religion, counselling and psychotherapy – complementary or controversial?' *Counselling and Psychotherapy Journal* 14(7): 18–22.

Wordsworth, W. (1960[1805]) *The Prelude*, ed. E. E. Reynolds, London: Macmillan & Co.

Worthington, E. L. (ed.) (1998) *Dimensions of Forgiveness: Psychological Research and Theological Perspectives*, London: Templeton.

Wright, F. (1980) *A Theology of Pastoral Care*, London: SPCK.

Wyatt, J. (2002) '"Confronting the Almighty God"? A study of how psychodynamic counsellors respond to clients' expressions of religious faith,' *Counselling and Psychotherapy Research* 2(3): 177–84.

Wyrostock, N. C. and Paulson, B. L. (2000) 'Traditional healing practices among First Nations Students', *Canadian Journal of Counselling* 34(1): 14–24.

Yusef, D. F. (2008) 'The body as a universal gateway', PhD thesis, Manchester University.

# Index

Note: Page numbers in *italics* denote a table.